VERSO
CLASSICS

The last few decades have seen an immense outpouring of works of theory and criticism, but, as the number of titles has increased dramatically, it has become more and more difficult to find one's way around this vast body of literature and to distinguish between those works of real and enduring value and those of a more ephemeral nature. The Verso Classics series will rise to the challenge by taking stock of the last few decades of contemporary critical thought and reissuing, in an elegant paperback format and at affordable prices, those books which genuinely constitute original and important intellectual contributions.

Many of these works are currently out of print or difficult to obtain: Verso Classics will bring them back into the public domain, building a collection which will become the 'essential left library'.

Black Macho
and
the Myth of the Superwoman

Black Macho
and
the Myth of the Superwoman

MICHELE WALLACE

VERSO

London · New York

First published by The Dial Press, New York
This edition, with new introduction and bibliography,
published by Verso 1990
Reprinted 1991, 1994, 1996
This Verso Classics edition published by Verso 1999
© Michele Wallace 1978, 1979, 1990, 1999
All rights reserved

Verso
UK: 6 Meard Street London W1V 3HR
USA: 180 Varick Street New York NY 10014–4606

Verso is the imprint of New Left Books

ISBN 1–85984–296–8

Printed and bound in Great Britain by
Biddles Ltd, Guildford and King's Lynn

For my mother, Faith Ringgold

Contents

ACKNOWLEDGMENTS

No (wo)man is an island. Corn, I guess, but true. A great many people helped to make this book possible. I would like to thank as many of them as I can. Most of all, I appreciate my family's unanimous, unwavering support, and I would like to extend a special thank you to my father, Earl Wallace, for his legacy of courage, rebelliousness, and creativity; my sister, Barbara; my grandmother, Willi Posey; and my stepfather, Burdette Ringgold, for adding immeasurably to the collection of experiences from which I have drawn many of my observations about black women and black men.

I met Pat Mainardi, Robin Morgan, and Kathy Sarachild—all young feminists then—when I was 18. Each contributed immeasurably to my early feminist thinking— Pat during those endless summers in Vermont when we discussed feminist theory, politics in general, art and history in particular; Kathy as my editor at *Women's World*; and Robin as an early fan of my poetry.

Perhaps there has been no one more important to the development of my writer self than Mark Mirsky, my preferred professor at City College, who became my mentor and one of my best friends. He gave me my critical eye and taught me how to write. Also Frances Louis, Jack Kroll, Donald Barthelme, Earl Rovit, and Faith Sale helped to make me the writer that I am.

For this book in particular, I have Marie Brown, Margo Jefferson, Alice Walker, Bob Miner, and Michael Wolffe to thank, all of whom took the time to read my manuscript at various stages and advise me.

I would also like to thank my agent, Maxine Groffsky, and my editor, Joyce Johnson, who extended herself above and beyond the call of duty and who is a marvelous editor besides.

I'm also grateful to Clayton Riley, Naomi Sims, Eartha Kitt, Henri Ghent, William T. Williams, Nelson Canton, and Barbara Knight, who kindly submitted to being interviewed, although I decided against using those interviews in this book.

And finally, I would like to thank Donald Brown for just holding my hand through most of the writing, and Una Ellman, who brought me through it all in one piece.

The author and publishers would like to make grateful acknowledgment of permission to use the following copyrighted material:

From *Against Our Will* by Susan Brownmiller: Copyright © 1975 by Susan Brownmiller. Reprinted by permission of Simon & Schuster, a Division of Gulf & Western Corporation.

From *Soul on Ice* by Eldridge Cleaver: Copyright © 1965 by Eldridge Cleaver. Used by permission of McGraw-Hill Book Company.

Lyrics from "Dr. Feelgood" by Aretha Franklin: © 1967 Pronto Music, Inc., and 14th House Music. Used by permission.

From *Black Feeling, Black Talk-Black Judgement* by Nikki Giovanni: Copyright © 1968, 1970 by Nikki Giovanni. By

". . . I say that the strongest principle of growth lies in human choice. The sons of Judah have to choose that God may again choose them. The Messianic time is the time when Israel shall will the planting of the national ensign. The Nile overflowed and rushed onward: the Egyptian could not choose the overflow, but he chose to work and make channels for the fructifying waters, and Egypt became the land of corn. Shall man, whose soul is set in the royalty of discernment and resolve, deny his rank and say, I am an onlooker, ask no choice or purpose of me? That is the blasphemy of this time. The divine principle of our race is action, choice, resolved memory. Let us contradict the blasphemy, and help to will our own better future and the better future of the world—not renounce our higher gift and say, 'Let us be as if we were not among the populations': but choose our full heritage, claim the brotherhood of our nations, and carry into it a new brotherhood with the nations of the Gentiles. The vision is there; it will be fulfilled."

—George Eliot, *Daniel Deronda*

INTRODUCTION

How I Saw It Then, How I See It Now

Early in 1978 there was a series of articles in *The New York Times* on the changes in the black community since 1968. It covered the Civil Rights Movement, the Black Movement, the economic and social situation for blacks today. Never once did it mention the contribution black women made to the Civil Rights Movement. The article spoke of three Americas: one white, one middle-class black, one poor black. No particular notice was given to the fact that that poor black America consists largely of black women and children. It was as if these women and children did not exist.

The history of the period has been written and will continue to be written without us. The imperative is clear: Either we will make history or remain the victims of it.

In 1978, I concluded *Black Macho and the Myth of the Super-woman* with these words. It is impossible for me to look back at this book without the conviction that the significance of black women as a distinct category is routinely erased by the way in which the Women's Movement and the Black Movement choose to set their goals and recollect their histories.

At that time the difficulty was that you weren't supposed to talk about both racial oppression and women's oppression at the same time. Now, with the success of Alice Walker and *The Color Purple*, and the virtual institutionalization of multicultural feminist inquiry in the U.S. (thanks to the work of June Jordan, Adrienne Rich, Barbara Smith, Audre Lorde and Bell Hooks), such dualism would appear to be less of a problem.

Yet the mainstream media still make this basic error on a daily basis, giving combinations of racism and sexism additional power to do their dirty work. In the realm of the dominant discourse, viewing women's oppression and black oppression as mutually exclusive areas results in the myth of a color-blind society and the myth of gender equality. Except for the occasional mainstream focus on "racism" or "sexism," both of which are very narrowly defined and delimited to suggest that in most cases whites are blind to race or gender difference, the charade goes on that anybody who tries can become happy and rich in the U.S.

Moreover, these myths further serve to mystify the structural inability of the mainstream to admit that women's oppression and racial oppression sometimes are seen in combinations which create a third and entirely different category of problems with regard to the black woman or woman of color. There is the further presumption that women of color are somehow too small a "minority" to conceptualize. But what it is really impossible to conceptualize in the realm of the dominant discourse is that women of color are actually a majority in the world.

It seems telling now that I drew my final example of how black women were being metaphorically disenfranchised by the Women's Movement and the Black Movement from an article in *The New York Times*, a paper which I now regard as the quintessential historical document in the white phallocentric tradition. *The New York Times* is the key voice of this brand of liberal humanism—although it is still not unusual among white males on the left in the U.S. to think that to talk about "race" is automatically "racist;" to see or acknowledge color difference is "racist."

Such feelings are vestiges of earlier stages of anti-racism. But what worries me is that such people don't realize that they thus become the instruments of the "invisibility" that Ralph Ellison described so well, although I don't suppose he thought it was ideological. Not only do I see "invisibility" as a problem of ideology; I also see it as the final, and most difficult to combat, stage of racism. The fact that it involves conjunctions not only of racism and sexism but also conjunctions of capitalist exploitation and compulsory heterosexuality makes it even more difficult to diagnose. I suspect that such conjunctions cannot be resolved at all. Rather they must be unpacked, examined and disarmed.

Today I understand the problem as one of representation. My view then was that blacks had been systematically deprived of the continuity of their own African culture not only by the oppression of slavery and the racism and segregation that followed it, but also by integration and assimilation, which had denied them the knowledge of their history of struggle and the memory of their autonomous cultural practices. In the process of assimilation, integration and accommodation, blacks had taken on the culture and values of whites in regard to sexuality and gender. This did more than make it inevitable that black men would be sexist or misogynistic: it also made inevitable black women's completely dysfunctional self-hatred.

For me, then, to say that black men hated black women or vice versa was simply an extension of saying that black people hated themselves. The resulting mythology was really an extension and reversal of the white stereotypes about black inferiority. It dictated that black men would define their masculinity (and thus their "liberation") in terms of superficial masculine characteristics—demonstrable

sexuality; physical prowess; the capacity for warlike behavior. Black women would define their femininity (or
their "liberation"—which was not, however, a movement) in
terms of their lack of these same superficial masculine
characteristics—precisely because the myth of their inferiority, the black female stereotype, had always portrayed
them as oversexed, physically strong and warlike. One of
the myths I called "Black Macho" and the other I called
"The Superwoman."

The arguments by which my book is best known—that
Black Macho and interracial relationships helped to
destroy the political effectiveness of the Civil Rights Movement and the Black Power Movement; that black men and
women hated one another, were all minor points in my
larger argument, which was really about black nationalism
with a feminist face and black female self-determination. I
now feel that the biggest failure of the book was that I
didn't understand the problems inherent to nationalism as
a liberationist strategy for women. I thought that the men
were simply leaving women out because it hadn't really
occurred to them to do otherwise. I didn't see that it comes
automatically to nationalist struggles to devalue the contributions of women, as well as gays or anybody else who doesn't
fit the profile of the noble warrior or the elder statesman.

I had already come to see that what a lot of people were
referring to as revolutionary concepts were not revolutionary at all, but reactionary. What I didn't understand was
just how hard it really is to even conceptualize effective
revolution, the kind of revolution that might really change
our present global inhumane and inegalitarian economic
and political arrangements.

I used history, literature, sociology, autobiography and
journalism to support my argument, although I didn't then
recognize that none of them offers a transparent window on

the world, but rather that they are all discursive modes, and as such intrinsically given to lapses into "fiction." Consequently, whereas then I spoke of black women making history and being written about, I now think it is more important that black women "write" their own histories, since the power to write one's own history is what making history appears to be all about.

If I had to do it over again, I would no longer maintain that Black Macho was the crucial factor in the destruction of the Black Power Movement, not because I no longer think it is true at least in some sense—and certainly it was true in the world I inhabited then—but because it was a claim that was impossible to substantiate at the level of sociological, historical or journalistic data. While it may be a valid interpretation of events to say that a brand of black male chauvinism contributed to the shortsightedness and failure of the Black Power Movement, there are other interpretations equally valid—for instance, that police and CIA repression were also factors in the demise of the movement. Moreover, from another perspective (although not necessarily my own) the Black Liberation Struggle can be viewed as never ending or beginning but rather waxing or waning, usually invisible to the dominant discourse, virtually since blacks became slaves in the Americas.

My critique of the Black Power Movement was based upon a limited perception of it taken primarily from the mainstream media; through my reading of literature written by white writers such as Norman Mailer and Tom Wolfe; and, more importantly, by black writers such as Richard Wright, Ralph Ellison, James Baldwin, Amiri Baraka and Eldridge Cleaver. What I learned from this perspective was more important than many of my critics have been willing to allow.

Media analysis has never been a focus of Black Studies, or of the most visible black intellectuals. But it is impossible to imagine the accomplishments of the Civil Rights Movement and the Black Power Movement without the technological innovation of the 7 o'clock evening news, which continually brought into all of our homes the footage from the latest Civil Rights encounter between police and protesters in the South. And, although black male writers have become somewhat unfashionable as a group (as opposed to black women writers), it was the black male writer who established the intellectual foundation of Black Liberationist thought, to the extent that such a thing existed. In fact, the heavily anti-intellectual impulse of Black Power rhetoric (which I described as Black Macho) was one of its greatest weaknesses. But my arguments were completely rooted in readings of literature, popular culture and the media.

My perspective on such matters has shifted from a preoccupation with "what really happened"—I will never really know about most of the events of the Civil Rights Movement and Black Power since I wasn't there—to a preoccupation with the politics of interpretation, specifically with who writes the history of the 60s and how that knowledge of "the past" determines power in "the present." For the most part, it is the white male left that is writing the history of the 60s.

The most important historical documentation of the 60s coming from the perspective of black participants has been the "Eyes on the Prize" Series of PBS television documentaries, and the books that have followed them, by *Washington Post* reporter Juan Williams. Not surprisingly, this version of events underplays the contribution of women, and the story of how the Women's Movement, the Peace Movement and the white male left emerged from the

Civil Rights Struggle. But what did surprise me is how heavily these documentaries followed what the networks had already established to be important in their initial coverage of the movement. Since "Eyes on the Prize" relied heavily on available footage and made no real attempt to subvert that context, what little interpretation there was (as against the "transparent window on the past" approach) was intensely phallocentric, elitist, and exclusionary.

As it happens, I like the story about heroism, sacrifice and courage in the black community, North and South, that "Eyes on the Prize" tells. But if one believes, as I do, that the purpose of historical narrative is to help us to understand the present, then the "Eyes on the Prize" story is simply inadequate to that task.

If *Black Macho* gives the impression that I felt as though interracial dating constituted a turning point in the Civil Rights Movement, I need to say that is no longer my conviction—if it ever was. I had meant to point it out as symptomatic of an aspect of my changing environment as a young black woman in New York. Again, the crucial matter is what it can tell us about interpretation. For instance, interracial dating is scarcely mentioned in most official black or white (male) histories of the sixties. Rather it is black or white women—Susan Brownmiller in *Against Our Will* (1975); Alice Walker in *Meridian* (1976); Sara Evans in *Personal Politics: The Roots of Women's Liberation in the Civil Rights Movement and the New Left* (1980); Paula Giddings in *When and Where I Enter: The Impact of Blacks on Race and Sex in America* (1981)—who take seriously such issues for what they can tell us about the lives of ordinary women and their access, or lack of access, to power and fulfillment.

As for the quote that adorned the cover of the book, and that caused so much stir:

xxiii

I am saying ... there is a profound distrust, if not hatred, between black men and black women that has been nursed along largely by white racism but also by an almost deliberate ignorance on the part of blacks about the sexual politics of their experience in this country.

I stand by it only to the extent that it is also possible to say that there is a profound distrust, if not hatred, between Jewish men and women, or Italian men and women, or Irish men and women, or Puerto Rican men and women, or Asian men and women, that has been nursed along largely by anti-Semitism, or anti-Catholicism, or orientalism, or cultural intolerance, but also by an almost deliberate ignorance on the part of Jews, or Italians, or the Irish, or Puerto Ricans, or Asians, about the sexual politics of their experience in this country. Only to the degree that such sexual hatred is true of other ethnic groups as well, is it true of Afro-Americans.

The assertion is not so ridiculous as it may sound on the surface. I think it is true to some degree that as the men of an ethnic group become middle-class, educated and prosperous in America, they may grow to resent in an unconscious way the working-class women of a prior generation—more specifically their mothers—who remain behind and who may come psychologically to represent to them the old ways before assimilation and success. They may try to the best of their ability to marry a woman as unlike this figure as possible. In the case of the successful black male, she might not be black, just as in the case of some successful Jewish males, she isn't Jewish, in the case of some successful Italian males, she isn't Italian—and so on. But thanks to the Civil Rights Movement, this is no longer a crime.

Also, there are many black men who love black women,

and vice versa, although I didn't know it at the time I wrote *Black Macho*.

Black Macho was criticized for the idea that becoming American means becoming a kind of imitation "white" person and, therefore, self-hating. I don't believe that anymore either. Rather I share James Baldwin's and Henry Louis Gates's (in *"Race," Writing and Difference*) view that racial difference is essentially mythological and highly ideological. Although blackness is something we can legitimately say we've experienced in a variety of concrete ways, it is not an essential category that we can empirically or biologically distinguish from other racial experiences. It only makes sense if we view it archeologically (after Michel Foucault in *The Archeology of Knowledge* and Houston Baker in *Blues, Ideology and Afro-American Culture*), as a discourse or a series of discourses concerning a matrix of material conditions, social relations, economic, political and cultural issues—beginning with the onset of the African slave trade in the seventeenth century and continuing until today.

In this context, whiteness, more than any other racial designation, is an invention of American ideology; a way of combating the fear of "the other" within, or the dread of polysemous and polyvocal selves through various social policies. Wanting to be "white," therefore, is an ideological fantasy, socially constructed and yet utterly impossible to achieve, like wanting to be without sin. Nevertheless, as long as there are white people who want to be white, it seems probable to me that there will also be black people who want to be "white" or, more to the point, black people who *don't* want to be "black" or "other." As for wanting to be "black," this has always been played out as a more heterogeneous phenomenon.

In regard to whether or not we should be concerned specifically to establish the relationship between our present cultural behavior and previous African cultural patterns, I still think such activity is worthwhile. Although I am strongly attracted to and persuaded by the postcolonial arguments of Edward Said, Homi Bhabha, Gayatri Spivak and Trinh Minh-ha, I don't think they begin to exhaust what we can possibly say about our relationship to "other worlds" beyond the hegemony of the West.

What they've done for me is to problematize the notion of a "homeland" or an indigenous culture. Afro-Americans, after all, are not immigrants, although we have always counted recent arrivals from the Caribbean and from Africa among us. As a group, we have been in the Americas longer than anyone apart from the Indians. Moreover, the question of whether or not our "homeland" in Africa should be a crucial factor in our culture, or in our discourse, has been a controversial issue among Afro-American intellectuals since the nineteenth century and perhaps before.

The more important issue to me is that historically, we have continued to create alternative cultural formations which not only interrogate and subvert the dominant discourse but which also continue to contest the viability of an institutionalized and commodified dominant discourse. Whether such activity stems from our experience of slavery, segregation and oppression, or from cultural precedents in previous African societies, or some combination of the two, is not the most crucial issue here. What's most important is the opportunity it seems to offer to think in counter-hegemonic ways about the function of culture.

Since I wrote *Black Macho*, there have been enormous changes in the availability of materials on the history and literature of white and black women during slavery, Reconstruction, the Civil Rights Movement and the Women's Movement. Not only have we seen the emergence of Black Women's Studies: since 1979 Women's Studies and Black Studies have become prominent academic and intellectual discourses. When criticisms of the book left me feeling uninformed, I went back to graduate school at Yale in 1980, first in Afro-American Studies and then in American Studies. Although my primary interest had always been in literature, the emphasis on literary studies there was on deconstruction and theory, so I focused on history.

The biggest thing I learned about history, or linear historical narrative at Yale was that it is always written by someone in particular and, therefore, never quite "true" in the factual sense. In order to be "true" in any sense that is usable to the present, "history" has to be dialogic; it has to find innovative strategies for taking into account contradictory voices and interpretations. The fact that literature had always probably been better at doing this than "history," which generally likes to hold on to its status as a Master Narrative, gave me a renewed interest in literature. I had written and continued to rewrite a novel that no one would publish, which was a story about the experiences I had had in publishing *Black Macho.* So I was enormously interested in knowing more about the criteria of literary value.

While teaching writing and Afro-American Literature, I read a lot in the fields of cultural studies; literary criticism; and feminist film, TV and art criticism. Since then, I've finally completed a Master's in Afro-American Literature and Literary Criticism at the City College of New York where I am now, also, an Assistant Professor of English. I don't necessarily feel much smarter or older than when I wrote *Black Macho* but I understand better the relation between my personal history and History. Although I don't love it anymore, I still want people to read it.

If the truth be told, I think the thing that most attracted me to feminism in the beginning was its implicit critique of the family. Backed up by the Moynihan Report and other authoritative sources, the conventional wisdom was that black families were entirely different from white families. If I had read such material when I wrote *Black Macho and the Myth of the Superwoman*, Wilhelm Reich's warnings about family repression as laying the foundation for political authoritarianism, and R.D. Laing's picture of how certain families almost automatically produced schizophrenic children, would have best summarized my most frightening intuitions about how the family functioned, regardless of race.

I had read little Freud, Reich or Laing then, or even Juliet Mitchell's 1974 *Psychoanalysis and Feminism*, which has since helped make this material accessible to me. It was *New Yorker* humorist James Thurber's hysterically funny version of uptight eccentric New England white families, in which disparate personalities are constantly clashing and never listening to one another, that best filled in what I saw when I thought of "the family."

I then thought of the conventional family as a torture chamber designed to oppress and repress women. I have never understood why American feminists weren't more interested in how the family in particular, and personal relationships in general, fulfill a crucial role in reconciling women especially to our station in life. More specifically, our parents, who were broken in by their parents, must break us in. It is their painful duty to be the first to make us realize what we can realistically expect to accomplish in this life and to help us understand what is impossible. If anything, this is even more true in the "minority" or black family. For me, this is what August Wilson's play *Fences* is really about. The most suggestive model that history offers us is less than one hundred-and-fifty years old: it is of the slave family in the antebellum South in which a slave mother beat her children in order to prepare them for the Master's whip and, perhaps, in the case of the girls, to prepare them for the Master's caress.

I have taught autobiographical writing to women of my own age and older at the Center for Worker Education (which is a branch of CCNY) in New York. Their struggle to write their own stories is, invariably, the struggle between their mothers, and sometimes their fathers, and themselves. Most of them can see their parents' side in any early childhood incident better than they can see their own side. They find it difficult to even remember having feelings of their own as children. All they can remember is what their parents felt; what their parents insisted they should feel. Autobiographical writing may partly be about reclaiming that childhood self; acknowledging her blamelessness. Yet this is almost impossible for many women to do in their writing about their earlier lives. Instead, they insist that there is no point in looking back; that, yes, their parents were strict or mean but the more important thing is that they are not raising their children as they were raised. They talk with their children. They defend them when they are wrongly accused. They love them openly. Or so they say.

It is my conviction that the only way to avoid repeating the mistakes of the past is openly to discuss them. Whether in nations, families or individuals, the practice of being on speaking terms with your past lives is the only thing that makes it possible to trust yourself or anybody else. Freedom, liberation, happiness and fulfillment don't come "naturally." Rather they must be struggled for, moment by moment, against the tide of institutionalization, commodification and repression.

In *The Myth of the Superwoman,* the much more difficult half of the book to write, I talk about the conflict between my mother and myself and my stay in a juvenile home when I was seventeen. Using this story as my foundation, I come to a variety of conclusions regarding the feasibility of feminism in the black community.

The thing that still remained to be worked out was my relationship to my family as a writer and as a woman. At the time, the hard thing for me to admit was that my family life was a seriously troubled one. I conceded only that relationships between men and women, and between mothers and daughters, in the "black community" were plagued by the intimidating shadow of normal "white" American life, as it was projected through the media and popular culture. While this was indeed true, I now think that the scope of the problem is much wider. The problem was not with the black family but with the family; not with "black" or "white" culture but with the fact that in the U.S. cultural diversity is thought of as something superficial that we need to get rid of. What's helped to clarify this situation is the way in which "family" and traditional values are repeatedly defended by the right in order to build its opposition to progressive changes—from abortion rights to Civil Rights (for blacks, gays, Latinos and Asians) to welfare rights to the right of free expression.

Not only wasn't I knowledgable enough then to support such a thesis; I hadn't yet put my life together with what I had learned, what I properly understood to be my knowledge of the world. This was partly because I was still denying my life; denying the exceptions and contradictions it raised to what then were my views as a feminist. Perhaps the crucial deception was painting a picture of myself as a child of the black middle class who had grown up in all the middle-class security of my white counterpart in Scarsdale, a place I'd never been but which I found fascinating to imagine as presenting precisely the same dangers as life on Sugar Hill in Harlem.

At this stage of my life, I have often mentioned in writing how my father was addicted to heroin and died of a drug overdose when I was thirteen years old. Yet it was a story I was incapable of telling when I wrote *Black Macho*. I had learned to be so ashamed of who and what my father was that very few of my friends even knew about him. What I was taught to say, and what I said in the book, was that he was a classical and jazz musician, and that he had died in a car accident. Of my stepfather, who was an assembly-line worker at General Motors and who was really the man who had shaped my conception of men, I said as little as possible.

In the fifties, when they were still in college, my father Earl, who was a jazz musician, and my mother Faith, who was an artist, were secretly married. They had grown up on Sugar Hill in Harlem together, their mothers sewed downtown in the factories together, and they had been going together since Faith was sixteen. But my grandmother Momma Jones was so strict with Faith, although she was twenty, that Faith didn't tell Momma Jones she was married until she came home so late one night, Momma Jones threatened to beat her. After that, Faith and Earl, who had very little money, spent some time living in Brooklyn, some time living at Momma Jones's house, and some time living at the house of my other grandmother Momma T. A little over two years later, Earl and Faith had borne two children: my sister Barbara and myself. Meanwhile, Earl's drug habit, which was fashionable in the jazz musicians' circle he frequented (Sonny Rollins, Jackie McLean, Max Roach, Abbie Lincoln, Bud Powell), had grown much worse. She finally divorced him because of it after four years of marriage, when I was two.

We then lived with my grandmother Momma Jones, whose house was on Edgecombe Avenue, directly next to the apartment building in which my other grandmother, Momma T, lived. My father often visited Momma T, so there would have been a great deal of opportunity for me to see him had I not been forbidden to by my mother—although she felt she could not explain to me why I wasn't supposed to see him until I was about six. Yet I still saw him almost every time I was allowed to visit Momma T, though I never got to know him. I don't think the knowledge I've gathered over the years about drug addiction, jazz musicians, racism and black male alienation in the 50s will ever fill the void created by his absence. I didn't realize that I loved him until he was dead. Or rather, I could not not love him.

When my uncle, who was also addicted to drugs, came to live at my grandmother's house, after having spent some time in jail, we moved again to a "middle income" project in the Bronx called St. Mary's so that we wouldn't get a chance to know him either.

The man I did get to know was my stepfather Birdie, who had been a friend of my father since he was a teenager. He, too, grew up on Edgecombe Avenue, but he never finished high school and he never went to college. He dated my mother from the time we left my father's house and, in fact, it had been him who had moved us from Momma T's house to Momma Jones's house across the roof of the two adjacent apartment buildings. He was there at Christmas with the tree and the presents. He took us to the library and the movies and the park, while my mother kept up with her studies in college and then graduate school. He was kind, funny, and he liked to take us for walks through the old neighborhood and tell everybody that we were his daughters. This was actually quite amusing since he was very light and looked white, and we were just the opposite.

In May 1962, when I was ten years old, Faith married Birdie and he began to live with us. Almost from the very first day, I remember it as being a kind of a nightmare that wouldn't end. His own childhood had been hellish— although that wasn't the way he talked about it. He talked about it as though it was a joke and he had deserved the treatment he had gotten. His mother had left him at the hospital because she couldn't pay the bill. She had not come back to get him. His aunt had raised him with the help of her husband who worked in the post office. She was a violent alcoholic who went in and out of the mental hospital. Periodically, she would get drunk and put him out in the middle of the night. He would sleep in the hallway or on the roof. With a life like this, it should come as no surprise that he quit high school when he was sixteen and got a job, although he always said he was stupid for leaving school.

After he married my mother, I came to know him as very unpredictable and vulgar. Although he wasn't violent, I always thought he could be. I was very much afraid of him. I had never heard anyone curse the way he did and I now think that when the carload of men that he rode with stopped at a bar on their way back to Manhattan from Tarrytown, he, too, would drink too much, which would explain his erratic behavior. When I grew older, I learned by drinking with him that his mood could change radically when he drank.

He had very specific rules and regulations about how the house should be kept. My sister and I were not supposed to go in my parents' bedroom; we weren't supposed to eat in the livingroom; we were supposed to wash and dry all the dishes (my mother didn't do housework); we were supposed to have gone to bed hours before he got home. He worked the night-shift at General Motors and when he would get home about 3 a.m., he would often wake us all up, including my mother, if he thought his rules weren't being kept. Cursing and screaming, he would then chase my mother around and threaten to beat her or threaten to beat us. Eventually he would calm down and just want to talk. Sometimes, if it wasn't a school night or if it was in the summer, he would go out to get ice cream or some other snack for us. Then he would tell stories about his childhood and how he was treated. He would tell us how lucky we were.

I had my first sexual experience not long after Faith and Birdie were married while riding to school on the elevated train that passed in front of our building. A man, whose face I never saw and whose race I can't remember, felt me up. I was too terrified to protest and he never said a word.

I don't remember ever talking about sex with my mother. On the other hand, my stepfather rarely talked about anything else. The way he talked about it was to tell us stories, often quite humorous, about his own tendency as a young man to exploit unsuspecting females. The point of these conversations, which he was only too happy to make explicit, was that men could not be trusted: they only wanted one thing and we would be better off to never let them have it. If we insisted upon having sex though, we should use a condom, which he called a raincoat.

During those years he and my mother often broke up but they always went back together again. It was my mother's idea that she needed his financial support and his "firm hand" to raise us. Although she was and is a brilliant artist and a feminist, I'll admit I never understood this attitude. Admittedly, since those times (the worst of which I have not described), he has slowly changed, even mellowed. I suspect he's sorry now for the way he acted then, although he has never said so. Perhaps because of this, it has taken a long time to finally concede that he has become a different man, no longer the man that terrorized me.

When I began to date as a teenager in Harlem, I expected and found no better men than my father and step-father had been. I expected and found hostility, anger, competition, violence, dishonesty, misogyny and ignorance. These experiences had a lot to do with my "theories" about black men and black male/female relationships as a black feminist. The story I've told doesn't make those "theories" any less true or untrue. It simply makes them less global. I am not saying that there aren't some black men out there who are mean to women and, indeed, I see this meanness as a political issue in our community. What I am saying is that I was not actually aware then that there was any other kind of man.

When I wrote *The Myth of the Superwoman*, I was warned by my agent and editor that it was extremely risky for me to tell the story of my confinement at seventeen in a juvenile home. Indeed, it would have been risky, or at least trans-gressive, if I had told the whole story of the family turbu-lence that led to my being placed there. Needless to say, it was a much more complicated and important affair than I talked about in the book. Only in recent years, have I begun to come to the defense of that little girl, to listen to her story instead of taking my mother's side against her. This is not so easy to do because, through fear, I had been learning for years to ignore and discount her.

I made some kind of realization in that Catholic home that allowed me to become a feminist. I think it had to do with listening to the little girl inside of me in the form of other little girls who clearly had been abused, neglected and deprived. I was quite certain that I had never been abused, neglected and deprived; that whatever had happened was my fault entirely. Now I am no longer convinced of that. It is my own story I want to listen to now, but I am only at the beginning of doing so. Meanwhile it seems almost impossible to get many black women to believe this is important despite the success in the marketplace of black women's writing. Historically, it is not at all unusual for black women to find their stories difficult and embarrassing to tell.

The first novel by a black woman was Harriet Wilson's *Our Nig*, written in the 1860s about the racist way she was treated as an indentured servant in the North. Feeling that she couldn't afford to give offense to white abolitionists who insisted that the enemy was the slave-owning class of the South, she handled the problem by writing a "novel" about a character named Frado. Her autobiographical account is thus translated into the third person and, by her own admission, she "purposely omitted what would most provoke shame in our good anti-slavery friends at home." Frado's white, unmarried mother had abandoned her as a child. As an adult, Frado married a fake fugitive of slavery, who abandoned her as well. These "realistic" features broke with the sentimental conventions of women's fiction in the nineteenth century, and thus helped to doom her work to obscurity. When I wrote *Black Macho*, Wilson's book was completely unknown. It wasn't until 1983 that Afro-American literary critic Henry Louis Gates, Jr. rediscovered it and helped to get it republished in a new edition.

I find myself much more sympathetic now to two other black female writers of the same period whom I mention extensively in *Black Macho*: Harriet Jacobs and Charlotte Forten Grimke. While I then criticized them both for Victorian scruples unnatural and self-contemptuous in black women, Afro-American literary criticism has enabled us to see them in an entirely different way now.

In the introduction to an annotated edition of *Incidents in the Life of a Slave Girl*, Jean Fagin Yellin establishes that Jacobs did, in fact, write her own narrative instead of having dictated it to the white abolitionist Lydia Maria Child, as was once thought. This makes her the only black female to have actually written her own slave narrative in the tradition of Frederick Douglass and so many other black male ex-slaves. When we think about this, we begin to see the sentimentalism of her text in another light. Harriet Jacobs had no alternative other than to publicly acknowledge that she had willingly had sex with a man outside of marriage, in order to tell the story of her life as a slave and her escape. It was precisely the signs of her reluctance—her use of a pseudonym, her deployment of the tactics of conventional nineteenth-century women's fiction and her insistence that she managed to escape the lust of her cruel master—that made black literary scholarship denigrate the value and authenticity of her narrative for so many years.

Charlotte Forten Grimke, too, was until recently lost to us as the middle-class black girl of the nineteenth century of Ray Allen Billington's invention, via his 1953 condensed edition of her journals. The more complete journals were only made available in 1988 in *The Schomburg Library of Nineteenth Century Black Women Writers*, again edited by Henry Louis Gates, Jr. Brenda Stevenson's sensitive introduction to that edition, and the expanded text, shows Forten to have been a sad young woman whose mother died when she was a baby and whose father virtually abandoned her as a child. Although she was produced by the union of two of the best abolitionist families in black Philadelphia, she was for most of her life barely able to scrape by financially. She suffered from respiratory ailments and was almost always too sick to work. Her ambition was to be a poet but financial necessity dictated that she be a teacher, work that she didn't much like although it was still a rare privilege for a black woman then. Her interesting black abolitionist family seems to have caused her as much grief as comfort but it should come as no surprise that Charlotte, who was deeply religious and self-sacrificing, rarely allowed herself to write about their problems in detail. The only person she ever really criticizes is herself.

It has been my intention in writing this new introduction to *Black Macho and the Myth of the Superwoman* to talk about why my views have changed and how I came to write some of the things I wrote in 1978. It has been much harder than I expected. When I first re-read the book in preparation for writing this, my immediate gut response was to destroy the book so that no one would ever read it again. How many black women writers, in the twentieth, nineteenth, or even eighteenth centuries have thought and done precisely this?

I wanted to destroy the book because my desire for something more from life than my marginal status as a black woman writer could ever offer was so palpable in its pages. In obsessively repeating the stereotypes of black women and black men, I wanted to burst free of them forever. However, this has only been slightly more possible for me than it was for Harriet Wilson, Harriet Jacobs and Charlotte Forten. But perhaps if we can begin to claim our own words and our own feelings within the public sphere, we will seize the means of re-producing our own history, and freedom will become a possibility in a sense that it never has been before.

New York, 1990

PART I

Black Macho

They face each other, the Negro and the African, over a gulf of three hundred years—an alienation too vast to be conquered in an evening's good-will, too heavy and too double-edged ever to be trapped in speech. This alienation causes the Negro to recognize that he is a hybrid. Not a physical hybrid merely: in every aspect of his living he betrays the memory of the auction block and the impact of the happy ending. In white Americans he finds reflected—repeated, as it were, in a higher key—his tensions, his terrors, his tenderness. Dimly and for the first time, there begins to fall into perspective the nature of the roles they have played in the lives and history of each other. Now he is bone of their bone, flesh of their flesh; they have loved and hated and obsessed and feared each other and his blood is in their soil. Therefore he cannot deny them, nor can they ever be divorced.

(James Baldwin, "Encounter on the Seine: Black Meets Brown," *Notes of a Native Son,* New York: Dial, 1955.)

1

You could have called the New Lincoln School in New York a radical integrationist's dream. Small and private, with about five hundred students from third to twelfth grade, it was located on the very boundary of the ghetto—110th Street, Central Park North—sandwiched between black Harlem on the west and Puerto Rican Harlem on the east. The teachers were mostly well-intentioned Wasps. For a while there was a black principal. The student body was predominantly Jewish—a hodgepodge of performers', intellectuals' and ordinary capitalists' children. A quarter of the kids were black, mostly middle class with a sprinkling of semighetto bunnies on half and full scholarships. The blue jeans uniform was worn by one and all. Everyone rode the city buses—some going south toward the doormen and canopies of Park Avenue, others to destinations farther north deep into the bar and storefront-church haven of the slums.

I entered New Lincoln in 1963, in the seventh grade, and got along passably well. There was, of course, racism, but it tended to be the subtlest kind. New Lincoln's attitude was quite casual about certain things that might have provoked the outright racist. During any given year, for example, at least a handful of black girls were dating white boys. Only the black students seemed to be occasionally disturbed by this. The spec-

3

tacle of black girls fawning over white boys was perhaps rightly seen as an indication of white fever; even then it was considered bad form to make such tastes conspicuous. When gossip was scant, the subject was hotly debated by the blacks. But mostly, interracial dating was tolerated in silence, if not totally ignored, by everyone.

But then we had no black consciousness. The Civil Rights Movement had been going on for most of our lives but it had not yet challenged the notion of white superiority. By suggesting that it was better to be near whites than not to be, that the morality of whites was not substandard but merely sluggish and in need of awakening, the Civil Rights Movement had condemned itself to the category of more-of-the-same in our book. The Movement had yet to intrude upon the frustration of our daily lives. Even at the exemplary New Lincoln, black kids still refused to eat watermelon when it was served for lunch. We weren't black—the word was still an insult—we were just second-class white kids. During class discussions of race, we still squirmed in our seats and referred to ourselves as *colored*. Otherwise we did not refer to ourselves at all.

It was especially difficult for my classmates and me to identify with the struggle for the privilege of sitting at lunch counters and attending school with whites, since we were inclined to take such privileges for granted. Passive resistance also baffled us, perhaps because we and our families had been engaged in a lesser form of it up North for years and it had won us only the dubious distinction of being tolerated by whites— if we were well behaved. Or it may have been that the Civil Rights Movement only served to reinforce our sense of guilt, to aggravate the already painful awareness that other, poorer, less educated blacks were suffering in our stead.

The increasingly regular news coverage of blacks in the Civil Rights Movement—the bombings of churches and of buses full of black school children served to break through our surface sophistication about social intercourse with whites. The now highly visible plight of blacks in the South and the courage with which they fought became more immediate to us. The Civil Rights Act was passed in 1964 and the Voting Rights Act in 1965. Our position had changed. We black kids at New Lincoln began to gain something we had never had: an identity, beyond being the in-residence representatives of the losing side in Tarzan movies, beyond being the butt of endless suntan jokes. We were no longer spooks, but martyrs. If we looked evil, it wasn't because we hadn't had our daily pigfoot, or because "niggas just get that way sometimes," it was because we were victims of racism—a word that had never really been in our vocabularies before. If we were grinning, it wasn't because niggas were happy-go-lucky, but because of our moral superiority.

Nevertheless it wasn't the spectacle on the evening news so much as the appearance of a strangely related phenomenon that, more than anything else, made us aware that a new day was coming. Black boys at New Lincoln started dating white girls. And in the streets we could see interracial couples composed of black males and white females much more frequently.

1968 was the year that would revolutionize the way blacks were viewed in this country. SNCC, the nonviolent integrated student organization for peace and brotherly love, would become the all-black, nationalistic Snick for Black Power. SNCC had been founded by black students in 1960 at Shaw University in Raleigh, North Carolina, and was best known throughout its Civil Rights career for its dramatic style in grassroots organizing. By 1964 its membership had grown from sixteen to one hundred eighty, of whom half were white. Besides the more visible black male leadership, black women played an important role, as they did generally in the Civil Rights Movement. Yet women, both black and white, handled an inordinate

5

amount of typing, coffee making, housework, in addition to their other duties. Black and white women might have fought this inequality together if a certain situation had not rendered them mutually antagonistic. During the summer of 1964 hundreds of middle-class white women went South to work with the Movement and, in a fair number of cases, to have affairs with black men. Some of the women were pressured into having these affairs (anything to avoid the label of being racist), others freely chose to do so. The black men, by all accounts, were not unwilling and often eager. Occasionally the relationships were lasting or at least loving. Often they were abusive. Whatever the case, black women felt they were being shut out. Cynthia Washington, director of a freedom project in Mississippi in 1964, wrote about her experiences in SNCC:

We did the same work as men—organizing around voter registration and community issues in rural areas—usually with men. But when we finally got back to some town where we could relax and go out, the men went out with other women. Our skills and abilities were recognized and respected, but that seemed to place us in some category other than female. Some years later, I was told by a male SNCC worker that some of the project women had made him feel superfluous. I wish he had told me that at the time because the differences in the way women were treated certainly did add to the tension between black and white women. (Cynthia Washington, "We Started from Different Ends of the Spectrum," *Southern Exposure*, IV, 1964.)

Shortly after that summer, black women in SNCC complained to the male leadership that they could not develop relationships with black men as long as black men could so easily turn to involvement with white women. Ruby Doris Smith Robinson, a powerful black woman in SNCC, participated in and perhaps led a sit-in earlier that year in SNCC offices protesting the relegation of women to typing and clerical work. She is said to have written a paper on the position of black women in SNCC. The paper was lost and no one is quite certain of its content because Robinson died of cancer in 1968, but reputedly it prompted Stokely Carmichael to respond, "The only position of women in SNCC is prone."

With freedom presumably on the horizon, black men needed a movement that made the division of power between men and women clearer, that would settle once and for all the nagging questions black women were beginning to ask: Where do we fit in? What are you going to do about us? It was the restless throng of ambitious black female civil rights workers— as much as any failure of the Civil Rights Movement—that provoked Stokely Carmichael to cry "Black Power!"

On August 11, 1965, riots erupted in Watts, a black section of Los Angeles. The next morning an aide of Chief William H. Parker of the L. A. police said, "It was just a night to throw rocks at policemen." Five days later, thirty-five were dead, four thousand more had been arrested, and the major part of Watts was in ashes.

On May 29, 1966, Rep. Adam Clayton Powell of Harlem, then Chairman of the Education and Labor Committee, said at Howard University:

Human rights are God-given. Civil rights are manmade. . . . Our lives must be purposed to implement human rights. . . . To demand these God-given rights is to seek *black power*—the power to build black institutions of splendid achievement. (Chuck Stone, "The National Conference on Black Power," *The Black Power Revolt,* ed. Floyd B. Barbour, New York: Macmillan, 1968.)

One week later SNCC's chairman, Stokely Carmichael, was down in Greenville, Mississippi, where James Meredith, one of the first black graduates of Ole Miss, had begun his own march

7

from Memphis to Jackson, Mississippi, "to show courage and inspire it in other blacks." He was pretty much alone until someone took a shot at him. He immediately found himself surrounded by a motley crew of civil rights leaders: Dick Gregory, Martin Luther King, Floyd B. McKissick, and Carmichael. A struggle ensued among the principals. Carmichael had won by the time they reached Canton, Mississippi. The eyes of the world were upon him and he made the most of it. "Black Power," he said. "It's time we stand up and take over. Take over. Move on over or we'll move on over you."

Next Powell convened a Black Power Planning Conference on September third in Washington, D. C., which was attended by one hundred and sixty-nine delegates from thirty-seven cities, eighteen states, and sixty-four organizations. On March 1, 1967, the House of Representatives unseated Powell because of his refusal to face up to a libel conviction in New York.

Carmichael spoke at Nashville on April seventh and eighth. The second night, students at Fisk University rioted, crying, "Black Power." At Mississippi's Tougaloo College, Carmichael spoke of the "Nashville Rebellion." A month after his Mississippi tour black students at Jackson State rioted for several days. Four days later a gunfight between black students and police at Texas Southern University ended with one policeman dead, and three policemen and one student wounded. Four hundred and eighty-eight students were arrested.

On July thirteenth, that summer, Newark picked up where Watts had left off. After four days, twenty-six were dead, a thousand and four injured. Another four days later, on July twenty-first, the National Conference on Black Power convened in that city. One thousand black people from twenty-six states, two hundred and eighty-six different organizations and institutions and two foreign countries came together to discuss and define Black Power. Although such notable Civil Rights figures as Roy Wilkins, Philip Randolph, and Martin Luther

8

King either refused to come or were excluded, those who assembled were more than just a group of militant extremists. Just about every important labor union and religious, political, and social organization in the black community was represented. Given the diversity of the groups that participated, what they came up with was rather astounding. Only one resolution was officially passed—the Black Power Manifesto, part of which read:

It is, therefore, resolved that the National Conference on Black Power sponsor the creation of an International Black Congress, to be organized out of the soulful roots of our peoples and to reflect the new sense of power and revolution now blossoming in black communities in America and black nations throughout the world. (Stone, "The National Conference on Black Power," *The Black Power Revolt*.)

The Black Power Conference also adopted "in spirit" a resolution to "initiate a national dialogue on the desirability of partitioning the U. S. into separate and independent nations, one to be a homeland for white America and the other to be a homeland for black Americans" and it "proclaimed" the "right to self-defense."

On July 23, 1967, rioting began in Detroit. Forty-three people died, hundreds more were injured, seven thousand were arrested and five thousand left homeless. H. Rap Brown, the recently appointed chairman of SNCC, called the riots a "dress rehearsal for revolution."

That same fall the streets of New York witnessed the grand coming-out of black male/white female couples. Frankly, I found this confusing. I was enough of a slave to white liberal fashions to believe that two people who wanted each other had a right to each other, but was that what this was about? It all seemed strangely inappropriate, poorly timed. In '67, black was angry, anywhere from vaguely to militantly anti-white; black was sexy and had unlimited potential. What did the black man want with a white woman now?

The thing that convinced me that this situation had a broader meaning was the amazing way people were taking it. Some white women were quite blunt: They wanted black cock because it was the best cock there was. Educated, middle-class liberal white men, the very people who tended to be the first to make pronouncements on everything, were maintaining a curious silence whenever possible. Otherwise, they seemed to feel it was their duty to condone relationships between white women and black men because that would mean they weren't racist. Even the lower-class white man tended to simply look the other way. Black men often could not separate their interest in white women from their hostility toward black women. "I can't stand that black bitch," was the way it was usually put. Other black men argued that white women gave them money, didn't put them down, made them feel like men. And black women made no attempt to disguise their anger and disgust, to the point of verbal, if not physical, assaults in the streets—on the white woman or the black man or on both. Some black women would laugh low in their throats when they saw a black man with a white woman and make cracks about his high-water pants or his flat head or his walk, anything that might suggest that he was inadequate: "Only the rejects crawl for white pussy." Others feigned incredulity: "I mean really. How could he want a white woman when black women fuck better, cook better, dance better, party better. . . ."

Meanwhile 1967 got away from us and it was 1968. Dr. Martin Luther King, in a move that was definitely ahead of his time, was beginning to shift his emphasis from civil rights to economic issues and was planning a Poor People's March on Washington. In April Dr. King marched with a band of striking sanitation workers in Memphis. The garbage men wore signs that read, "I am a man."

On April 4 King was shot and the rioting began again, worse than ever. Praying, waiting, singing, and everything white were out. Rioting was viewed as urban guerrilla warfare, the first step toward the complete overthrow of the honky, racist government. On the cultural level everything had to be rehauled. Black poems, plays, paintings, novels, hairstyles, and apparel were springing up like weeds in Central Park. Brothers, with softly beating drums in the background, were talking about beautiful black Queens of the Nile and beautiful full lips and black skin and big asses. Yet the "problem" with the white sisters downtown persisted.

Some of the more militant sisters uptown would tell you that the "problem" was that white women were *throwing* themselves at black men and that if they would just let the man be, he'd come home. And, furthermore, there was this matter of a black matriarchy. Everybody wanted to cut Daniel Moynihan's heart out and feed it to the dogs, but he did have a point after all. The black woman had gotten out of hand. She was too strong, too hard, too evil, too castrating. She got all the jobs, all the everything. The black man had never had a chance. No wonder he wanted a white woman. He needed a rest. The black woman should be more submissive and, above all, keep her big, black mouth shut.

And the black woman started to do just that. She grumbled quietly to herself about the black man and the white woman. The Women's Movement came along, and she went right on trimming her Afro, having her babies for the revolution. Admirably thorough about not allowing a word of feminist rhetoric to penetrate their thinking, some black women even attacked the Women's Movement out of their feelings of inadequacy, shame, and hatred for white women. Others cleaned house and fried chicken. They just knew that their man, the black man, would not stand for no backtalk from no white girl. He was on his way home for sure. But they were wrong.

In retrospect, their mistake seems obvious. That young, educated, upwardly mobile, politically active and aware black men were taking an interest in white women had nothing to do with whether black women or white women were more docile, compliant, or attractive. White fever, which is no more than the love of white skin, had something to do with it, but even that didn't really get to the heart of the matter. That black women had for many years been overtly and covertly available to white men contributed to the fury with which some black men pursued white women, but that wasn't the whole story either.

There was a misunderstanding between the black man and the black woman, a misunderstanding as old as slavery; the I.O.U. was finally being called in. Apart from some occasional drunken ranting on a street corner, the black man had held his silence admirably for centuries. The Moynihan Report, as preposterous a document as it was, combined with the heady atmosphere of the times to loosen the black man's tongue. The Moynihan Report said that the black man was not so much a victim of white institutional racism as he was of an abnormal family structure, its main feature being an employed black woman. This report did not *create* hostility. It merely helped to bring the hostility to the surface. The result was a brain-shattering explosion upon the heads of black women, the accumulation of over three hundred years of rage. The black woman did not, could not, effectively fight back. No one had written a report for her. It was a man's world. And guilt had silenced her. What could she say when the black man cried that the black woman had never believed in him, had hated him in fact? It wasn't entirely untrue. She could not completely deny it. And even her response that she was his mother, that she had made his survival possible, was made to sound feeble and was turned against her.

Now that freedom, equality, rights, wealth, power were assumed to be on their way, she had to understand that manhood was essential to revolution—unquestioned, unchallenged, unfettered manhood. Could you imagine Ché Guevara with breasts? Mao with a vagina? She was just going to have to get out of the way. She had had her day. Womanhood was not essential to revolution. Or so everyone thought by the end of the 1960s.

I am saying, among other things, that for perhaps the last fifty years there has been a growing distrust, even hatred, between black men and black women. It has been nursed along not only by racism on the part of whites but also by an almost deliberate ignorance on the part of blacks about the sexual politics of their experience in this country.

As the Civil Rights Movement progressed, little attention was devoted to an examination of the historical black male/female relationship, except for those aspects of it that reinforced the notion of the black man as the sexual victim of "matriarchal" tyranny. The result has been calamitous. The black woman has become a social and intellectual suicide; the black man, unintrospective and oppressive.

It is from this perspective that the black man and woman faced the challenge of the Black Revolution—a revolution subsequently dissipated and distorted by their inability to see each other clearly through the fog of sexual myths and fallacies. They have gone on alternately idealizing and vilifying their relationships, very rarely finding out what they are really made of. This has cost them a great deal. It has cost them unity, for one thing.

Though I am a black feminist, and that label rightly suggests that I feel black men could stand substantial improvement, I still find it difficult to blame them alone. Black men have had no greater part than black women in perpetuating the ignorance with which they view one another. The black man, however, particularly since the Black Movement, has been in the position to define the black woman. He is the one who tells her whether or not she is a woman and what it is to be a woman. And therefore, whether he wishes to or not, he determines her destiny as well as his own.

Though originally it was the white man who was responsible for the black woman's grief, a multiplicity of forces act upon her life now and the black man is one of the most important. The white man is downtown. The black man lives with her. He's the head of her church and may be the principal of her local school or even the mayor of the city in which she lives.

She is the workhorse that keeps his house functioning, she is the foundation of his community, she raises his children, and she faithfully votes for him in elections, goes to his movies, reads his books, watches him on television, buys in his stores, solicits his services as doctor, lawyer, accountant.

She has made it quite clear that she has no intention of starting a black woman's liberation movement. One would think she was satisfied, yet she is not. The black man has not really kept his part of the bargain they made when she agreed to keep her mouth shut in the sixties. When she stood by silently as he became a "man," she assumed that he would subsequently grant her her long overdue "womanhood," that he would finally glorify and dignify black womanhood just as the white man had done for the white woman. But he did not. He refused her. His involvement with white women was only the most dramatic form that refusal took. He refused her across the board. He refused her because he could not do anything else. He refused her because the assertion of his manhood required something quite different of him. He refused her because it was too late to carbon-copy the traditional white male/female relationships. And he refused her because he felt justified in his anger. He claimed that she had betrayed him.

14

And she believed that, even as she denied it. She too was angry, but paralyzed by the feeling that she had no right to be.

Therefore her strange numbness, her determination, spoken or unspoken, to remain basically unquestioning of the black man's authority and thereby seemingly supportive of all he has done, even that which has been abusive of her. She is in the grip of Black Macho and it has created within her inestimable emotional devastation.

The black woman's silence is a new silence. She knows that. Not so long ago it would have been quite easy to find any number of black women who would say with certainty, "A nigga man ain't shit." Perhaps more to the point, there has been from slavery until the Civil Rights Movement a thin but continuous line of black women who have prodded their sisters to self-improvement. These women were of the opinion that being a woman did not exempt one from responsibility. Just like a man, a woman had to struggle to deliver the race from bondage and uplift it. In their time a woman's interest in herself was not automatically interpreted as hostile to men and their progress, at least not by black people. Day to day these women, like most women, devoted their energies to their husbands and children. When they found time, they worked on reforms in education, medicine, housing, and their communities through their organizations and churches. Little did they know that one day their activities would be used as proof that the black woman has never known her place and has mightily battled the black man for his male prerogative as head of the household.

The American black woman is haunted by the mythology that surrounds the American black man. It is a mythology based upon the real persecution of black men: castrated black men hanging by their necks from trees; the carcasses of black men floating face down in the Mississippi; black men with their

bleeding genitals jammed between their teeth; black men shining shoes; black men being turned down for jobs time and time
again; black men watching helplessly as their women go to
work to support the family; black men behind bars, persecuted
by prison guards and police; jobless black men on street cor-
ners, with needles in their arms, with wine bottles in their hip
pockets; black men being pushed out in front to catch the
enemy's bullets in every American war since the Revolution of
1776—these ghosts, rendered all the more gruesome by their
increasing absence of detail, are crouched in the black woman's
brain. Every time she starts to wonder about her own misery,
to think about reconstructing her life, to shake off her devotion
and feeling of responsibility to everyone but herself, the ghosts
pounce. She is stopped cold. The ghosts talk to her. *"You*
crippled the black man. *You* worked against him. *You* betrayed
him. *You* laughed at him. *You* scorned him. *You* and the white
man."

Not only does the black woman continue to see the black
man historically as a cripple, she refuses to take seriously the
various ways he's been able to assert his manhood and capabilities in recent years. Granted that many of his gains of the past
decade have been temporary and illusory; but he is no longer
a pathetic, beaten-down slave (if indeed he ever was only that).
He's grown, progressed, developed as a man, and if one recog-
nizes him as a man he must begin to carry some measure of
responsibility for what happens to him. But none of this matters to the black woman. Whether he is cast as America's latest
sex object, king of virility and violence, master of the ghetto
art of cool, or a Mickey Mouse copy of a white capitalist,
she pities him. She sees only the masses of unemployed black
men, junkies, winos, prison inmates. She does not really see
the masses of impoverished, unemployed black women,
their numerous children pulling at their skirts; or, if she
does, she sees these women and children only as a further

humiliation and burden to that poor, downtrodden black man.

She sees only the myth. In fact what most people see when they look at the black man is the myth.

American slavery was a dehumanizing experience for everyone involved. Both black men and women were forced to labor without compensation, to live in an environment totally controlled by their owners, and to live with the fact that their children could not expect any better. They were compelled to accept the quasibenevolence of the Anglo-Saxon patriarchy that was the plantation system, and the relentless deculturalization process that eventually rid them of most of the apparent manifestations of their African origin. In addition, many blacks, male and female, were underfed, overworked, and physically abused. Yet somehow the story goes that the black man suffered a very special and particularly debilitating kind of denigration because, as a slave, he was not permitted to fulfill his traditional role as a man, that is as head of his family, sole provider and protector. Here are some versions of this story:

For the Negro child, in particular, the plantation offered no really satisfactory father-image other than the master. The "real" father was virtually without authority over his child, since discipline, parental responsibility, and control of rewards and punishments all rested in other hands; the slave father could not even protect the mother of his children except by appealing directly to the master. Indeed, the mother's own role loomed far larger for the slave child than did that of the father. She controlled those few activities—household care, preparation of food, and rearing of children—that were left to the slave family. For that matter, the very etiquette of plantation life removed even the honorific attributes of fatherhood from the Negro male, who was addressed as "boy"—until, when the vigorous years of his prime were past, he was allowed to assume the title of "uncle." (Stanley Elkins, "Slavery and Personality," *Slavery: A Problem in American Institutional and Intellectual Life,* Chicago: University of Chicago Press, 1959.)

After black women were brought over to the New World, they served as breeders of children who were treated as property, and as the gratifiers of white plantation owners' carnal desires. More importantly, they became the central figure in black family life. The black man's only crucial function within the family was that of siring the children. The mother's role was far more important than the father's. She cleaned the house, prepared the food, made clothes and raised the children. The husband was at most his wife's assistant, her companion and her sex partner. He was often thought of as her possession, as was the cabin in which they lived. It was common for a mother and her children to be considered a family without reference to the father. (Robert Staples, "The Myth of the Impotent Black Male," *Contemporary Black Thought: The Best from The Black Scholar*, ed. Robert Chrisman and Nathan Hare, New York: Bobbs-Merrill, 1973.)

The black man in America has always been expected to function as less than a man; this was taken for granted, and was the ugliest weight of his enslavement. The liberal white man has always promised the de-testicled black some progress to manhood. In other words, "We will let your balls grow back . . . one day! Just be cool." In slavery times, theoretically, the slave master could make it with any black woman he could get to. The black man was powerless to do anything to prevent it; many times he was even powerless to keep his woman with him, or his children. One effect of this largely one-sided "integration" was to create a very deep hatred and suspicion in the black man for any black woman who had dealings with white men. This is a feeling that still exists. (LeRoi Jones, "American Sexual Reference: Black Male," *Home*, New York: William Morrow, 1966.)

The picture drawn for us over and over again is of a man who is a child, who is the constant victim of an unholy alliance between his woman and the enemy, the white man. It is an emotional interpretation but it has also been used by the contemporary black man to justify his oppression of the black woman, to justify his getting ahead by walking over her pros-

18

trate body. "I don't owe you anything, black woman because (1) you sold me out and (2) you've always been ahead anyway." The facts are a good deal more complicated and ambiguous.

The slave family was constantly subject to disruption by sales of children, of father and mother. Black women did have sex with and bear children for their white masters. The slave father did lack traditional authority over his family. He could not control the destinies of either his wife or his children. For the most part he could not provide for them and protect them. But to accept these features of slavery as the entire picture is to accept that the character of life in the black slave community was solely a product of white oppression.

Despite the obstacles, the slave family was often a stable entity. Herbert Gutman points out in *The Black Family in Slavery and Freedom* (New York: Random House, 1977.) that most black families were headed by a stable male/female partnership, by a husband and a wife. Slaves were not usually required by their masters to form permanent unions, but they did nevertheless exist in great quantities. That fact suggests that blacks, both males and females, took traditional marriage and all it entailed, including male authority, quite seriously.

Yes, black men were called boys. Black women were also called girls. But the slaves thought of themselves as "mens and womens." That so many slave narratives show evidence of great attachment for fathers would indicate that the father/child relationship was not taken lightly. Both male and female children were frequently named after dead or sold-away male relatives.

Eugene Genovese suggests in *Roll, Jordan, Roll* that despite the persistence with which whites insisted that blacks were not human, blacks continually found ways to exert their own humanity. There were cases of black women who were raped as their husbands looked on, powerless to do anything about it. There were also cases of men who fought to the death to prevent such things. Most of the women who engaged in interracial unions were probably single. And, although many were unwilling, some were not. Some won certain advantages by it. A large percentage of the free class of blacks were products of such unions. It is impossible to say just how often black women and white men had sexual relations during slavery. There can't be any doubt that it was fairly often but not all of it was strictly abusive. There was also some sexual contact between black male slaves and white women. White men did not seem to become obsessed with preventing such relations until much later.

The slaves were bound by a system that denied them the right to perpetuate their sexual relations and family life in the way they might have liked. But there were certain limitations to the abuse, even laws that slaveholders put on the books in order to better state their case that slavery was beneficial to blacks. Blacks frequently expanded upon these "rights" and turned them to their own advantage. Genovese, who is the author of this thesis, is quite convincing on the subject. There were also ways in which blacks were able to exercise a limited authority and to project an image of black accomplishment. These were available to both men and women.

A slave woman really had four ways in which to distinguish herself. The first way was by excelling at physical labor. The reports tell us of women who could pick cotton faster, haul more, and so on, than any man for miles around. The ability to do heavy labor was of paramount importance on the old Southern plantation. Whereas women who were sensitive, delicate, and fragile suffered a great deal in slavery (and there were a great many such women), women who were physically strong and robust were highly valued by the slave community.

Secondly, there were women who rose above the common lot by becoming the sex partners of their masters. Sometimes their white owners lived openly with them as wives. More often they and their children were given their freedom upon the master's death. But this path was also fraught with risk. Such women were sometimes the victims of special abuse, were sold away to avoid scandal in the larger white community and embarrassment to the master's wife.

The third way a black woman slave might achieve some status was as a mammy. The mammy is a hated figure in black history and perhaps with good reason. Legend has it that she often controlled the household, its white members as well, that she was sometimes overly loyal to her master and guarded his wealth and position with great vigor. But she also served a function that was useful to the slave community. She might intercede in behalf of a slave and prevent his being punished, and she often provided much of the information from the big house.

The fourth way for a black woman to be set apart from the ordinary slaves was as a house servant with a special skill. She might be a laundress, a weaver, a spinner, and, as a good worker, she might come to be greatly valued by the master. But here again the record also shows that she was often the victim of special abuse and suffered under the constant eye of her mistress.

The distinctions available to black male slaves were actually somewhat more impressive and more varied. First, men might become artisans, craftsmen, mechanics. These men were among the most respected members of the slave community and were frequently allowed to take some percentage of their wages when they were hired out. Second, black men might become drivers or even de facto overseers. The black driver, another hated figure in black history, had the job of seeing that the slaves performed well in the fields. Sometimes he was vicious. On occasion he might force some of the slave women to have sex with him. But sometimes he was lenient. Clearly he was an important tool of the master class, but he also benefited the slave community in that he was a living example of a black man in a position of authority, and he helped counter the notion of the black man as a boy.

A black male slave might also distinguish himself in ways comparable to those available to women slaves. For example, he might become the body servant, butler, or coachman of his master. As such, he might, over the years, win a great deal of trust and subsequent authority. And of course it was often the black male, not the female, who won prestige through his achievements in field labor. In addition black men won influence in the slave community by fighting in the American Revolution and then in the War of 1812. Many slaves reported proudly that some male ancestor had fought for his country.

Lastly, it was the men, in all cases, who planned and/or led the slave revolts. Although women participated, every known slave plot or actual rebellion was the result of male initiative.

Viewing American slavery with any kind of objectivity is extremely difficult, mostly because the record was unevenly and inconsistently kept. Nevertheless we can surely doubt the assumption that the black man was totally robbed of his manhood and divested of his authority over the black woman. The system of slavery did much to undermine that authority, but there were certain loopholes in the system; these, combined with the black man's strength and the black woman's determination to maintain what she saw as her role as a woman, left the black man with a challenged but very much intact "manhood." To suggest that the black man was emasculated by slavery is to suggest that the black man and the black woman were creatures without will. Slave men and women formed a coherent and, as much as possible, a beneficial code of behavior, values, and mores, a culture, a way of seeing and dealing with life, that was based upon the amalgamation of their African past and the forced realities of their American experience —in other words, an African-American culture.

Yet the myth of the black man's castration in slavery, or at least the joint participation of the white man and the black woman in a ruthless attempt to castrate him, has been nurtured over a century—along with the black man's contempt for the mostly imaginary self-sufficiency of the black woman. But the presumed dominance of the black female during slavery would not be quite enough to explain the full extent of black male anger, especially since it was more untrue than not, and at some point the black man must have known that. Rather his actual gripe must be, at least in part, that the black woman, his woman, was not *his* slave, that his right to expect her complete service and devotion was usurped. She *was*, after all, the white man's slave.

There can be no doubt that the role of patriarch was made virtually impossible for the black man during slavery and ex-tremely inconvenient afterward. Nevertheless, the record shows that black men and black women emerged from slavery in twos, husbands and wives. It was mostly after slavery that the fear white men had of black men began to take some of its more lascivious forms. It was then that the myth of the black man's sexuality, the myth of the black man as sexual monster, as a threat to pure white womanhood, began to gain force. After the ill-fated Reconstruction period came the rise of the Ku Klux Klan, the thousands of lynchings, and the group effort on the part of white men to sever the black man's penis from his body and render him economically unable to provide for his family, despite his legal freedom.

How did the black family respond to this pressure? For the most part it continued its two-by-two stride, husbands and wives, solid families. And they continued the tradition of adap-tation that had marked the evolution of the Afro-American family from slavery. There was the pressure of the American white standard but there was also the standard that black Americans had set for themselves; they understood very well that they were not white. Slave rule, as described by Gutman, provided for trial marriage, for pregnancy followed by marriage —for some degree of sexual experimentation prior to settling down. All of which had precedents in African societies, as well as in most precapitalist agrarian societies. After marriage, however, adultery was considered intolerable. If possible the man worked and provided for all. If not the woman also worked. But at no point in American history have more black women been employed than black men.

Only as American blacks began to accept the standards for family life, as well as for manhood and womanhood embraced by American whites, did black men and women begin to resent one another. And as time went on their culture, under constant attack from the enemy, became more impoverished and dependent and left with fewer self-regenerating mechanisms.

The Americanized black man's reaction to his inability to earn enough to support his family, his "impotence," his lack of concrete power, was to vent his resentment on the person in this society who could do least about it—his woman. His problem was that she was not a "woman." She, in turn, looked at the American ideal of manhood and took the only safe course her own fermenting rage and frustration could allow her. Her problem was that he was not a "man." But neither the black man's nor the black woman's view of their own or their mate's inadequacies was uniform, absolute, or suddenly arrived at. Both continued to feel a substantial group identity. For a long time their own unique Afro-American standard served to reinforce their sense of self-worth, but over the years blacks began to lean more and more toward Americanization —in their case, another word for self-hatred.

Slowly, as the black man began to see himself as America had defined him, he began to accept America's interpretation of his experience. Donald Bogle, the author of *Toms, Coons, Mulattoes, Mammies & Bucks: An Interpretive History of Blacks in American Films* (New York: Viking Press, 1973.), advances an intriguing theory. According to him, *Uncle Tom's Cabin* and the later *Birth of a Nation* gave us a set of black stereotypes out of which have come all subsequent characterizations of blacks in American film.

The male stereotypes were Toms, Coons, and Bucks. We are all familiar with Uncle Tom. He is devoted to whites, religious, hard working, loyal, trustworthy, patient, and restrained. The Coon is happy-go-lucky, a clown, a buffoon, a child, clever and witty but unable to perform the most simple task without guidance. He's a trickster, cunning and resourceful. The third stereotype, the Buck, made his last appearance prior to the seventies in *The Birth of a Nation*. The Buck is the only black stereotype that is sexual. He is brutal, violent, virile, tough, strong—and finds white women especially appealing. By constitution he is unable to smile and grovel like the Coon and the Uncle Tom. He is the personification of the black threat to white womanhood and, more importantly, to white male authority and dominance. The Buck is the stereotype, the nightmare, that whites could not handle, and thus he disappeared and did not make his appearance again, Bogle tells us, until the black movies of the seventies such as *Shaft, Superfly,* et al. In other words, rebellion as well as compliance had been determined by whites.

A similar thing occurred in the day-to-day life of the black man. As his Americanization became more and more total, he was conditioned to define his rebellion in terms of the white nightmare. He accepted as appropriate the white man's emphasis on his sexuality. And he accepted as sincere the white man's reasons for trying to abort his sexuality.

The Ku Klux Klan, the lynch mob, and Jim Crow legislators said their task was to prevent the black man from violating sacred white womanhood. In pursuit of this mission, thousands of black men were lynched, murdered, degraded, their homes destroyed. Sacred white womanhood had been an economically necessary assumption under the slavery system. It had also been necessary to assume that black women were promiscuous and fickle and gave no more thought to their offspring than pigs did to their litters. Therefore whites might sell black children with impunity. But the white woman would be the mother of the little man who would inherit the white man's fortune. One had to be certain of the child's origin. Thus the white woman's purity, like the black female's promiscuity, was based upon her status as property. After slavery, when the lynching began, white men could not with any kind of dignity admit their sexual fears of black men. But there was good economic reason to perpetuate those fears. The less there was for black men, the more for them. There were many fewer penises cut off than there were men who were kept out of jobs and prevented from making a living. But all of this, the black man was to believe, was in order to protect the white woman.

Thirty Years of Lynching in the United States (New York: Arno Press, 1970.), compiled by the NAACP, reported that between 1889 and 1918, 3,224 persons had been killed by lynch mobs; 2,838 of the killings were in the South and 78 percent of the victims were black. It also pointed out that "less than one in five of the colored victims have been accused of rape or 'attacks on women.' " Despite this, Susan Brownmiller points out in *Against Our Will,* her study on rape in America, that the effort mounted to stop the lynching of blacks aimed much of its venom at that hysterical, frigid, masochistic Southern white woman.

. . . it took a woman, a Viennese disciple of Freud who had probably ventured no farther south than Boston, to provide the clincher. . . . Once Dr. Helene Deutsch laid down her dictum of the hysterical, masochistic female, it was adopted with astonishing speed by those who wanted, or needed for their own peace of mind, to dilute white male responsibility for the Southern rape complex. . . .

The fact that the white men believe so readily the hysterical and masochistic fantasies and lies of the white women, who claim they have been assaulted and raped by Negroes, is related to the fact that they (the men) sense the unconscious wishes of the women, the psychic reality of these declarations, and react emotionally to them as if they were *real*. The social situation permits them to discharge this emotion upon the Negroes.

With this kind of argument the Left fought successfully to eradicate mob lynching and the institutional murder of black men in the South, but there were some undesirable side effects. As Susan Brownmiller pointed out, the fallacy was perpetuated that the charge of rape was almost never justified, because women who charged rape were having masochistic fantasies.

As Southern white men continued to round up black men, lynch them or try them in a courtroom and give them the maximum sentence for the holy purpose of "protecting their women," Northern liberals looking at the ghastly pattern through an inverted prism saw the picture of a lying white woman crying rape-rape-rape. (Susan Brownmiller, *Against Our Will*, New York: Simon & Shuster, 1975.)

But more importantly, the notion of the black man's access to white women as a prerequisite of his freedom was reinforced. These ideas shaped the minds of both those white women who came South as part of the Civil Rights Movement and the black men who met them.

The Till case became a lesson of instruction to an entire generation of appalled Americans. I know how I reacted. At age twenty and for a period of fifteen years after the murder of Emmett Till whenever a black teen-ager whistled at me on a New York City street or uttered in passing one of several variations on an invitation to congress, I smiled my nicest smile of comradely equality—no supersensitive flower of white womanhood, I. . . . After all, were not women for flirting? Wasn't a whistle or a murmured "May I fuck you?" an innocent compliment? And did not white women in particular have to bear the white man's burden of making amends for Southern racism? (Brownmiller, *Against Our Will.*)

I saw in a magazine a picture of the white woman with whom Emmett Till was said to have flirted. While looking at the picture, I felt that little tension in the center of my chest I experience when a woman appeals to me. I was disgusted and angry with myself. Here was a woman who had caused the death of a black, possibly because, when he looked at her, he also felt the same tensions of lust and desire in his chest—and probably for the same general reasons that I felt them. . . . I looked at the picture again and again, and in spite of everything and against my will and the hate I felt for the woman and all that she represented, she appealed to me. I flew into a rage at myself, at America, at white women, at the history that had placed those tensions of lust and desire in my chest. . . . (Eldridge Cleaver, *Soul on Ice*, New York: McGraw-Hill, 1965.)

So the black man's Americanization meant more for him than just his coming to view the deviation of his woman from the American ideal as an affront to his manhood. Since he had also come to think of himself in largely physical terms, the inaccessibility of the white woman represented a severe limitation of his manhood.

Around the time that Shirley Chisolm was running for President in 1972, Redd Foxx, the black comedian and television star, made a joke about her. He said that he would prefer Raquel Welch to Shirley Chisolm any day. The joke was widely publicized, particularly in the black community, and thought quite funny. There was something about it that made black men pay attention, repeat it, savor it.

Shirley Chisolm was the first black woman to run for the office of President of the United States. She had shown by her congressional record, her fiery speeches, and her decision to run a spunk that America hadn't seen in a black woman since Fannie Lou Hamer. The black political forces in existence at the time—in other words, the black male political forces—did not support her. In fact, they actively opposed her nomination. The black man in the street seemed either outraged that she dared to run or simply indifferent.

Ever since then it has really baffled me to hear black men say that black women have no time for feminism because being black comes first. For them, when it came to Shirley Chisolm, being black no longer came first at all. It turned out that what they really meant all along was that the black man came before the black woman. And not only did he come before her, he came before her to her own detriment. The proof is that, as soon as Shirley Chisolm announced her intention to run, black men pulled out their big guns and aimed them at her. They made every attempt to humiliate her, not only as a political being but also as a sexual being.

That blacks fought against Chisolm was a setback for all black people, but it was even more of a setback for black men. The reaction of black men to Chisolm's campaign, a reaction they made no attempt at all to conceal, marked the point at which the Black Movement breathed its last as a viable entity. Black male hostility to Chisolm exploded any illusion that blacks might actually be able to sustain a notion of themselves apart from America's racist/sexist influence, a notion essential to their autonomy and inner direction.

Redd Foxx's joke expressed the comparisons black men were making between black women and white women: responsibility, always tiresome, versus the illusion of liberation and freedom. In some sense, every ethnic group of men wishes to be free of its women for similar reasons. However, although Jewish male comedians are famous for making fun of what is, essentially, the "Jewishness" of their wives, it would never have occurred to a Henny Youngman or an Alan King to make a crack about preferring Raquel Welch to Golda Meir, at least not in public. We black men, Redd Foxx's joke seemed to say, are more interested in going to bed with Raquel Welch than we are in having a black president.

Redd Foxx was at the time NBC's shining star as the lead character in *Sanford and Son.* And I am told that he was financially crucial to them then. Week after week he presented his characterization of the black man as wine guzzling, lazy, idiotic, and strongly contemptuous of all black women except his wife, who was conveniently dead. He felt comfortable enough with white racist Americans to laugh with them about the comparative sexual merits of Shirley Chisolm, his leading black woman politician, and Raquel Welch, a white sex symbol. Surely the white man was laughing all the way to the bank.

The black man of the 1960s found himself wondering why it had taken him so long to realize he had an old score to settle. Yes, yes, he wanted freedom, equality, all of that. But what he really wanted was to be a man.

America had made one point painfully clear. As long as the black man did not have access to white women, he was not a man. The lynchings, murders, beatings, the miscegenation laws designed to keep the black man and the white woman apart while the white man helped himself to black women, created in him a tremendous sense of personal urgency on this matter. America had not allowed him to be a man. He wanted to be one. What bothered America most? The black man and the white woman. Therefore if he had a white woman, he would be more of a man. And as it became more and more apparent that white America would regard any serious bid for social, economic, and political equality as a declaration of full-scale war, the white woman/black man version of freedom began to make a great deal of sense.

But there was more to keep him busy. In 1965 the Moynihan Report on the black family said that the problem with blacks was not so much white racism as it was an "abnormal family structure." This abnormal family structure made it nearly impossible for blacks to benefit from and participate in the American power structure. And the primary feature of this abnormality was the "matriarch," the "strong black woman," the woman who had nearly as much or more education than the black man, who worked more frequently than the white woman, who had a greater percentage of professionals among her rank, though they were mostly nurses, teachers, and social workers, not doctors, lawyers, and Indian chiefs. In other words, Moynihan was suggesting that the existence of anything so subversive as a "strong black woman" precluded the existence of a strong black man or, indeed, any black "man" at all.

In books and articles the black man ripped into this argument and tore it apart. But it had brought his resentment to the surface. Moynihan had hit just the right note. Many might argue that the average black person has no idea of what is contained within the Moynihan Report. But just about any black person, when asked who is more oppressed, the black man or the black woman, would respond with some version of "Well, the black woman has always been liberated because she was able to find work when the black man couldn't get any." There were blacks who would have said that before Moynihan's report but they would have been more difficult to find; they would have been uncertain and willing to argue the point with you. Now they were certain, resolute in their conviction, and they presented this opinion with pride because they were saying something for which they knew there was full support in the black community. Moynihan did that. Moynihan bared the black man's awful secret for all to see—that he had never been able to make his woman get down on her knees.

Come 1966, the black man had two pressing tasks before him: a white woman in every bed and a black woman under every heel. Out of his sense of urgency came a struggle called the Black Movement, which was nothing more nor less than the black man's struggle to attain his presumably lost "manhood." And so America had tightened the noose, although it did not know it yet; by controlling the black man's notion of what a black man was supposed to be, it would successfully control the very goals of his struggle for "freedom."

But how was he to achieve those goals? By passive resistance, by sitting in at the Barbizon Hotel for Women, by laying his body down in front of the buses that carried black domestics to work? Theoretically the Civil Rights struggle was won with the passing of various kinds of civil rights legislation, but it had cost so many black lives. Blacks still couldn't sit down and eat a decent meal in a white restaurant because they couldn't pay for it. Their vote meant nothing because they had no one to vote for. And, as the final kick in the pants, the white man's mind had not changed one iota. The white man still saw the black man as "a nigga with a big dick" who was after his daughter. Rap Brown had not been wrong when he said that "violence is as American as cherry pie." When the black man had tried restraint, compassion, patience, cautiousness, peaceful means—those good old standards of dear Uncle Tom—the white man had responded in violence and hatred, as if to say "Nigga, you can't fool us. We know what you have in your pants. We know what you're really after." Sex. Violence. The two are really inseparable, aren't they? Who had the white man always been afraid of? Uncle Tom? No. Coon? No. It was that brutal buck who would come to get his daughter and his wife. And how would he come to get her? By ringing the front doorbell and inquiring politely? No. By force. What had that woman always symbolized to the white man? Everything that he owned, his domination. And it was that simple.

Certainly some black men continued to pursue a more decent and humane existence for all black people, and perhaps a majority continued to believe that that was what it was all about. But as far as the leadership was concerned, the struggle for human rights was more or less left behind with the Civil Rights Movement. To some degree this was because the Movement was largely shaped by those flamboyant aspects of it that particularly interested the white media. But black leadership played to the media and so did many black men on the corner. That was the message of Tom Wolfe's "Mau-Mauing the Flak Catchers" (*Radical Chic & Mau-Mauing the Flak Catchers*, New York: Farrar, Straus & Giroux, 1970.). There was more to the protest and furor of the sixties and seventies than an attempt to correct the concrete problems of black people. The real key was the carrot the white man had held just beyond the black man's nose for many generations, that imaginary resolution of all the black man's woes and discontent, something called manhood. It was the pursuit of manhood that stirred the collective imagination of the masses of blacks in this country and led them to almost turn America upside down.

2

It seems odd now that so many advocates of Black Power criticized the Civil Rights Movement for its romanticism. The Black Power Movement was probably one of the most fiercely romantic in America's history. Its agenda was quite simple. All economic and political control over the black communities was to be demanded and, if not given, taken by force out of white hands and delivered into black hands where, it was assumed, it would naturally begin to benefit black people. Methods for handling this control were hotly debated but generally thought to be less important than the control itself. Planning and organizing were sporadic at best. The most highly organized group the Movement had to offer was the Black Muslims, and even they were dependent upon the presumed righteousness of the Honorable Elijah Mohammed, a rather dubious presumption after the murder of Malcolm X.

We want what you owe us, Black Power leaders said. On the surface it sounded rational enough, but underneath a blind rage was working. Human fallibility among blacks was relegated to the realm of the impossible. If it was black, it was right. If it was white, it was wrong.

The driving force behind the movement had really very little to do with bread and butter needs. The motive was revenge. It was not equality that was primarily being pursued but a kind of superiority—black manhood, black macho—which would combine the ghetto cunning, cool, and unrestrained sexuality of black survival with the unchecked authority, control, and wealth of white power.

As Norman Mailer had predicted in his essay "The White Negro" (1957), the expectant emergence of this super black man threw the country into chaos:

Since the Negro knows more about the ugliness and danger of life than the white, it is probable that if the Negro can win his equality, he will possess a potential superiority, a superiority so feared that the fear itself has become the underground drama of domestic politics. Like all conservative political fear it is the fear of unforeseeable consequences, for the Negro's equality would tear a profound shift into the psychology, the sexuality, and the moral imagination of every white alive.

With this possible emergence of the Negro, Hip may erupt as a psychically armed rebellion whose sexual impetus may rebound against the antisexual foundation of every organized power in America, and bring into the air such animosities, antipathies, and new conflicts of interest that the mean empty hypocrisies of mass conformity will no longer work. A time of violence, new hysteria, confusion and rebellion will then be likely.... (Norman Mailer, *The White Negro*, San Francisco: City Lights, 1957.)

The headlines about the Black Muslims in 1964 left me with the impression that a resurrected Hannibal was marching upon New York with an army of seven-foot Watusis to eat all whites alive. The press—white men as sexual beings reacting to the threat of black men as sexual beings—was clearly swept up in that "new hysteria" Mailer had described. According to Stokely Carmichael, Black Power meant "Where black men have a majority, they will attempt to exercise control . . . where Negroes lack a majority, Black Power means proper representation and sharing of control. . . ." But that wasn't what Black Power meant to most of us.

To most of us Black Power meant wooly heads, big black fists and stern black faces, gargantuan omnipotent black male organs, big black rifles and foot-long combat boots, tight pants over young muscular asses, dashikis, and broad brown chests; black men looting and rioting in the streets, taking over the country by brute force, arrogant lawlessness and an unquestionable sexual authority granted them as the victims of four hundred years of racism and abuse. The media emphasized this definition. It was their selective image of Stokely Carmichael that I fell in love with as a teenager, not the cautious, rational man who defined Black Power as "proper representation and sharing of control."

To see Carmichael back then, his shiny black face contorted in anger and outrage across the television screen, was to know immediately in the gut that here was a black spokesman unlike any other that had come before him. Here was a black man with an erect phallus, and he was pushing it up in America's face. No one was much in the mood for listening to what he was actually saying. Attention was focused on the unlowered head, the unfaltering speech, the disturbing absence of a shit-eating grin. It was as though, without a buck and wing, America could not comprehend Stokely's flawless English. Stokely was the nightmare America had been dreading—the black man seizing his manhood, the black man as sexual, virile, strong, tough, and dangerous.

Or was there a conspiracy to keep the focus on the visible, romantic manifestations of manhood, the Black Macho? To keep everybody's mind on rippling ebony muscles and screwing a black buck and off stocks and bonds?

Carmichael, as media figure and America's new sex symbol, was the embodiment of the impending revolution, but Malcolm X was its lifeblood; without him revolution would have been unthinkable. He was the dream. White men may speak of Martin Luther King with misty eyes but to black men, at least black men under thirty-five, King represented a glaring impossibility—a dream of masculine softness and beauty, an almost feminine man—and they took his murder as the final warning to rally to the other side: Men must be hard, knock down whoever is in their way, and take what they want "by any means necessary."

Malcolm was virile, strong, and generated a powerful, fearsome presence. (Carmichael would have seemed positively wishy-washy beside him.) He had spat in the faces of the white woman and the white man. He needed neither. He'd gone through the hatred of whites and passed through to the other side. He didn't ask or plead. He demanded. He didn't bargain. He fought. Malcolm was the supreme black patriarch. He would provide for his women and children and protect them. One felt certain of that. He would stand toe to toe with the white man. He would gain economic and political control of the black community. And he wouldn't take any shit in the process. The great black father was finally in our midst. But in 1965 black men murdered Malcolm, and with him died the chance for a black patriarchy. Malcolm X was their only hope. No black man would ever fill Malcolm's shoes. Everyone knew it. But that didn't stop some people from going through the *motions.* Eldridge Cleaver in *Soul on Ice* quotes Ossie Davis as saying in a eulogy to Malcolm X:

If you knew him you would know why we must honor him: Malcolm was our manhood, our living, black manhood! This was his meaning to his people. And, in honoring him, we honor the best in ourselves. . . . Consigning these mortal remains to earth . . . secure in the knowledge that what we place in the ground is no more now a man —but a seed—which, after the winter of our discontent will come forth again to meet us. And we will know him then for what he was and is—a Prince—our own black shining Prince—who didn't hesitate to die; because he loved us so. (Cleaver, *Soul on Ice.*)

If Malcolm had lived, if white America had been able to calm its racist paranoia, if black women had grabbed what was rightfully theirs from the beginning, if the groundwork for a profoundly deep hatred of himself and his woman had not been so well laid in the black man's soul by four hundred years of relentless conditioning, the years that followed 1965 might have been very different and perhaps more constructive. Or if the world had stood still, if women had stayed in their place and if black men had remembered that a man was first and foremost a patriarch, black men might have established a little black America in the heart of this country, a carbon copy of its daddy, and the liberation of black women would be hundreds of years away. But hindsight is cheap. When Cleaver closed his chapter on the assasination of Malcolm X with "We shall have our manhood. We shall have it or the earth will be leveled by our attempts to gain it," he was making a promise which history had demanded of him, but which America would make damned difficult to keep.

In 1957 Norman Mailer wrote "The White Negro," which was ostensibly about the then recent phenomenon of "hip" whites who used black language and fancied themselves in touch with the realities of black music.

Back then, when I was five years old, if you were the average white person, blacks still didn't exist for you. You could watch television, read every book and every magazine and newspaper on the newsstand, haunt every movie theater in town, walk down the endless tree-lined tranquil streets of a thousand neighborhoods across the country and still never be aware that there were actually people who were black. From time to time you might catch a glimpse of some shuffling dark-colored creatures of indeterminate sex and age shaking out the living-room rug, or hanging out the wash, or shining shoes, but these creatures were hardly more thought-provoking than the patterns of the linoleum on the nearest floor, and certainly less obtrusive.

And blacks had become accustomed to not existing. The unruly ones learned to vent their anger on other blacks and on themselves. More "mature" types contented themselves with being (white) man's best friend, next to the dog. During no period in America's history had racism been better internalized by the victims of it than it was in the fifties. At no time had blacks a greater resolve to accept and bow before their oppression. It was, after all, the great and vast calm before the storm. Yet there was one refuge from all of this. Jazz, black music, was more resistant to the dominant culture than ever. Black musicians took to wearing strange and grungy-looking clothing, or turning their backs on audiences. Even their language, always a code to exclude whites, become more difficult to decipher.

There was a definite rumbling in the slave quarters. Whether Mailer heard that rumbling and understood its import, or whether he just happened to hit on something by accident in "The White Negro" is hard to say. At any rate, he was one of a select group of white intellectuals that allowed blacks some measure of existence, with a small number of blacks (usually in rotating shifts) acting as consultants. These whites seemed to enjoy no end of speculation on what might be in the heads of those faceless masses. What were they really thinking? What might they do next? The sky was the limit because it was plain to see that they weren't doing anything except trying to stay alive. Mailer came up with an interestingly accurate idea about a peculiar phenomenon—the intersection of the black man's and the white man's fantasies, that is to say, their frustrations. As a result, I think he had a profound effect on such black leaders as LeRoi Jones and Eldridge Cleaver.

Within the greater Black Movement during the sixties, there was a smaller movement among my generation and class toward returning to ghetto life. I had lived in Harlem since my birth but I lived on Sugar Hill. More importantly, I lived in an extremely protected environment. I was not allowed to know anything about the streets. Every summer when I had free time on my hands, I was sent away to camp or taken to Europe or the Cape. Which is not to say that certain of the gross realities around me did not penetrate my consciousness, but in most respects I was a true child of my class—naïve, innocent, unworldly. I probably knew a good deal less about sniffing glue than most white children in Schenectady. As I've said, middle-class black children of my generation were plagued by a gnawing guilt. We were certain that there were other poorer blacks who were taking our punishment in our stead. That was in part what made us rather uncomfortable about the attention that was given to the Civil Rights Movement; it made us all the more conscious of that guilt.

When the emphasis shifted to blackness, to exploring and exalting the experience of blacks in the ghettos, we knew we were certainly not what anyone meant when they said that blacks were beautiful. We either had to get in on the black experience immediately or forever be confined to that purgatorylike state between black and white that was being middle-class and black. In our simplemindedness we had completely fallen for the popular definition of ghetto life: It was erotic, wild, free, intense, and liberating in its poverty and in the violence of its extremes. We did not go to the streets to contribute; we came to pay penance and to extract, finally, a definition of ourselves—not unlike whites, even whites of Mailer's ilk. Most of us chose to examine our roots in one of two ways. For many who had been raised in white neighborhoods and taken whites too seriously, drugs seemed the fastest way to wipe off that stinking black middle-class polish. Others, like myself, despite our naïveté, knew enough of the ghetto to have been close to people who had died of drug overdoses. We got involved in relationships with men from the streets.

A good number of us are still floundering in that realm of rediscovery, for one thing because drugs don't let go very easily and, for another, because babies one didn't really mean to have cannot be simply disposed of as one crosses the borders of the ghetto. I got out when I realized that there was nothing beautiful or worth saving about living in the ghetto, that its violence was not an indication of liberation, but rather of the restrictions that pervaded all areas except the purely physical.

The really entrenched ghetto dweller is one who is brutalized, so brutalized, in fact, that his every action, thought, word, emanates from a sense of his own affliction, from the consciousness of having been deeply and irreparably wounded.

Surrounded by such human wreckage, one fears each day that the unbearable will occur, that finally one will be anesthetized, become a vegetable unable to recognize one's own pain. In other words, with the whole package of hunger and poor medical treatment, dirty hallways, roaches, and rats, spareribs, chittlins and Duke Ellington, Count Basie and "Hey, what's hap-in-in, ma man," and "Let's do tha thang," dancing and partying, comes a desperate and passionate anger, which is usually contained, but which may strike out, usually at someone close, and kill or maim at any time for the most unlikely reason. (See the emergency room of Harlem Hospital on a Saturday night for details.) It is quite simply what my mother meant when she told me, "Grass roots stink." It is quite simply the reason I made the decision to move myself as far away as possible, economically and socially, from being poor and black, because being poor and black means nothing so much as it means that one has no control over when or for what reason one may live or die, and this is not in any way an enriching experience.

Now, to some limited degree Mailer grasped this and saw fit to parallel it with the situation of modernized civilized man. He too, thanks to the A-bomb, chemical warfare, industrialization, had no way of knowing when he might draw his last breath and under what circumstances. Therefore, Mailer reasoned, if the blacks had survived this state of perpetual anxiety, then perhaps they had a lesson to teach us all about such living. Hadn't they been rendered more human by it? And this is where the distortion came in. He failed to differentiate between the impulse of blacks to destroy themselves and their impulse to perpetuate themselves. When he said that they were more human, he meant in their murderousness and in their creativity alike.

He did not see that the two impulses had entirely different, even opposing, origins. The murderousness of the black community (besides that which was inflicted by outsiders, police, and politicians) was an attempt to come to terms with the hideous reality that white America proposed for blacks. It was their greatest concession to it. Whereas black music, language, ways of cooking and dressing, even of walking, came into being despite oppression—to circumvent and ease oppression. Black creativity came out of an understanding and acceptance on the part of black people of themselves as a unique culture within America, a culture which had a right to exist and to continue to exist. In other words, the two impulses were at war with each other. When the murderousness really took over in the seventies, the musicians, along with the other beacons of creativity, all but disappeared from Harlem. Creativity and violence simply could not thrive in each other's company. Interestingly enough, despite what historians of the area maintain, my grandmother insists that Harlem was in no sense a dangerous place to live in before the fifties, and it has never been nearly as dangerous as it has become in the seventies.

But Mailer was in the grip of a bad case of the I've-got-the-pseudo-anglo-saxon-technological-male menopausal-twentieth-century-civilized man's blues. He needed an antidote; or rather, in order to maintain his reputation as seer for the uptight white world, he needed to propose an antidote, and quickly. Blacks, Mailer said, are psychopaths, and he further said that that was good. Since I've never found any indication in Mailer's work that he considered black women, in fact, human beings, I'm going to assume that what Mailer meant was that black *men* were psychopaths.

When one lives in a civilized world, and still can enjoy none of the cultural nectar of such a world because the paradoxes on which civilization is built demand that there remain a cultureless and alienated bottom of exploitable human material, then the logic of becoming a sexual outlaw . . . is that one has at least a running competitive chance to be physically healthy so long as one stays alive. It is therefore no accident that psychopathy is most prevalent with the Negro. Hated from outside and therefore hating himself, the Negro was forced into the position of exploring all those moral wildernesses of civilized life which the Square automatically condemns as delinquent or evil or immature or morbid or self-destructive or corrupt. . . . The Negro, not being privileged to gratify his self-esteem with the heady satisfactions of categorical condemnation, chose to move instead in that other direction where all situations are equally valid, and in the worst of perversion . . . the Negro discovered and elaborated a morality of the bottom. . . . (Mailer, *The White Negro.*)

Oppression heightens sexuality, not a very original thesis. But Mailer does not stop there. First, not only is the black man sexual, he is a sexual outlaw, a chronic rapist. And not only is he a sexual outlaw, he's a psychopath, a pathological criminal.

By labeling the black man a psychopath, Mailer meant to place him closer to the original man, primitive man, a savage who knew how to beat his women when they gave him trouble and who dealt with shit when it occurred not by pressing a button in some emasculated way, but with his fists or by whipping out his switchblade. Living in an environment of total fear, Mailer's psychopath is past fear, and thus does not have

43

the restraints and reservations that encumber modern man. He is able to be what men were intended to be, to deal with the world with his brawn, his muscles, and his penis. This black psychopathy, this supposed antithesis of everything the overly civilized modern white American male holds dear, Mailer reasoned, is the white man's only salvation. And look, Mailer said, the invigorating, rejuvenating process had already begun. Psychopathy, what the black negro gave the white negro, was at the root of hip.

The Hip ethic is immoderation, childlike in its adoration of the present (and indeed to respect the past means that one must also respect such ugly consequences of the past as the collective murders of the State). It is this adoration of the present which contains the affirmation of Hip . . . the nihilism of Hip proposes as its final tendency that every social restraint and category be removed, and the affirmation implicit in the proposal is that man would then prove to be more creative than murderous and so would not destroy himself. . . . Hip, which would return us to ourselves, at no matter what price in individual violence, is the affirmation of the barbarian, for it requires a primitive passion about human nature to believe that individual acts of violence are always to be preferred to the collective violence of the State; it takes literal faith in the creative possibilities of the human being to envisage acts of violence as the catharsis which prepares growth. . . . (Mailer, *The White Negro.*)

It may be one of the signs of a truly decadent society when major so-called radical voices begin to romanticize oppression. Mailer had, in "The White Negro," become such a voice. Since the new, sanitized, civilized man was killing us off, Mailer exhorted us to return to that brave and noble primitive creature of the jungle. Never mind that such a man had never really existed, except in the warped imagination of Western males, and certainly did not exist in Harlem. Mailer was determined to have his Garden of Eden, to preserve the myth that

44

there was a way to get out of male history without surrendering
the notion of male supremacy. Technology had robbed the
white man of his vitality and inspiration, his creativity. Put
your slide rules and graphs aside and contemplate the infrequency and poor quality of your orgasms, the noble bestiality
of man straining at the bit and saddle of civilization, the
feminization process. Look at the black man and take a lesson.

The psychopath is a rebel without a cause. His rebelliousness is aimed
to achieve goals satisfactory to himself alone; he is incapable of
exertions for the sake of others. All his efforts, hidden under no
matter what disguise, represent investments designed to satisfy his
immediate wishes and desires. . . . (Psychiatrist Robert Lindner's
definition of psychopathy from *The White Negro.*)

No signs of Malcolm's patriarch here. This man really has
no time for women and children, for home and community; he
cares little for education, for anything like a state of prepared-
ness or comfort. He is self-absorbed, he is violent, he is narcissistic, he is virile, he is a child. Such a black man, Mailer told
us, would be in the vanguard.

But what did this have to do with the Black Movement? It
should have had nothing to do with it. If one compares Malcolm's design for a revolution to Mailer's, the major difference
is that Mailer's was formulated to meet the needs of the white
community. Mailer, as do most white men who write about
black men, insisted that the major function of blacks was to
produce a better white America, to humanize white men. Malcolm insisted that the black man's function was to produce a
better black America. And the twain, I'm afraid, shall never
meet, as long as a better black America means an America in
which the black man maintains a right to preserve and perpetuate his uniqueness, his own culture, something the belligerence
of white America will not allow.

45

What Malcolm was talking about would have meant nothing less than full-scale war, a war blacks could never win, mostly because they were unable to understand why it should be fought. So Mailer won. The black man he had told us about, whom white oppression and racism had created, was in the vanguard.

It was not the accuracy of Mailer's prophecy that was so important, but that he had articulated so well the nature of the white man's fantasy/nightmare about the black man; that fantasy/nightmare, through an Americanization process of several hundred years, had become, to a great extent, the black man's as well.

In 1968, after Black Power had arrived and been around for a little while, Mailer seemed to become more cautious.

Black Power moves then, obviously, against the technological society. Since the Negro has never been able to absorb a technological culture with success, even reacting against it with instinctive pain and distrust, he is now in this oncoming epoch of automation going to be removed from the technological society anyway. His only salvation, short of becoming a city brigand or a government beggar, is to build his own society out of his own culture, own means, own horror, own genius. Or own heroic, tragic, or evil possibilities. For there is no need to assume that the black man will prove morally superior to the white man. Schooled in treachery, steeped in centuries of white bile, there are avalanches and cataracts of violence, destruction, inchoate rage, and promiscuous waste to be encountered—there is well a question whether he can build his own society at all, so perverse are the conduits of his crossed emotions by now. But the irony is that the White would do well to hope that the Black can build a world, for those well-ordered epochs of capitalism which flushed the white wastes down into the Black heart are gone—the pipes of civilization are backing up. The irony is that we may even yet need a Black vision of existence if civilization is to survive the death chamber it has built for itself. So let us at least recognize the real ground of Black Power

—it is ambitious, beautiful, awesome, terrifying, and has to do with nothing so much as the most important questions of us all—what is man? why are we here? will we survive? (Norman Mailer, *Existential Errands,* New York: New American Library, 1973.)

Mailer was backing off. He was beginning to have doubts. In the face of an actual Black Movement, he had crept to the sidelines, contenting himself with trying to orchestrate things in a fervent stage whisper: "Okay, now you're in motion. Now what you have got to do is rebuild us, rebuild white America. Help us out of our trap. Only if you want to, you understand. But don't you think it would be nice? Sure you do." But just precisely how well did blacks follow Mailer's instructions?

American blacks are no more psychopathic, as a group, than are white Americans, and the evidence would indicate that they're a good deal less so. But there is the matter of that kind of violence I have described, typical of all ghettos, specifically black ghettos, and devastating not because of its frequency but because of its unpredictability, and if one thinks carefully one will realize that it was precisely this kind of violence—not Mailer's psychopathy, which was an invention in any case— that actually occurred during the Black Movement. The rest was bravado, mouth, a form of intimidation as popular in black ghetto streets, if not more so, as any overt violence. That is to say that there was very little actual violence directed at the so-called enemy. But then there is more to the psychopath than his willingness to take lives. And if one accepts a psychopath as one who is "incapable of exertions for others," and accepts that "all his efforts . . . represent investments designed to satisfy his immediate wishes and desires," one would have to say that there did seem to be a curiously psychopathic energy at work in the black man's pursuit of his manhood (Black Power) during the sixties. But then one would also be guilty of oversimplification. Because, as Mailer points out, being a "rebel without a cause" was not a position that the black man *freely* chose but one he'd been forced into. That is, in the face of a machine that limited and confined his existence to the most purely physical, that had perfectly worked out and planned his helplessness, what other choice had he but to focus upon those things that could be his advantage alone—unpredictability, virility, and a big mouth, which is all any kind of macho really is when you come down to it. One could say, in fact, that the black man risked everything—all the traditional goals of revolution: money, security, the overthrow of the government—in the pursuit of an immediate sense of his own power.

He pursued the white woman though it might mean, and had meant, his life, because he understood that she was a piece of the white man's property that he might actually obtain. He turned his back on the white man and degraded the black woman because that produced much faster and surer effects than a sit-in at GM. The riots, the most overt violence on the part of blacks this country saw during the Black Movement days, were spontaneous and largely ineffective outbursts of rage that were directed inward and hurt the ghetto dweller most. For the most part black men bad-mouthed whites on television, in print, and live, frequently and belligerently. But they didn't go out and kill whites because, for all their "psychopathic" frenzy, they had not been programmed to do that. Instead they joined groups like the Panthers, where they could slowly and safely pick one another off, or they joined the CIA, the FBI, the local police force, as the greater emphasis on "equal opportunity" opened up jobs. Meanwhile America stockpiled weapons and trained men as if in preparation for a Third World War.

And appropriately enough the manhood America finally conceded to blacks was the manhood of a psychopath or, changing the skin color and motivation here and there, of a

James Bond movie. It was flashy and attention-attracting like a zoot suit. Black men kicking white men's asses, fucking white women, and stringing black women along in a reappearance of the brutal Buck on the silver screen. Black men in big green hats, high-heeled shoes, and mink, with "five white bitches" around the corner turning tricks for them.

A black man can walk down the street with a white woman unmolested. What a victory for a black revolution. He can marry a white woman, *if he's got the money,* and no one will try to stop him. And he doesn't have to take any lip from black women either. He is the figurehead king of his own special jungles. Black men make white women and black women tremble on the streets all over the country and America has hardly had to make any adjustment at all to accommodate the "difference."

In *The Fight,* a book which Mailer wrote about the match between Foreman and Ali in Zaire, he said this about his own feelings toward blacks.

But his love affair with the Black soul, a sentimental orgy at its worst, had been given a drubbing through the seasons of Black Power. He no longer knew whether he loved Blacks or secretly disliked them, which had to be the dirtiest secret in his American life. Part of the woe of the first trip to Africa, part of that irrationally intense detestation of Mobutu . . . must be a cover for the rage he was feeling toward Blacks, any Blacks. Walking the streets of Kinshasa on that first trip while the Black crowds moved about him with an indifference to his presence that succeeded in niggering him, he knew what it was to be looked upon as invisible. He was also approaching, if not careful, the terminal animosity of a Senior Citizen. How his hatred seethed in search of a justifiable excuse. When the sheer evidence of Africa finally overcame these newly bigoted senses . . . then it became impossible . . . not to sense what everyone had been trying to say about Africa for a hundred years, big Papa first on line: the place was so fucking sensitive! . . . Then

he could no longer hate the Zairois or even be certain of his condemnation of their own Black oppressors, then his animosity
switched a continent over to Black Americans with their arrogance,
jive, ethnic put-down costumes, caterwauling soul, their thump-
your-testicle organ sound and black new vomitous egos like the slag
of all of alienated sewage-compacted heap U.S.A.; then he knew
that he had not only come to report on a fight but to look a little
more into his own outsized feelings of love and—could it be?—
sheer hate for the existence of Black on earth. (Norman Mailer,
The Fight, Boston: Little, Brown & Co., 1975.)

Really quite sad. They had let him down. He was disappointed
though he had no right to be. It was, indeed, a sentimental
orgy. Mailer said in 1957:

Hip sees the context as generally dominating the man, dominating
him because his character is less significant than the context in which
he must function. . . . (Mailer, *The White Negro.*)

What an accurate way of accounting for the difference between the African who came here over three hundred years ago
and the American black male who came to the fore during the
Black Movement. The latter man could never make a new
world. He was too much a mirror of what already existed.

It is 1978. Up until recently Stokely Carmichael was married
to a famous South African singer named Miriam Makeba and
was living with her in Guinea. He made yearly appearances
on American college campuses, preached fervently of Pan-
African socialism and the evils of Zionism, grabbed his
money, and ran. Makeba has now initiated divorce proceedings and Carmichael has quietly taken up residence in Washington, D. C. Imamu Baraka (LeRoi Jones), his operation
based in Newark, has packed his dashikis and his hatred of
whites in mothballs and now sports a T-shirt and scruffy

jeans, and can be found encouraging both blacks and whites to join in a socialist struggle to overthrow the government. George Jackson is dead. Huey Newton has returned from exile in Cuba, where he was avoiding trial for the murder of a sixteen-year-old black woman in a street fight. He says he was framed. He is leading the Black Panther Party again. Though the party's aim is still a socialist America, their immediate goal is full employment, and they view the growth of black capitalism as useful in terms of aiding and strengthening the black community. Bobby Seale is an entertainer again. Elijah Mohammed is dead and has been succeeded by his son Wallace Mohammed. Some of you may remember that Wallace briefly denounced his father as a racist and a manipulator immediately following the murder of Malcolm X back in 1965. He has changed the Muslims significantly. The women can now wear pants, and whites are now permitted to join. Rap Brown has been released after having served a sentence for a stick-up in a Manhattan bar. Roy Inniss was last seen publicly recruiting American blacks to fight on the South African side in Angola.

Two years ago Eldridge Cleaver turned himself over to the United States police authorities, after having been in exile in Cuba, China, Algeria, and France, where he made pants with codpieces. The man who once called for the overthrow of "the American nightmare" now claims to have a renewed confidence in American justice and says that he'd rather stand trial in America than live in any communist or Third World country. "I'm having a love affair with the U. S. military," Cleaver said in *The New York Times Magazine* in January 1977. And, though once an atheist, he now seems to have gotten religion. His religious rebirth occurred in France while he was "watching a full moon over the Mediterranean. There appeared in the moon in sequence the faces of all my former heroes—Mal-

colm X, Ché, Castro, Mao. Gradually the face of Jesus appeared. I found myself reciting the 23rd Psalm."

In early 1976 an *Ebony* editorial mourned the passing of
the days of black militancy, when guilt-ridden whites poured
their blood money into moderate black organizations. On August 8, 1977, an article by Orde Coombs, subtitled "The
New Civil War Begins," appeared in *New York* magazine.
The subject was the growing distance between middle-class
blacks and street blacks. During a New York power failure,
street blacks had looted LeMans, an elegant men's clothing
store under black ownership, first of all the stores on Amsterdam Avenue. "We've got to tell the brothers that if they
can't make it in America, they can't make it anywhere," one
defender of the realm is quoted as saying. "I used to laugh
when I heard white people say that. Now I find that I am
saying it, but I have to bust my ass every day to do it. Yet too
many people won't try and then are angry at people like me
for trying."

The New York Times of February 28, 1978, reported on its
front page a split in the black community along class lines.
"One of the most striking developments in American society
in the last decade has been the abandonment of the ghetto by
millions of upwardly mobile blacks . . . some . . . live side by
side with white families in similar economic circumstances.
More often, they have moved to middle-class black neighborhoods, which have expanded in almost every American city.
The houses and yards are indistinguishable from those in afflu-
ent white communities. And, in many instances, so are the
attitudes of the residents."

Black leadership with the ability to inspire has disappeared.
The men who supplied it are either dead, in jail, or doing other
things. "Black Power" exists only as a historical reference. The

revolution is over. But what of Cleaver's promise, "We shall have our manhood . . ."?

Between 1966 and 1976 the annual gross income of blacks increased by fifteen billion dollars. According to *Ebony* (1976), the bulk of that increase went to a relatively small percentage of people, about 5 percent: the black middle class and the aspiring black middle class.

The unemployment rate for blacks as of 1977 was 13.2 percent, twice that of whites; the unemployment rate for black youth, about 40 percent. Bernard E. Anderson of the Urban League asserts that if you include those who have never been employed the rate skyrockets to 25.3 percent, as opposed to 11.7 percent for whites.

In 1966, 41.8 percent of blacks were below the poverty line. As of 1976, 31.1 percent of blacks were below the poverty level.

Ever since the Moynihan Report and the Kerner Commission Report on Civil Disorders of 1968, not only *has there appeared to be an emphasis* upon supplying blacks with greater educational and employment opportunities, but also, unofficially, upon giving the black man, as opposed to the black woman, the best breaks. The reasoning was that better employed black men would marry black women, reduce the numbers of women who were heads of households, and thereby improve the situation of the black race as a whole.

From 1965 until 1976 the percentage of black families with female heads increased from 23.7 percent to 33 percent. During that time, among black families headed by women, the percentage below the poverty line went from 56.3 percent to 52.2 percent, only a slight decrease. Black families headed by men, however, went from 25.3 percent below the poverty level in 1967 to only 13.5 percent as of 1976. And the unemployment rate for black men with families is 6.7 percent, only 2.2 percent higher than whites in this category.

■

The median black family income went from $4,875 in 1967 to $9,264 in 1976, which seems a dramatic increase until one learns that the median white family income went from $8,234 to $15,571 in the same period; 54.6 percent of white families gross over $15,000 a year, whereas the comparable figure for black families is 30 percent. A small proportion of black families, 7.5 percent, make over $25,000 a year.

■

There are about six million black families in America. Of these, about 334,000, as of 1976, were headed by persons who had more than four years of college.

This was the 5 percent that won. Their median income is $20,733. A great many blacks, especially women, are still very poor. The evils that the "positive black male image" proposed to cure remain uncured. And Stokely's call for "representative control" has gone totally unrealized. There are a sprinkling of blacks in the government, thirteen in Congress, one in the Senate, one in the President's Cabinet, Andrew Young is Ambassador to the United Nations. Although a few blacks now sit on the boards of major corporations, blacks do not have even "representative control" over any major American industry or business.

But was Cleaver's promise kept—"We shall have our manhood . . ."? That depends upon how you look at "manhood."

If you accept the definition America force-fed the black man —access to white women sexually and the systematic subjugation and suppression of black women—then the answer is an unequivocal yes. But if we consider America's actual standard of "manhood"—control of the means of production and power; in other words, money—the answer has got to be no.

Richard Wright's *Native Son* was the starting point of the black writer's love affair with Black Macho. Bigger Thomas, the product of a black Chicago ghetto, is employed as chauffeur by an upper-middle-class white family. His first night on the job he drives the daughter of his employer and her socialist boyfriend to a political meeting. They try to befriend Bigger, drink with him, go with him to a black restaurant. Later Bigger takes the drunken young woman home, barely escapes raping her, murders her accidentally, and burns her in the furnace in the basement. Lest we should doubt his viciousness, he then rapes his own black girl friend and throws her out of a window. Bigger, Wright would have us believe, had gained an identity and realized himself as a man for the first time in his life through these acts of violence.

Bigger Thomas was nothing more than the American white males's fantasy/nightmare/myth of the black man thinly disguised, expanded upon (albeit brilliantly), endowed with the detail of social reality and thrust back in the white man's face in a form recognizable enough to connect with the old terror.

In inventing such a protagonist, Wright seemed much more concerned with making a lasting impression on whites than he was with self-revelation or self-exploration. The black man could only come to life in the act of punishing the white man or, in other words, the black man could only come to life by losing his humanity. It would be some years before this view would become common currency; later writers, such as

Norman Mailer, turned back to *Native Son* for confirmation.
Finally, Baldwin was right about *Native Son*.

Recording his days of anger he has also nevertheless recorded, as no
Negro before him had ever done, that fantasy Americans hold in their
minds when they speak of the Negro: that fantastic and fearful image
which we have lived with since the first slave fell beneath the lash.
This is the significance of *Native Son* and also, unhappily, its over-
whelming limitation. (James Baldwin, "Many Thousands Gone,"
Notes of a Native Son.)

Bigger's tragedy is not that he is cold or black or hungry, not even
that he is American, black; but that he has accepted a theology that
denies him life, that he admits the possibility of his being sub-human
and feels constrained, therefore, to battle for his humanity according
to those brutal criteria bequeathed him at his birth. (Baldwin, "Everybody's Protest Novel," *Notes of a Native Son*.)

I began reading James Baldwin when I was about twelve and
he remains one of the black writers whom I respect most, not
because I agree with everything he has to say or even the way
he says it, but because he has paid more attention to black
women, to the actual mechanics of the black male/female
relationship and to the myths that have been working on it,
than any other black male writer (except Thomas Wideman
and, perhaps, John A. Williams). At least in his earlier essays
and novels, Baldwin did, in fact, explore "the disquieting com-
plexities of ourselves." In that sense, reading him is still an
education.

Baldwin seemed wiser than Wright because he maintained
a sense of the double reality of being black: the white man's
vision of the black man and the man the black man had to be
for himself. Baldwin had in mind a more humane manhood,
a manhood that would take into account the expensive lesson
the black man had learned from oppression, a manhood that

would perhaps turn even America's corrupting influence into something beneficial.

Negroes are Americans and their destiny is the country's destiny. They have no other experience besides their experience on this continent and it is an experience which cannot be rejected, which yet remains to be embraced. If, as I believe, no American Negro exists who does not have his private Bigger Thomas living in the skull, then what most significantly fails to be illuminated here is the paradoxical adjustment which is perpetually made, the Negro being compelled to accept the fact that this dark and dangerous and unloved stranger is part of himself forever. Only this recognition sets him in any wise free and it is this, this necessary ability to contain and even, in the most honorable sense of the word, to *exploit* the "nigger," which lends to Negro life its high element of the ironic and which causes the most well-meaning of their American critics to make such exhilarating errors when attempting to understand them. To present Bigger as a warning is simply to reinforce the American guilt and fear concerning him, it is most forcefully to limit him to that previously mentioned social arena in which he has no human validity, it is simply to condemn him to death. (Baldwin, "Many Thousands Gone," *Notes of a Native Son.*)

Baldwin had no way of knowing in 1951, when he said, "it is quite beyond the limit of possibility that Negroes in America will ever achieve the means of wreaking vengeance upon the state . . . also . . . it cannot be said that they have any desire to do so," that there would indeed be those who would want to and who would try to before long.

Ralph Ellison, like Baldwin, expressed a horror of the white man's nightmare, and the realization of the inevitable lack of humanity it afforded the black man. The white man's own nightmare could not be used to conquer him. But then Ellison was more obsessed than Baldwin with the way blacks were seen, or rather not seen, by whites; with

57

the extent to which they only existed, even for one another, if whites recognized that existence. And although I fully realize what an important literary accomplishment *Invisible Man* was, I am often tempted to wonder if that concern with white perception did not help to make it such a huge success. Ellison's hero takes the coward's way out. He retreats because he cannot deal with a world in which his existence as an individual is never allowed but must be taken —a dilemma that seems almost naïve. Ellison tells us little about how blacks relate to one another, except to the extent that whites intrude upon that intercourse. It's not surprising that he has never successfully completed another novel. There was no place for his hero to go, no reason for him to come up from underground.

Baldwin, in contrast, plunges headlong into the intricacies of the black relationship. He does not propose a solution outright, but he is clearly working out of a specific set of values, and the values are those of patriarchy. It strikes me as very appropriate that he and Martin Luther King should have been close friends. Both seemed to believe in the notion of man as God on earth in the Christian sense. This notion of man, while unacceptable to me from a feminist perspective, as well as on religious and philosophical grounds, presumed some emotional and material responsibility towards black women and children. The ideal man was distinguished by both power *and* compassion, for he would be held accountable to God for his actions towards his charges. He thus had a moral responsibility for the destiny of the entire race.

Baldwin is an emphatically moralistic writer. He has never been able to adequately justify the actions sometimes taken by black men regarding women and children. His continual struggle in print with his father testifies to that. He tells us that his father was frightened because he was unable to support the family he had created, that he was beaten down, driven mad by this society. Yet Baldwin remains unable to completely excuse his father's acts of insensitivity and cruelty toward his mother, his siblings, and himself. Throughout his earlier work there is evidence of his interior struggle over the question of whether the black man had been more right or wrong in his exploitation of the black woman; that is, in using her as a target for his anger. A tenet of patriarchal morality is the conviction that men must rule because they are more often right about what's best for everybody.

That very uncertainty was why Amiri Baraka and Eldridge Cleaver singled Baldwin out for such vicious attacks. In his novels *Go Tell It on the Mountain* and *Another Country*, Baldwin told the black woman's story with far too much empathy to ever be accepted into the ranks of the militant black male intellectuals in the Black Power days.

Now I talked to many Southern liberals who were doing their best to bring integration about in the South, but met scarcely a single Southerner who did not weep for the passing of the old order. . . . But the old black men I looked at down there—those same black men that the Southern liberal had loved . . . they were not weeping. Men do not like to be protected, it emasculates them. . . . It is not a pretty thing to be a father and be ultimately dependent on the power and kindness of some other man for the well-being of your house.

But what this evasion of the Negro's humanity has done to the nation is not so well known. The really striking thing, for me, in the South was this dreadful paradox, that the black men were stronger than the white. I do not know how they did it, but it certainly has something to do with that as yet unwritten history of the Negro woman . . . (James Baldwin, "Nobody Knows My Name: A Letter From The South," *Nobody Knows My Name,* New York: Dial, 1961.)

Like Martin Luther King, Baldwin was an anachronism come the sixties; but unlike King he was not conveniently murdered, so they had to dispose of him some other way.

Ironically, Baldwin's love affair with the tragic details of the black man's life, and his romanticization of them, laid the groundwork for the deification of the genitals that would later characterize the prose of the Black Movement. That is, to a degree, Baldwin, too, admired what was characterized as the brutal masculinity of the black man, also saw it as an affirmation of his existence. The biggest difference between Baldwin and the others really was that Baldwin saw in the black man as much potential for a sense of responsibility as any tendency toward brutal sexuality.

Because he is in partial agreement with Mailer, Baldwin's criticism of "The White Negro" is oddly evasive. He does not come right out and accuse Mailer of making a racist argument.

"Man," said a Negro musician to me once, talking about Norman, "the only trouble with that cat is that he's white." This does not mean exactly what it says—or, rather, it *does* mean exactly what it says, and not what it might be taken to mean—and it is a very shrewd observation. What my friend meant was that to become a Negro man, let alone a Negro artist, one had to make oneself up as one went along. This had to be done in the not-at-all-metaphorical teeth of the world's determination to destroy you. The world had prepared no place for you, and if the world had its way, no place would ever exist. Now, this is true for everyone, but, in the case of a Negro, this truth is absolutely naked: if he deludes himself about it, he will die. . . . (Baldwin, "The Black Boy Looks at the White Boy," *Nobody Knows My Name.*)

Baldwin is patting Mailer on the head and sending him back to play with the little kids. He is saying, anybody who isn't black shouldn't dare to presume to understand why black men do the things they do.

The language is ambiguous not only because it is Baldwin's style to be so but also because he wants to make Mailer aware that black men and white men move, and must move, in different directions and toward different ends. But there is, as well, an implicit affirmation of the right of the black man to assert himself sexually, the right of the black man to be a sexual outlaw if he finds it necessary to his survival. "To become a Negro man . . . one had to make oneself up as one went along. . . ." Nor does Baldwin deny outright that black men are psychopaths or that theirs is what Mailer calls a "morality of the bottom." Rather he asks, "Why malign the sorely menaced sexuality of Negroes in order to justify the white man's sexual panic?"

Then things changed. The rhetoric of Black Power became loud and not a little idiotic. Baldwin was repeatedly attacked. He was singled out to represent everything younger blacks didn't like about the solutions and evasiveness of their parents. Cleaver, who had his own peculiar love-hate relationship with Baldwin, accused him of waging "a war . . . against black masculinity." LeRoi Jones accused him of doing "the Martyr's Shuffle in cocktail time."

In 1967, Baldwin returned to America from his long self-imposed exile in France to take his punishment, to say what other black writers wanted him to say, perhaps because he, too, desperately wanted to believe in the quixotic virility of the black man.

If Beale Street Could Talk was published in 1974. It was a novel about a young black ghetto girl. She falls in love with and becomes pregnant by a young black boy who is falsely accused of rape and imprisoned. The boy's father is an impotent drunkard. Nevertheless, he is portrayed as noble, even kindhearted, driven to drink and despair by his domineering, malicious, frigid, churchgoing wife. The girl's parents and sister, who are very poor, are curiously overjoyed to hear of the girl's pregnancy and are thoroughly supportive of the unmarried couple. All of the characters positively gush the dogma

of the Black Movement, except the boy's mother, who is the
perfect caricature of the man-eating black woman. Earlier, in
1972, Baldwin had said:

Every black man walking in this country pays a tremendous price for
walking: for men are not women, and a man's balance depends on
the weight he carries between his legs. All men, however they may
face or fail to face it, however they may handle, or be handled by it,
know something about each other, which is simply that a man without balls is not a man. . . . (James Baldwin, *No Name in the Street*,
New York: Dial, 1972.)

And so, by whatever means, Baldwin had finally seen the
light, arrived at the theoretical premise that made the Black
Movement a vehicle for Black Macho: Black males who
stressed a traditionally patriarchal responsibility to their
women and children, to their communities—to black people—
were to be considered almost sisified. The black man's sexuality
and the physical fact of his penis were the major evidence of
his manhood and the purpose of it.

LeRoi Jones was the Black Movement's leading intellectual
convert, having deserted success in the white world for the
uncertainty of the Black Revolution. He had lived in Greenwich Village. His friends were Gregory Corso, Allen Ginsberg,
Frank O'Hara, Larry Rivers. His wife was white. His poetry
was individualistic, well-crafted, and lauded by the critics.
Those who knew him then described him as gentle, "the nicest
man you ever met."
Then one day—it seemed to happen all of a sudden according to his white friends—he was among the angriest of black
voices. His new hatred of whites led him to leave his white wife
and his two half-white children to marry a black woman and
start a nationalist organization called New Ark in Newark, New
Jersey. Now Imamu Amiri Baraka, his poetry—and he was the

father of the entire 1960s black poetry movement—advocated violence, the death of all whites, the moral and physical superiority of the black man, Black Macho.

But before he severed all ties with the white world, he remained with one foot in and one foot out for a period of a few years during which he wrote an essay called "American Sexual Reference: Black Male" (1965). According to Jones the struggle of black against white was the purity of primitivism against the corruption of technology, the noble savage against the pervert bureaucrats, the super macho against the fags.

Most American white men are trained to be fags . . . they devote their energies to the nonphysical, the nonrealistic . . . even their wars move to the stage where whole populations can be destroyed by *pushing a button* . . . the purer white, the more estranged from, say, actual physical work . . . can you, for a second, imagine the average middle class white man able to do somebody harm? Alone? Without the technology that at this moment still has him rule the world? Do you understand the softness of the white man, the weakness. . . . (Jones, "American Sexual Reference: Black Male," *Home.*)

Whites labeled him racist, but there turned out to be no cause for worry. In time Jones would prove himself neither a politician nor a general. He was first and last a writer. As a writer, even in his essay, he was most concerned with compelling images. What did it matter whether they were real or imagined? He would frequently pass up the moderate when there was an extreme within reach. Black Macho was the stuff of which stirring, gut-spilling prose was made and Jones seized the opportunity.

. . . the black man and the white woman were not supposed to have any connections, even in anybody's wildest fantasies. This was (is?) the great taboo of the society. This taboo did a number of things. For one, it created for such a possible blackman-white-woman union an

63

aura of mystery and wild sensuality that could provoke either princi-pal to investigate, if either were intrepid or curious enough.

The reason the white woman was supposed to be intrigued by the black man was because he was basic and elemental emotionally (which is true for the nonbrainwashed black, simply because there is no reason he should not be; the black man is more "natural" than the white simply because he has fewer *things* between him and reality, fewer wrappers, fewer artificial rules), therefore "wilder," harder, and almost insatiable in his lovemaking. (Jones, "American Sexual Reference: Black Male," *Home.*)

He admonishes black men for being taken in by the trap of pursuing white women—which is not to say that black men should spurn white pussy but that they should seize it rather than grovel for it. Whereas Mailer's rallying cry to the primi-tives seemed half tongue-in-cheek, Jones's seemed deadly seri-ous.

The most heinous crime against white society would be . . . the rape, the taking forcibly of one of whitie's treasures . . . the average ofay thinks of the black man as potentially raping every white lady in sight, which is true, in the sense that the black man should want to rob the white man of everything he has . . . for most whites the guilt of the robbery is the guilt of the rape. That is, they know in their deepest hearts that they *should* be robbed, and the white woman understands that only in the rape sequence is she likely to get cleanly, viciously popped. . . . The black man, then, because he can enter into the sex act with less guilt as to its results, is freer. Because of the robbery/rape syndrome, the black man will *take* the white woman in a way that does not support the myth of The Lady. (Jones, "American Sexual Reference: Black Male," *Home.*)

Jones had transformed Mailer's "sexual outlaw" into the role model for the black revolutionary—"the black man as robber / rapist (take it further, it is murderer . . .)". A compelling fictional character, he is a fascist in real life. Black men, with the help of Jones and others like him, would take the prototype of man as warrior, as conqueror blind to the rights of all but himself, as rapist and psychopath turned soldier, and use it as the English settler had used a similar form of macho to place the American continent at his feet.

That Jones wrote with such fanaticism and hatred does not surprise me. First, Jones as an individual had to negate his former love affair with whites. Second, throughout the so-called calm period of his earlier poetry there repeatedly emerges the voice of a man who has a tremendous amount of anger bottled up inside of him. In *Dutchman*, which was written in 1964, Clay, a young black man, says to Lula, a white woman who's been hassling him for being stiff, uptight, middle class:

. . . If I'm a middle class fake white man . . . let me be. And let me be in the way I want. I'll rip your lousy breasts off! Let me be who I feel like being. Uncle Tom. Thomas. Whoever. . . . You don't know anything except what's there for you to see. An act. Lies. Device. Not the pure heart, the pumping black heart. You don't ever know that. And I sit here, in this buttoned-up suit, to keep myself from cutting all your throats. I mean wantonly. . . . All the hip white boys scream for Bird. And Bird saying, "Up your ass, feeble-minded ofay! Up your ass." And they sit there talking about the tortured genius of Charlie Parker. Bird would've played not a note of music if he just walked up to East Sixty-seventh Street and killed the first ten white people he saw. Not a note! And I'm the great would-be poet. Yes. That's right! Poet. Some kind of bastard literature . . . all it needs is a simple knife thrust. Just let me bleed you, you loud whore, and one poem vanished a whole people of neurotics, struggling to keep from being sane. And the only thing that would cure the neurosis would be your murder . . . all it needs is that simple act. Murder. Just murder! Would make us all sane. Ahhh. Shit. But who needs it. I'd rather be a fool. Insane. Safe with my words, and no deaths, and clean, hard thoughts, urging me to new conquests. . . . (Le Roi Jones, *Dutchman and the Slave*, New York: William Morrow, 1964.)

A recurring theme in his work is this one of masks, of "Cold air blown through narrow blind eyes. Flesh, / white hot metal. Glows as the day with its sun. / It is a human love, I live inside. A bony skeleton / you recognize as words or simple feeling. / But it has no feeling. As the metal, is hot, it is not / given to love. / It burns the thing / inside it. And that thing / screams." (LeRoi Jones, "An Agony As Now," *The Dead Lecturer*, New York: Grove Press, 1964.)

No, I cannot consider Jones's verbal violence a surprise. To some degree it was predictable that he would crack under the pressure of the kind of extreme role playing he was doing. And it was also predictable that a man like that, a black man whose father was a postal employee and whose mother was a social worker, who was born in Newark and who wrote a book called *The Systems of Dante's Hell* (New York: Grove Press, 1965.) which according to a writer in the *Village Voice*, "sent critics scurrying off to examine his sources in Homer's *Odyssey*, Dante's *Inferno*, Tennyson's 'The Lotus-Eaters,' and Joyce's *Ulysses*," would ultimately swing so violently in the other direction. But that he was taken so seriously seems to me a sad comment on the Black Movement. Just how long had it been since a race of black conquerors had marched into town, looted the churches of the enemy, smashed their gods, and raped their women!

Cleaver, Jones's ideological other half, was an even more effective voice for Black Macho. A former rapist, he described himself as a student of Norman Mailer's "The White Negro." Their definitions of a revolutionary were similar. His raping was not a crime against women but a political act. The white man's culture rendered the white impotent, but the black man a super stud. Yet Cleaver was perhaps closer to the truth than

Jones. He understood that, sexually, black women and white women were victims of America's history and that the white man was a victim of his own Frankenstein monster.

Cleaver did a lot to politicize sexuality in the Black Movement. One of his most dubious contributions was the idea that black homosexuality was synonymous with reactionary Uncle Tomism. This is particularly clear in his attack on Baldwin. He describes Baldwin's criticism of Mailer's "The White Negro" as "schoolmarmish" and then turns, none too subtly, to an examination of the black male homosexual.

... it seems that many Negro homosexuals, acquiescing in this racial death-wish, are outraged and frustrated because in their sickness they are unable to have a baby by a white man. The cross they have to bear is that, already bending over and touching their toes for the white man, the fruit of their miscegenation is not the little half-white offspring of their dreams but an increase in the unwinding of their nerves—though they redouble their efforts and intake of the white man's sperm. . . .

The white man has deprived him of his masculinity, castrated him in the center of his burning skull, and when he submits to this change and takes the white man for his lover as well as Big Daddy, he focuses on "whiteness" all the love in his pent up soul and turns the razor edge of hatred against "blackness"—upon himself, what he is, and all those who look like him, remind him of himself. He may even hate the darkness of night. . . . (Cleaver, "Notes on a Native Son," *Soul on Ice*.)

Soul on Ice was a book that appealed to the senses. Cleaver was violent and advocated violence. Cleaver was macho and the sixties were years in which macho heroism was highly exalted and taken seriously by many people of all sorts of political and intellectual persuasions (whites did not scorn Jones's macho but his racism, assuming it is possible to separate the two). People yearned for the smell of blood on a page and Cleaver provided it.

If one is to take Cleaver at his word, the black homosexual is counterrevolutionary (1) because he's being fucked and (2) because he's being fucked by a white man. By so doing he reduces himself to the status of our black grandmothers who, as everyone knows, were fucked by white men all the time.

However, it would follow that if *a black man were doing the fucking* and the one being fucked were a white man, the black male homosexual would be just as good a revolutionary as a black heterosexual male, if not a better one. Black Macho would have to lead to this conclusion. If whom you fuck indicates your power, then obviously the greatest power would be gained by fucking a white man first, a black man second, a white woman third and a black woman not at all. The most important rule is that *nobody* fucks you.

Finally, if homosexuals are put down, even though they're males, because they get fucked, where does that leave women in terms of revolution? Black Macho allowed for only the most primitive notion of women—women as possessions, women as the spoils of war, leaving black women with no resale value. As a possession, the black woman was a symbol of defeat, and therefore of little use to the revolution except as the performer of drudgery (not unlike her role in slavery).

The white man had offered white women privilege and prestige as accompaniments to his power. Black women were offered no such deal, just the same old hard labor, a new silence, and more loneliness. The patriarchal black macho of Malcolm X might have proven functional—black women might have suffered their oppression for years in comparative bliss—but black men were blinded by their resentment of black women, their envy of white men, and their irresistible urge to bring white women down a peg. With patriarchal macho it would have taken black men years to avenge themselves. With the narcissistic macho of the Black Movement, the results were immediate.

And when the black man went as far as the adoration of his own genitals could carry him, his revolution stopped. A big Afro, a rifle, and a penis in good working order were not enough to lick the white man's world after all.

3

Imagine for a moment that there was a part of your body, an organ, that by the very nature of the society in which you lived, existed under immense pressure. Imagine that this organ, placed in a conspicuously vulnerable position on your body, was to expand, rise, and remain erect at will. Imagine that your status in society depended upon your ability to control this organ. Imagine that if you couldn't get the damn thing to work, the importance of your existence would be questioned.

Suppose further that some other overly oppressive race of people confined your "freedom of expression" almost exclusively to the manipulation of this organ. And then suppose that this race was always threatening to cut it off, to sever this organ from your body and leave you with nothing!

Suppose your peers started a movement to obtain your equality to this oppressive race. Suppose you took it upon yourself to prove your ability to use other parts of your body such as your heart and your mind. Suppose your great heart enabled you to endure enormous suffering and still love your enemy. Suppose your clever and resourceful mind enabled you to prepare eloquent and moving speeches and to write exhaustive and lengthy papers that gave evidence beyond doubt that you were the equal of any man.

But then suppose your enemy's response was to spit in your

face, to waterhose you, to bomb your homes and school buses loaded with your children, and suppose the whole nation in which you lived watched the abuse of your people on national television but still did nothing to end your misery. And suppose that one of the main reasons they didn't was because they were afraid you would use this organ on their daughters. Suppose the enemy race continued to define you only in terms of this organ (meanwhile making the function of this organ a dirty thing, illegal to describe or photograph), giving even greater emphasis to your by now legendary ability to manipulate it. And finally suppose that this enemy race's ability to manipulate this organ was assumed, by the popular culture, to be extremely doubtful at worst, unreliable at best.

Isn't it just possible that, under these circumstances, you might begin to fantasize about this organ? Couldn't you begin to bestow all sorts of magical powers on it that it might or might not have? Couldn't this organ begin to represent the very essence of your struggle against the oppressive race? Isn't it possible that you would begin to feel, since its manipulation was your one absolute strength and your enemy's one absolute weakness, that with the operation of this organ lay the solution to all your problems? How else could you react to centuries of attack on this part of your body, this organ that separated you from nonexistence, from extinction, from nonmanhood—from death?

For hundreds of years white men had written and spoken about how the black man was "hung like an ape," about how he fucked like an animal. The big black prick pervaded the white man's nightmare. Why? In a male chauvinist society each man is somewhat threatened by every other man's virility. Because white men were the oppressors and black men were oppressed, white men had an even greater cause to fear the black man's virility.

It was really quite simple. As long as black men were virile, black people would continue to exist (assuming the women were willing) and as long as black people existed, there would be the possibility of their liberation, their taking what was theirs—the products of their labor—even of their conquering the white man.

On one level, the emotional, hysterical level and the level on which most powerless white men react, white men feared the black man's sexual dexterity, the black man's sexual appeal, and the black man's attraction for the white woman. But on another level, on the level at which actual power changes hands, white men feared the black man's penis as the starting point of black families, of the strength of numbers, of the perpetuation of the race, and the resourcefulness gained from centuries of oppression.

The Civil Rights Movement occurred when black men and black women could not be terrified into silence any longer. A black woman, Rosa Parks, set the wheels in motion. Both black men and black women had grown weary of suffering, were ready to struggle, and thought they had discovered techniques that would soon lead to their freedom. But white men would not budge an inch. Despite the Civil Rights Movement's dedication to the methods of "passive resistance," white men saw the speaking out of black men as a combined threat to their own virility, to their money, and their power.

Under pressure the white man enacted meaningless legislation. He continued to debate the inferiority of the black race. He gave blacks the right to vote and nothing to vote for, the right to buy but no money to buy with, the right to go wherever they wanted but no transportation to get there. And lastly he told the black man to keep his penis tucked between his legs or there would be nothing at all. With good reason, the black man grew blind with rage. He decided he would do exactly what he thought the white man wanted him to do least. He would debase and defile white women. He would also show the white man that black women had no influence over him and that they would have to pay for fucking white men for all those years. He too would make his woman submissive, but he would not be the chump the white man had been. He'd give his woman nothing for her submissiveness.

Yes, white men were perversely obsessed with the black man's genitals but the obsession turned out to be a communicable disease and in the sixties black men came down with high fevers. Richard Wright was the first to present the white nightmare, Black Macho, as a vehicle of liberation. Then Mailer spoke of the nobility of the primitive within America's center and described how if that primitive was ever to realize his equality—equal education, wealth, political representation, and couple it with his sheer physical magnificence, his awesome virility, and stone-age sexual morality, he would rule the earth.

Black men began to harp on the white man's obsession with their genitals and that was the very point at which their own obsession began to take hold. Baldwin, under pressure, Jones, Cleaver, and many others began to glorify the primitivism of the black man, to take his macho out of the category of human error and place it in the category of divine destiny.

An assertion of his selfhood and sexuality, a rejection of the all-importance of fear, was very probably essential to the black man's development at the stage he found himself in the sixties. Perhaps it was necessary for Huey Newton and the Black Panthers to make a public display of arming themselves. Their actions represented an unprecedented boldness in the sons of slaves and had a profound and largely beneficial effect on the way in which black men would regard themselves from then on. Yet the gains would have been more lasting if an improved self-image had not been so hopelessly dependent upon Black Macho—a male chauvinist that was frequently cruel, narcissistic, and shortsighted.

Eldridge Cleaver describes a confrontation between the police and Huey Newton in February of 1967. Betty Shabazz, the widow of Malcolm X, escorted by an armed guard of Black Panthers including Newton, had arrived at *Ramparts* magazine offices in San Francisco in order to talk to Cleaver:

At that moment a big, beefy cop stepped forward. He undid the little strap holding his pistol in his holster and started shouting at Huey, "Don't point that gun at me! Stop pointing that gun at me!" He kept making gestures as though he was going for his gun. . . . Huey stopped in his tracks and stared at the cop.

"Let's split, Huey! Let's split!" Bobby Seale was saying.

Ignoring him, Huey walked within a few feet of the cop and said, "What's the matter, you got an itchy finger?"

The cop made no reply.

"You want to draw your gun?" Huey asked him.

The other cops were calling out for this cop to cool it, to take it easy, but he didn't seem to be able to hear them. He was staring into Huey's eyes, measuring him.

"O.K.," Huey said. "You big fat racist pig, draw your gun!"

The cop made no move.

"Draw it, you cowardly dog!" Huey pumped a round into the chamber of the shotgun. "I'm waiting," he said, and stood there waiting for the cop to draw. . . .

Then the cop facing Huey gave it up. He heaved a heavy sigh and lowered his head. Huey literally laughed in his face and then went off up the street at a jaunty pace, disappearing in a blaze of dazzling sunlight. (Eldridge Cleaver, *Post-Prison Writing & Speeches*, ed. Robert Sheer, New York: Random House, 1969.)

Cleaver said Newton's actions indicated he had "courage," and that would have to be the obvious conclusion. But I wonder.

It all sounds rather demented to me. And we now know for a fact that it was foolhardy. There were voices, such as Julius Lester's in *Revolutionary Notes,* that pleaded for more restraint, more calculation. "The revolutionary is very careful not to do anything that would call for a confrontation between him and the enemy as long as he knows he can't win that confrontation," Lester said in 1968. "The revolutionary does nothing that will serve only to unite the enemy against him. . . ." But no one listened.

The black revolutionary of the sixties calls to mind nothing so much as a child who is acting for the simple pleasure of the reaction he will elicit from, and the pain he will cause, his father. Is it possible that the contemporary black man is too dependent? And can we blame that dependency on slavery?

Some accepted slavery in fear of freedom; others in awareness of superior forces; others only because they were held down by the manifestation of that force. Almost all, however, with lesser or greater intensity, fell into a paternalistic pattern of thought, and almost all re-defined that pattern into a doctrine of self-protection. . . .

To the slave . . . the very meaning of paternalism shifted to one of interdependence. If the master had a duty to provide for his people and to behave like a decent human being, then his duty had to become the slave's right. Where the master preferred to translate their own self-defined duties into privileges for their people . . . the slaves understood duties to be duties. . . .

. . . the intersection of paternalism with racism worked a catastrophe, for it transformed elements of personal dependency into a sense of collective weakness . . . they had to wage a prolonged, embittered struggle with themselves as well as with their oppressors to "feel their strength" and to become "conscious of their responsibility and value." It was not that the slaves did not act like men. Rather, it was that they could not grasp their collective strength as a people and act like political men. The black struggle on that front, which has not yet been won, has paralleled that of every other oppressed people. It is difficult because it is the final struggle a people must wage to forge themselves into a nation. (Eugene Genovese, *Roll, Jordan, Roll: The World the Slaves Made,* New York: Pantheon, 1974.)

Genovese portrays the patriarchy as both harmful and beneficial. Beneficial in that it afforded the slave an opportunity to wrench from the slaveholders certain rights (i.e., the right to own his time on Sundays, to name his own children, to expect that his opinion of an overseer would be honored) as well as the opportunity to formulate a synthesis of African and American white culture. But this derived culture was harmful in that it was one of accommodation. It provided only for a situation in which the whites would be the ultimate controlling factor. Although black culture was subversive by nature, it had no way of providing for aggressive, organized, collective action, "the final struggle a people must wage to forge themselves into a nation." This may, indeed, be the case, but I would like to suggest something else.

The black man's tremendous struggle for education, for land, for political rights, for the right to protect his land and his children, can all be taken as signs that the black man was far from a helpless dependent at the time of the Emancipation Proclamation. And for that matter, probably, the infrequency of slave rebellions in the U.S. can be taken in the same way.

As Nathan Huggins suggests in his introduction to *Black Odyssey,* perhaps we have been too singleminded about discovering and proving the heroism of the minority of slaves who engaged in overt resistance, while devoting too little attention to the dignity and persistence of that majority of slaves who quietly and consistently insisted upon their own humanity in a thousand little ways against enormous odds.

. . . looking beyond the acts of defiance, rebellion, and escape, we will find a quality of courage still unsung. It is the triumph of the human spirit over unmitigated power. It raises no banners. It gained no vengeance. It was only the pervasive and persistent will among Afro-Americans to hold together through deep trauma and adversity. Much that was in their circumstances would have reduced them to brutes, to objects in the market. It would have been easy to become what many whites insisted they were: dumb, slow, insensitive, immoral, wanting in true human qualities. But slaves laid claim to their humanity and refused to compromise it, creating families where there would have been none, weaving a cosmology and a moral order in a world of duplicity, shaping an art and a world of imagination in a cultural desert.

It is exactly this triumph of the human spirit over adversity that is the great story in Afro-American slavery. . . . No black American, and certainly no white American, has cause to apologize for them. Modern history knows of no more glorious story of the triumphant human spirit. (Nathan I. Huggins, *Black Odyssey: The Afro-American Ordeal in Slavery*, New York: Pantheon, 1977.)

The black man knew that momentary acts of courage could mean the wholesale slaughter of his people, and nothing was more important to him than their preservation, not even the gratifying experience of a public manhood that whites would finally have to recognize. In this sense, the black man showed boundless courage. And it was probably the reason the move to crush Reconstruction, to bind him again to subservience, was so forceful. He was still very dangerous then, because he was still so close to that slave ship he had arrived in. But as he lost grip on a black perspective, as he lost track of his original intentions, and adopted a white perspective, a perspective from which he was seen as helpless, dependent, animalistic, he began to think the things he had done indicated that he was not a man. Once this process was set in motion, he would be allowed more and more freedom by the whites. You could say that the less he knew what to do with his privileges, the more the white power structure was willing to give him.

The black man's acceptance of a white perspective was gradual and it was only partially accomplished at the time of the abolition of slavery. Many newly freed slaves insisted that their women not work in the fields. Their material advancement was severely set back as a result. In this case black men had forgotten their priority, independent economic survival, and substituted for it a white priority that was totally inappropriate to their situation. But for the most part black men after slavery kept their own priorities in the foreground and that was why they were so maniacally feared and put down.

Contrary to what Genovese says, the danger for the slave was not dependency itself. Rather it was the danger of becoming dependent upon a foreign and essentially hostile culture: only then would the black man superimpose the values of the larger white society upon his own quite different needs. The black man post-slavery for the most part successfully avoided that danger. But today, more than a hundred years later, he seems closer to a destructive dependency upon white culture than he has ever been before.

Can you imagine what the newly emancipated slaves would have done with the opportunities that are now available to blacks in this country? Would they have needed to parade before white police with rifles to prove that they were men? Would it be possible to explain to them why blacks destroy their own neighborhoods, rape and abuse their own women, drink too much liquor, inject heroin into their veins?

Civil Rights Movement tactics were deserted because they depended too much upon the goodness of whites. But the Black Movement turned out to be even less independent in its notion of freedom. There was a great deal more marching around with rifles and combat boots, of badmouthing and

78

threatening whites, than there was of actual revolutionary planning and action. What did this son of a slave actually expect whites to do? Did he expect, like the boy who is throwing a tantrum because he can't have something he wants, that Big Daddy would finally buy it for him just to shut him up? The black man had forgotten who he was. He had come to believe that his universe was really as the whites had defined it. The most important thing was no longer the welfare of his family, his people, but white racism.

White racism is the white man's problem, not the black man's. His task is rather—and the black man post-slavery knew it—to ameliorate the manifestations of racism, his own poverty, deprivation, and unhappiness; to remove by whatever means necessary the restraints that exist on his health, his productivity, his creativity, and the perpetuation of his culture, the way of life that will allow him to live, survive, and flourish.

But the contemporary black man no longer exists for his people or even for himself. He has made himself a living testament to the white man's failures. He must continue to suffer, to be brutalized, and to brutalize his peers until whites are able to become the better people that will be required to deliver him from his condition. He has become a martyr. And he has arrived in this place, not because of the dependency inflicted upon him in slavery, but because his black perspective, like the white perspective, supported the notion that manhood is more valuable than anything else.

As long as he was able to hold onto his own black-centered definition of manhood, his sense of himself was not endangered. But it was inevitable, as the time that he had been in this country lengthened, that he would get the black and white perspectives confused. He is unaware that he has accepted a definition of manhood that is destructive to himself and that negates the best efforts of his past.

The Black Power Movement did yield certain gains—jobs, grants, scholarships, poverty programs, etc.—but many of these things are in the process of being lost, and weren't worth the price that was paid for them in any case. As long as black people are dealing in jobs and titles and grants, and not factories and land and department stores, anything they have achieved has got to be subject to the whims of the dominant white power structure and beneficial only for a select few. The majority of blacks are left with only the booby prize of an outmoded manhood that mocks their powerlessness.

It is interesting to note how various black male leaders are recouping in the aftermath of their abominable failure to effect any changes in the lives of the masses of black people. Each in his own manner is trying to shift away from the disastrous emphasis on "the beautiful black man," that is, the black man as formed by the white man's fantasy of him, and toward an emphasis on economics. Jones, now Comrade Baraka, Stokely Carmichael, and Huey Newton have all become socialists— Carmichael stressing the importance of organizing the Third World, Baraka and Newton stressing the organization of Americans, both black and white. On the other side of the political spectrum, there's Jesse Jackson, one of the most vocal advocates of black capitalism, of hardworking blacks who discipline their children and save their money and buy station wagons instead of Cadillacs. Then there's a level of newly corrupt black leadership such as Reverend Ike, the quintessential slick black preacher, who proudly tells his congregation that their donations go to pay for his expensive suits and his fleet of Rolls Royces. The Muslims have dropped their racist policy and have renewed their emphasis on economic autonomy the American way. Former President Ford's representative attended Elijah Mohammed's funeral. Money was nearly a dirty word among blacks in the sixties but no longer, and that's a good sign, since the definition of power in America is money.

But black leaders have emerged from the dream world of Black Power only to enter another. Before, they deluded themselves into thinking the white power structure could be defeated with bravado. Now they think that if they don three-piece suits and ties and behave in a gentlemanly fashion, they can join the white power structure. And, what is most disturbing, they refuse to realize that there is a choice to be made here. The choice is either to assimilate, which will mean the cultural annihilation of black people, or to pursue the struggle of their slave descendants for a decent existence for all black people and the continuation of their cultural and racial identity. Pursuing money, economic independence, does not mean that one has to become white.

Perhaps the single most important reason the Black Movement did not work was that black men did not realize they could not wage struggle without the full involvement of women. And in that sense they made a mistake that the blacks of the post-slavery period would have been least likely to have made. Women, traditionally, want more than anything to keep things together. Women are hard workers and they require little compensation. Women are sometimes willing to die much more quickly than men. Women vote. Women march. Women perform tedious tasks. And women cannot be paid off for the death and the suffering of their children. Look at how important women have been to the liberation struggles in Africa. By negating the importance of their role, the efficiency of the Black Movement was obliterated. It was just a lot of black men strutting around with Afros.

Black people, as a whole, seem trapped now in a curious group amnesia that is maintained, in part, by their lack of confidence in their leadership. But can anyone blame them? If leadership shows no courage in facing up to the mistakes of the past, why should anyone expect them to show courage in facing the possibilities of their future?

The middle-class black man—he may have a Master's Degree in business, he may only have a union card—believes that he has found some alternative to being black. He believes he can sneak in and raid whitey's piggy bank while whiteys' back is presumably turned, live in a white community or a suffocating black middle-class community with his white or nearly white wife, avert his eye when the company he works for wants to do something abusive to blacks, drive a Mercedes, wear expensive European suits, become indignant at blacks who are inelegant enough to nod out on the subway—he believes he can do all this and not die inside, completely and irreversibly.

It is interesting the levels of delusion he has incorporated. During the Black Movement he was the one who got away with all the goods. As blacks were rioting in the streets, troubling the sleep of whites in every suburban enclave in America, there he was, prepared, educated, trained, clean cut, with a well-groomed Afro, slightly menacing but negotiable. "I have only to wave my magic wand and all those angry blacks at your doorstep will disappear," he said. "Buy me out and I will be your black." Or even worse, as did the poverty players, he said, "Give me some money to work miracles in the ghetto." And either way, with or without his white wife, he used that money to escape from the ghetto, but also to escape from blackness. Because Black Macho, which had only the most perverted relation to blackness, had been a mistake, he decided he did not want to be black anymore.

He took his money and his energy and poured it back into the white community. He called it "working within the system." And he took the credit when blacks finally settled down, or rather were drugged and beaten into silence. Those blacks were proud—or should have been proud, he thought—of what he had been able to rip off. Then it got so he could no longer go into the ghetto to visit his mother or to have an occasional home-cooked meal for old times' sake because the "niggas" there, his former brothers, who had bought him his affluence with their blood, and their suffering, would steal the tires off his Mercedes, demand his wallet from behind the handles of their switchblades, or dribble their drug and alcohol deliriums all over his silk suit while they were talking to him.

Why couldn't they, he wanted to know, pull themselves up by their bootstraps? How dare they threaten the peace now? How dare they hate him because of his material wealth, because he was a traitor? How dare they be so conspicuously oppressed?

Middle-class blacks insist upon believing that the white man should take care of their poor, upgrade the prisons, stop sending blacks to jail, clean up the mess in the slums, improve the schools, make their children learn. I am not saying that white government and business, since they are partially sustained by black money, are not responsible and ought not to be tapped whenever possible, but that it is time to recognize that we cannot expect very much from them in the way of initiative or cooperation in the solving of our problems. That is just the way it is. Big Daddy is no relation.

Capitalism is dependent upon the notion of a Big Daddy. Genovese was right in that sense. You are supposed to give the principal part of your production, the fruits of your labor, to someone else and he will take care of you. Carl McCall (Councilman, N.Y.) has spoken about the dearth of black leadership. He said, basically, that there were black leaders but that people didn't know it because whites failed to give these leaders anything to give black people. That's my idea of dependency.

And the poor black man is implicated in this as well. Yes, forces conspire against him but he *allows* life to happen to him, he *allows* others to make the decisions for him, he trusts the white bureaucracy enough to allow them to put him behind bars, to allow them to take care of his wife and children. He acts as though he and the black woman are at war, as though he might win something by her destruction. He uses the debilitating game of sexual superiority as a substitute for establishing something worthwhile. He's got nothing else, he says. He's got to have some fun, he says. That's how he's kept in his place. And just as fast as he can enter the black middle class, he begins to turn white, or what he thinks is white. Slavery is a subject he never discusses, and about which he knows little. The Civil Rights and Black Movements have become nothing more than slightly amusing cocktail party conversation. And all because he's forgotten the hopes and aspirations of the slaves, forgotten what he's been through and all of the lessons of these four hundred years.

By so doing he is making a choice: the complete submergence of his cultural identity. After all, he is no longer African. His blood is mixed. He has no memory of the old ways, the life on the continent, the sense of outrage at the kidnap. The other experience that sets him apart, poverty and discrimination, will have to be eliminated if he is to survive. The question is simply this: If one removes the memory of his African past, and the experience of deprivation, is there an identity unique to the American black, an identity worth preserving beyond that of simply being an American, a slightly soiled white American?

I tend to think there is, there must be. From a purely objective point of view, miscegenation and assimilation are not at all bad things and they may, in fact, eliminate poverty, discrimination, and ignorance in this country. Full employment is not a national impossibility, even under capitalism. But there is always the chance, the considerable likelihood really, that white America will use the lack of racial consciousness on the part of the black middle class as an opportunity to formalize what already exists unofficially: a partitioning off of the undesirable black element into urban reservations. Also, the black man's skin is still black. Even conscious, planned miscegenation would take generations to make the difference invisible.

Furthermore, is there nothing worth preserving of the black experience? Our ancestors put a lot of energy into the formulation of a survival plan for displaced Africans, an Afro-American culture. Is uniformity the only cure for this country's ailments? Can white and black Americans only live in peace if blacks negate the importance of their contribution to American civilization?

It seems to me that what makes people valuable is whatever they have to offer that is unique. Black people have their blackness. They have their music, their dance, their manner of cooking, of walking, of talking, their dress and, most important, their story which cannot, must not be discarded like some old dress that can no longer be reworked with a different hemline to meet the current fashion. There is no reason to assume that losing all of that would get rid of the poverty and oppression. And even if it does, at what price? Surely it is at least worthwhile to note that there would indeed be a price.

Finally, it is the black man who has made this undeclared choice. The black woman is simply along for the ride. His actions in the sixties and in the Civil Rights Movement have made an indelible imprint on the quality of our lives. Do we like what he has done? Are we satisfied to ride the tide of the changing interpretations of black manhood? Can it sustain us and the nearly fifty percent of black children who depend upon us? Can we afford to sit by and allow him to orchestrate our future?

PART II

The Myth of the Superwoman

The cumulative effects of the way black women have been mistreated and sexually dehumanized in America, the way they have had to labor to earn a living and rear children and support both white and black men, from the days of slavery even until now, have produced in many Negro females a sort of "studism," which expresses itself in a strong matriarchal drive. Negro men complain that black women are too dominating, too demanding, too strict, too inconsiderate, and too "masculine"—so much so that the men get the feeling that they are being "castrated." Well, what can one expect?

(Calvin C. Hernton, *Sex and Racism in America*, New York: Grove Press, 1966.)

1

By the time I was fifteen there was nothing I dreaded more than being like the women in my family. I had been taught to be repelled by them as effectively as I had been taught to avoid women who wore men's trousers and smoked cigars. Their sharp tongues were able to disassemble any human ego in five minutes flat. Men always seemed peripheral to their lives. Nearly all had been divorced at least once. They all worked. Never as domestics and none had ever been on welfare. "Too proud," they said. All of them were haughty about having made their own way. They seemed to already know everything.

When I brought a young man to the house, I watched these women nervously, pleading silently with them not to submit him to the family X-ray. As soon as the door was closed behind him, they would begin to make pronouncements. "He's cheap," or, "He's very immature." They were always right, and that disturbed me. It seemed as though there were centuries between our perceptions of life. They told me that they were only trying to help me, that it was ever so difficult growing up to be a whole black woman. But I didn't want to hear that.

I can't remember when I first learned that my family expected me to work, to be able to take care of myself when I grew up. My mother was so extraordinarily career-oriented that I was never allowed to take lessons in anything unless I manifested a deep interest in a career in that area. "Will she ever be a musician?" she asked my piano teacher. "It's not very likely," he said, and my lessons stopped abruptly. It had been drilled into me that the best and only sure support was self-support.

The fact that my family expected me to work and have a career should have made the things I wanted very different from what little white girls wanted according to the popular sociological view. But I don't believe any sociologist took into account a man like my stepfather. My stepfather gave me "housewife lessons." It was he who taught me how to clean house and how I should act around men. "Don't be like your mother," he told me. "She's a nice lady but she's a bad wife. She was just lucky with me. I want you to get a *good* husband."

Although he never managed to fully domesticate me, it was him I finally listened to because he was saying essentially the same things I read in the magazines, saw in the movies, gaped at on television. Despite the lessons of the women in my family, I had no intention whatsoever of growing up to earn my own keep. I knew better than those women and everything in my environment supported what I knew. Didn't American media proclaim that with the right equipment, the appropriate quantities of femininity and sex appeal, I need not develop any other talents? Didn't my peers tell me not to listen to my mother? Older women are bitter because they were unable to measure up, they cautioned. Don't trust them. Growing up in Harlem, I listened to these messages no less intently than the little white girls who grew up on Park Avenue, in Scarsdale, and on Long Island. In a way I needed to hear them, to believe them, even more than they did. Their alternative was not eternal Aunt Jemimahood, Porgy-n'-Besshood. Mine was. I viewed work as no more than a contingency plan.

Then in 1968, the year I turned sixteen, blackness came to Harlem. In lofts, theaters, apartments, the streets, any available space—black artists, musicians, writers, poets, many of them fresh from the East Village, began to gather in response to the cries of "Black Power" and "kill whitey" that had echoed in the streets during the recent riots. They were the cultural wing come to entertain, to guide, to stimulate the troops of black rebels. And Harlemites, who had always been divided into two distinct categories—the black bourgeoisie, and the poor—now began to split into more factions.

The old categories were first renamed. The black bourgeoisie became the "knee-grows" and the poor became the "lumpen" or the "grass roots." The two new factions were the "militants" and the "nationalists." The militants had no patience with the singing, dancing, incense, and poetry reading of the black nationalists; with the black bourgeoisie's appeals for restraint; or the inertia of the poor. The nationalists could not abide the militants' insistence that everyone "hit the streets" or their Marxist rhetoric; the black bourgeoisie's loyalty to European culture; and the frequent cultural obtuseness of the poor about everything but rock, blues, and gospel. The black bourgeoisie was temporarily, but thoroughly, intimidated by everyone. And the poor thought they were *all* crazy. But all parties managed to agree on at least one issue: The black woman's act needed intensive cleaning up.

She was too domineering, too strong, too aggressive, too outspoken, too castrating, too masculine. She was one of the main reasons the black man had never been properly able to take hold of his situation in this country. The black man had troubles and he would have to fight the white man to get them solved but how would he ever have the strength if his own house was not in proper order, if his wife, his woman, his mother, his sisters, who should have been his faithful servants, were undermining him at every opportunity.

I was fascinated by all of this. Not by the political implications of a black movement in a white America. I quickly realized that was a male responsibility. But by how it would affect my narrow universe. To me and many other black women the Black Movement seemed to guarantee that our secret dreams of being male-dominated and -supported women were that much more attainable. If black men had power, as in Black Power, then we would become the women of the powerful. Surely this was more substantial food for fantasy than our previous fare. After all, Lucille Ball and Sandra Dee and Jane Fonda and Audrey Hepburn and Elizabeth Taylor and Shirley MacLaine and Kim Novak had not been black. Here was an opportunity that had real flesh and blood.

But first we had a hell of a history to live down. We had been rolling around in bed with the slave master while the black man was having his penis cut off; we had never been able to close our legs to a white man nor deny our breasts to a white child; we had been too eagerly loyal to our white male employer, taking the job he offered when he would give none to our man, cleaning his house with love and attention while our man was being lynched by white men in white hoods. We had not allowed the black man to be a man in his own house. We had criticized him interminably and questioned his masculinity. We had driven him to alcohol, to drugs, to crime, to every bad thing he had ever done to harm himself or his family because our eyes had not reflected his manhood.

I felt shocked by this history. My mother had done her best to keep all of it from me. I only knew that the men in my family had seemed to be very sweet, very intelligent, but a bit ineffectual and spineless. And the women had seemed to be relentless achievers, often providers.

It was the women who had pulled together to make sure my sister and I never knew a moment of loneliness or want. We attended private schools from the very first, were taken to camp or Provincetown or Europe in the summers. My mother was a teacher, then a college lecturer and an artist. Despite having two children at the age of twenty-two (my sister and I were born in the same year) and having separated from my musician father after four years of marriage, she was able to complete her B.S. in education and her M.A. in fine arts at CCNY. My aunt had entered NYU at sixteen and people used to come from all around Harlem to see the little girl who was going to the "big university." When I was small, she was already working on her Ph.D. at Hunter. My grandmother, Mama Jones, was a seamstress and an established neighborhood dressmaker and designer. Five feet tall in her stocking feet and with a bit of a tendency to play the Southern belle, she was, nevertheless, I slowly began to realize, a woman of fierce determination and an iron will; she absolutely refused to recognize anything but the best from any of us.

Yet in so many ways that I had not realized these women were just like other black women. I was woefully incapable when I was a child of seeing that their strength was just one facet of their humanity, their fallibility. When I found out that my mother had majored in education as an undergraduate, and had subsequently become a teacher, mostly because CCNY back then did not accept females in the School of Liberal Arts; that my aunt was never able to complete her Ph.D. because she, who had devoured books all of her life, had been repeatedly accused of illiteracy by her professors and had finally dropped out, I made little of it. When I was told that Mama Jones had wanted to be a dancer and was unable to realize her ambition because her parents considered that profession unfitting for a lady, somehow I thought that it must have been because Mama Jones wanted it that way. Later still I would find out that although she had shown much spirit when she had divorced my grandfather and taken back her maiden name, she never worked a day in her life until her youngest child was fourteen, and up until then she supported herself and her three children with alimony payments, payments for which she had to make frequent visits to the family courts. At one point she had tried to go back to school, to the Fashion Institute, but having come home one day from class to find my aunt and my mother talking with some boys in the hallway, she had promptly given it up. And it is said that she never made a single move without the approval of her older brother. That other paragon of strength, my father's mother, had given up her work completely to traipse around the world after my step-grandfather, who was an officer in the Army.

Both of my grandmothers and my grandfathers had come from solidly patriarchal backgrounds. My great-grandfathers were providers and protectors, men accustomed to unquestioned authority; the idea that their daughters might one day be considered Amazons and their sons dispensable and lightweight probably would have confounded them. There was even some evidence that my grandfathers' lackadaisical approaches to patriarchy were more in the nature of rebellions against their own fathers than rooted in their historical emasculation; that my grandmothers were so quick to divorce not because they couldn't abide the fetters of marriage but because every man was necessarily measured against their fathers. My great-grandfathers were a school principal and a preacher on my mother's side, a sea pilot and a plantation owner in Haiti and Jamaica on my father's side. My great-grandmothers, at least the fuzzy little women I knew from old photos, seemed hardly intimidating. One was even named Baby Doll. They were all housewives, except Ida Mae, whose husband was the principal—occasionally he allowed her to teach in his school.

But at sixteen I had no use for paradoxes. The women in my family could not be both strong and weak, both victimizers and victimized. I could hardly see the point in pursuing such an obviously unrewarding line of contemplation. It was much easier just to believe these women were the bloodless monsters the Black Movement said they were, and to reckon with my share in that sin. What must I do, I wondered, to atone for my errors and make myself more palatable? I must be, black men told me, more feminine, I must try to make myself more attractive, and above all more submissive, in other words a "natural woman."

It made me cringe to hear men refer to me as "strong," because I knew they were referring to the historical me, the monolithic me—the invincible black woman who made their penises shrivel up into their bellies, who reminded them they had no power to control their own destinies, much less hers, who made them loathe and want to destroy that woman. Never realizing how imaginary my "strength" really was, I swore never to use it.

But that didn't seem to be enough. I was not terribly convincing as a passive woman. The men seemed to go right through my fingers. I was overeager, too impatient, and somehow I could not stop getting angry from time to time. So I was left alone, unwillingly, with my limited resources, my private-school education, my good college board scores, my black bourgeois upbringing, my bright and promising career potential. The spring I graduated from high school, in 1969, the last thing on my mind was college. Against almost unanimous school and family protest, I decided to go to Howard University to be with black people, and because it was the next best thing to not going at all, and that was where I was scheduled to be the following September unless I could come up with something better during the summer.

In June my sister and I went to Mexico, a graduation present from my mother. She knew how desperately we longed to function as adults and perhaps she thought we would be able to pull it off without too much damage if she was in a different country. At the University of Mexico my sister and I met up with a group of upper-middle-class quasi-revolutionary Mexican students. The six revolutionaries lived in communal fashion in a kind of ranch house right outside of Mexico City, and we soon moved in with them. I quickly paired off with the most Indian looking one of the group, a twenty-six-year-old Guatemalan, and made up my mind just as quickly, as was my habit in those days, that I would be spending the next few years at his side. He was quite good-looking, had an aristocratic but pleasant and affectionate manner, and a master's degree in architecture. He spoke little English, which was a great boon to our relationship since I spoke practically no Spanish. When it was essential, my sister, who spoke Spanish, acted as translator or, in more personal matters, we made do with French.

Here seemed the answer to all my problems. I had formed the conviction that as soon as I could get a man, any man, to assume responsibility for me, I would no longer have to answer to my mother. Whenever she called to tell me to come home, I'd keep telling her, "We'll get married, just send permission." And my Guatemalan friend would nod eagerly, as if my mother could see him. How I wished she could. I couldn't understand how she could possibly worry. Wasn't this the way I was supposed to end up? If it had happened a little early, so much the better for everyone. Didn't she really mean me to have a career only if I couldn't find anything better? In the end, my mother put pressure on the American Embassy and I was forced to return to New York. As long as I was seventeen my mother could continue to control my movements, even on the international scale. As far as I was concerned I had received a serious marriage proposal from my Guatemalan revolutionary. As far as my mother was concerned I was a juvenile delinquent.

I was in no way prepared to understand what my mother was going through. At least partially, she was under the influence of what she had been hearing about communes in American media. She imagined I was sleeping alternately with at least four men, experimenting with new drugs every evening, and doing all sorts of degenerate things. That I was asking permission to marry simply meant that I had been drugged into submission, taken for all my money, and was being held captive. I think she expected the ransom demands at any moment. Little did she know how tame and Latin Roman Catholic the rebellion of my Mexicans was. Our commune was rigidly monogamous, although each couple used to trade bedrooms every week. Marijuana was the only drug permitted. There was a maid who came every day to do the cleaning and fix breakfast. The males took turns going to work for a very straight company in the city that was owned by one of their fathers. The group's ambition was to make movies. I even did a screen test, admittedly in the nude. It was a very domestic life. I would have been bored to tears, if I hadn't been high most of the time. Everyone except myself, after my sister went home, was over twenty-one and they're all probably staunch pillars of society by now. They were amazingly unnerved by my mother's phone calls. There were four males and two females in the commune besides myself—nice, ordinary, intelligent, educated kids who smoked too much pot. That was all. But how could my mother have known that? She told me later that she was very surprised by how healthy and happy I looked when I got back.

At that time bands of teenagers were roaming the East Village, barefoot, dirty, and glassy-eyed. LSD, mescaline, marijuana, hashish, heroin, speed were all easily available. The white kids were rebelling. And black kids, not to be outdone, were doing the same. I was big enough to pass for an adult; I could participate in almost any form of dissipation, if I wanted to. And worst of all, I believed that there was an impenetrable wall between me and anything like poverty and suffering.

All of this had the effect of accelerating my mother's paranoia. She had protected me and tried to render my childhood one extended fairytale of security, comfort, and happiness, and I had let her down.

It must be a difficult thing to be the mother of a teenage daughter in a black community. Some of the nice little old men who used to pat her on the head when she was a child begin to want to pat her on the ass when she is thirteen. The neighborhood pimps and hustlers begin to proposition her. They know that she is tired of the rules and regulations of family life, that her head is filled with escapist fantasies. Adolescence is also the point at which peer pressure begins to take over.

I can understand why my mother felt desperate. No one else thought it would be particularly horrible if I got pregnant or got married before I had grown up, if I never completed college. I was a black girl; I had done as well as could be expected under the circumstances. My mother has since explained to me that since it was obvious her attempt to protect me was going to prove a failure, she was determined to make me realize that as a black girl in white America I was going to find it an uphill climb to keep myself together. I did not have a solid and powerful middle-class establishment to rebel against—only an establishment of poverty and oppression thinly veiled by a few trips to Europe, a private school education, and some clothes from Bonwit Teller. She wanted to compel me to think for myself because she knew, whatever else she didn't know, that I would never be able to survive if I didn't. Little black girls who had a predilection for moving in with anyone who had a handsome face and a kingsize bed tended to end up dead, or with needles in their arms, or on welfare.

Now that I know my mother better, I know that her sense of powerlessness made it seem all the more essential to her that she take radical action. We agreed, upon the advice of a social worker at the Bureau of Child Guidance, that I was to enter a Catholic Home called the Sisters of the Good Shepherd Residence. I willingly went there because I thought at the time that I would rather live in hell than be with my mother. That she sent me was a calculated risk; it was her way of providing me with a peek at where I was inevitably heading. And I must say it worked.

Back in 1969 record numbers of white girls were running away from home and it made big news. But many more black girls were running away. Running away is a uniquely juvenile, and mostly female, crime. As with most crimes, you are usually incarcerated for it only if you are poor. When a middle-class child runs away and is picked up, the courts will usually let her parents take her back, if they are willing. But if a child has committed previous offenses—and such a child tends to come from a home where the mother has no husband and there are a lot of other children, where the income is scanty and/or provided by public assistance—the child is institutionalized.

The Sisters of the Good Shepherd Residence was one of the institutions which provided temporary shelter for many of these runaway girls, mostly black and Puerto Rican, although some were there because they were victims of child abuse. The function of the Residence was to administer psychological tests. The results were then used to help the court decide what to do with the child. Most children stayed in the Residence for no more than three weeks. I, however, had not come through the courts. I was a special case. I was a black middle-class girl who did not know how to behave and could not get along with her mother. Although I was middle class, my mother was determined not to put me in a private home; it would have been no more than an extension of my private-school experience. I was to remain in a public institution until it was time for me to go to college in the fall. My stay there was five weeks.

The first week I cried. The second week I became very depressed. I was totally unprepared, to say the least, for my situation. The head sister, who was far away in a main floor office, knew my circumstances, my family, how I had come to be there. The other sisters did not. As far as they were concerned I was just another filthy little black girl with sex and drugs on the brain. I spent a number of afternoons in solitary (an office with the door closed, no food, reading, or other

entertainment) for "making speeches." As far as I could deter-
mine, "making speeches" was defined as any kind of discussion
of ideas contrary to those of the presiding nuns. For example,
I remember one of my "speeches" was about how absurd it was
to condemn premarital sex, when dealing with a group of girls
who were already sexually experienced. The nuns seemed much
more comfortable when the girls were having wishful-thinking
chats about their boyfriends. As I began to realize that in-
dividuality and intelligence, in all their incipient forms, were
considered subversive, I stopped attracting attention to myself
and began to look around me, to become aware of the other
inmates.

Most of them were much younger than I. By the time most
black girls in the ghetto have reached seventeen, they have
either come to terms with their limited possibilities and settled
on careers as typists or nurses or, for the very ambitious, social
work and teaching, and/or quietly had their babies and sunk
into the background of the church; or become so much involved in the streets that they cannot be contained by a place
like the Residence and must be sent directly to the more
prisonlike "homes" for really "bad" girls.

The average girl at the Residence had at least four brothers
and sisters and a very young mother, who was either unmarried
or separated from her husband, and on welfare. The girl usually
had not done well in school, was bored by it. Her home was
small and unlivable. She frequently found the very clean and
well-equipped Residence, which had private rooms for many of
the girls, infinitely more desirable. She often felt she was in her
mother's way, or in her mother's boyfriend's way, that her
mother did not have time for her or that it was too crowded
in the house, especially in the summer, so she spent a lot of
time in the streets messing with the neighborhood boys, experimenting with her sexuality (she was always much ashamed of
this), until something bigger and better came along. This usu-

ally took the form of an older man, in his twenties, perhaps a pimp, a drug dealer, or just a small-time neighborhood punk, who she was convinced could offer her what she had been looking for ever since she could remember: an authority beyond her mother's; womanhood; in a word, marriage.

A few weeks after I arrived, the administration of the home changed hands. Sister Geraldine, a large, generous, down-to-earth young white woman, took over from the two nuns who had preceded her. These two sisters, also white, whom we all called Mutt and Jeff because one was huge and fat and the other one was almost a midget, had run a very tight ship. The brief and infrequent periods during which we were allowed to talk were signaled by the ringing of bells. Requests for special attention of any kind—an extra cigarette beyond the allotted six a day, a particular work assignment—were all flatly denied. Mutt and Jeff were the ones who called my ideas "making speeches." But the most important and devastating thing about them, to my mind, was their disdain for us; their haughty silence seemed a continual reminder that we were irredeemable, disreputable creatures, unworthy, by implication, even of God's attention. The thing to remember about the girls in the Residence is that they were children, twelve, thirteen, fourteen, even though many of them had taken a variety of drugs, were pregnant, or already had children of their own. Some of them even played with dolls. More than anything else, they seemed in need of love, unqualified love, and attention. Sister Geraldine seemed to know that from the first moment she came.

The first time I laid eyes on her I was in solitary and I was crying. Somehow I had always known that one of the biggest struggles of growing up would be to never allow anyone to make me think I was bad. By the time I was fifteen I had completely renounced the church because I had realized that as a black teenage girl I could not live with the standard it imposed. I had resolved that I would find my God in my own way. I first had sex after having made what I thought was a conscious and clear decision to do so, although later I would realize that I was not prepared at the time to make such a decision. But what was most important to me was the feeling, even though I was a child, that I was controlling my life and setting my own standards. I was very stubborn, perhaps too stubborn about this, but that day in solitary I was beginning to waver. How could I be right if everyone thought I was wrong? *Something* was wrong. Was it me? Sister Geraldine came into that barren office and sat beside me. She asked me why I was crying. I told her. I told her everything. Quietly she told me that she would soon send for me, that things would be changing at the Residence, that she would expect me to help her.

And she made good her word. Under Sister Geraldine there was always plenty of talk, even argument, lots of activity. Girls took turns sitting on her lap. She kissed them, held them, listened carefully to their problems both large and small. Perhaps no one had ever done such things for them before without attaching a price to it. She took us for rides in her car. And she did allow me to help her. I was assigned to take small groups of girls out on trips around the city. She put me to work as a kind of assistant. Under her administration the home became a kind of refuge for us, a vacation from the stressful pressures of sexual relationships that we were not grown-up enough to handle, from having to pretend that we were adults, sure of ourselves and what we were doing with our lives. She allowed us all time to think.

As the atmosphere of the Residence changed, I became more involved with my companions, with listening to their stories. Teenage girls are notoriously male-identified. I was no exception. It did not occur to me, right away, to feel any kinship with these females because they were black and young like me. Yes, I was for Black Power, but that didn't have anything to do with a bunch of little girls who had gotten themselves into trouble, now did it? But as they told me their stories, I began to recognize a pattern. Many of them had been in countless foster homes, sometimes they were brutally beaten. The mothers of a few of these girls would encourage them to spend the night out and then would send the police to pick them up. In court the mother's characteristic plea was, "I can't do nothin' with her." While white girls tended to run out of state, black and Hispanic girls could rarely imagine that, much less afford it. Usually they didn't run farther than a couple of blocks. They'd tell me about the boyfriends who had finally made them feel like someone, and the inevitable pregnancies, the babies they were determined to have because they needed something that belonged to them. Perhaps their own mothers had said the same things. "Don't you understand?" they insisted. "He wants to marry me." Weren't those my words? Was not their story in some way my own, despite my mother's efforts to protect me?

The fact is, we had all been born into a situation in which it was continually brought home to us that there was only one acceptable standard of womanhood: Doris Day, housewife and mother—pretty, attractive, sexy even, yet inaccessible and virginal; married to a prince who never cursed his wife, never raped his children, and always brought home more than sufficient bacon. The circumstances of our lives made that standard not only impossible to achieve, but masochistic to hope for. First of all, we were black and therefore we could never be Doris Day. Second, our needs were really quite different. We lived in a dangerous environment, the black community, which did not protect its girl children, and beyond that the United States of America, which viewed black women as beasts of burden and sex toys. To be innocent *and* sexy was nothing less than suicidal. We needed to stand up for ourselves, think for ourselves, formulate and maintain our own standards. Many of us might marry men who raped our children and cursed at us; all of us were sure to encounter a great many refutations of the fantasy. What would we do when we met with reality? Be destroyed by it?

Many of the girls at the home had already been brutalized. They had been taught that their very efforts to survive meant that they were bad. Nice girls simply did not survive such things. I remember once I took a girl on a trip. We went to Orange Julius on Eighth Street and sat at the counter. Perhaps because she was very pretty with huge eyes and long lashes, the man behind the counter took a liking to her and gave her an orange. As soon as he had turned his back, as quick as lightning, she had stolen two more oranges. I was amazed. She had no use for them and threw them away soon after we left.

One of the things I knew by the time I left the Residence was that many of the girls there would not survive, or rather they would survive but they would never really live. They were locked into the pattern, sealed into the little niche society had prepared for them, labeled "girls who do not know how to behave." Already their concept of themselves was too low. They saw any kindness to them as weakness. They seemed to wait for some male to take charge of their lives. And when there was no such male around, they stopped living. They went wherever the tide swept them. They were in limbo.

On a recent visit to the Residence, a black girl of sixteen told me, gleefully, of how she had run away with her boyfriend of seventeen who had robbed a bank. They had used the money to work their way across the country, partying. He was in Spofford serving a term of eighteen months. She was getting out in a few weeks. I asked her what was she going to do when she got out. "I'm gonna wait for my boyfriend." "You can't spend eighteen months just waiting," I said, and the other girls laughed nervously. "What else are you going to do?" "I'm gonna stay high," she said blankly. According to her society's oldest, most strictly enforced rules, she wasn't wrong. She was following the real prescription for womanhood. First, she'd found the man around her who had the most money and attached herself to him. Since he'd been detained, she would go into hibernation until he returned. Her life began and ended with him, belonged to him, even though he was only a child himself. He determined her moral character. If he had none, she had none.

In the world the black woman comes from, the best man is automatically defined as the man with the most money and "power" that he can get. In the ghetto, this is often the pimp, the drug dealer, the numbers runner, the common thief, but he might just as well be (and is for middle-class black girls) the public official; the highly paid executive in the poverty structure; the Scotch-drinking self-absorbed doctor, lawyer, professor, entertainer whose only concern is with his summer home, his Mercedes-Benz, his bank account, his Gucci shoes, and the lightness of his wife's skin.

This black woman can be poor but she can also be middle class, have attended private schools, summered not in the hot city streets but in Europe, or on the Cape; her father could be a doctor or a lawyer or a judge; her mother a housewife, a society lady, or a career woman. Whatever her status, she would have learned by the time she reached adolescence that black women were treated like animals during slavery, that somehow that means that to be a black woman is bad, that the archetypal black woman is Aunt Jemima or a whore, and that she must smile so that black men won't think she's tough and "matriarchal." And she need not end up in "trouble" necessarily, in prison, in a juvenile home, on drugs, on the streets as a prostitute, or having a baby at fourteen, but just in a dead-end job that she hates, in an unhappy destructive marriage, having children she doesn't want, or wasn't ready to have, or shouldn't have had. Or she might just become a quiet alcoholic, over-weight and with high blood pressure, or chronically depressed. The point is that the life of such a young woman is gone and she never once exercised any control over it.

In the girls I met at the Residence I could see generation after generation stretched out into infinity of hungry, brutal-ized, illiterate children. Born of children. Black women have never listened to their mothers. No black woman ever pays much attention to any other black woman. And so each one starts out fresh, as if no black woman had ever tried to live before. The Black Movement was unable to provide me with the language I needed to discuss these matters. I had no alter-native but to become a feminist.

■

. . . throughout the entire span of her existence on American soil, the Negro woman has been alone and unprotected, not only socially but psychologically as well. She has *had* to fend for herself as if she were a man; being black, even more so. I am not implying that the Negro woman has become frigid or "masculine." In fact, she is potentially, if not already, the most sexual animal on this planet. It is not frigidity that I am describing. It is *rigidity.* And it has been this quality of austerity in the Negro woman which has enabled her to survive what few other women have ever lived through. . . . (Hernton, *Sex and Racism in America.*)

Sapphire. Mammy. Tragic mulatto wench. Workhorse, can swing an ax, lift a load, pick cotton with any man. A wonderful housekeeper. Excellent with children. Very clean. Very reli-gious. A terrific mother. A great little singer and dancer and a devoted teacher and social worker. She's always had more oppor-tunities than the black man because she was no threat to the white man so he made it easy for her. But curiously enough, she frequently ends up on welfare. Nevertheless, she is more edu-

cated and makes more money than the black man. She is more likely to be employed and more likely to be a professional than the black man. And subsequently she provides the main support for the family. Not beautiful, rather hard looking unless she has white blood, but then very beautiful. The black ones are exotic though, great in bed, tigers. And very fertile. If she is middle class she tends to be uptight about sex, prudish. She is hard on and unsupportive of black men, domineering, castrating. She tends to wear the pants around her house. Very strong. Sorrow rolls right off her brow like so much rain. Tough, unfeminine. Opposed to women's rights movements, considers herself already liberated. Nevertheless, unworldly. Definitely not a dreamer, rigid, inflexible, uncompassionate, lacking in goals any more imaginative than a basket of fried chicken and a good fuck.

From the intricate web of mythology which surrounds the black woman, a fundamental image emerges. It is of a woman of inordinate strength, with an ability for tolerating an unusual amount of misery and heavy, distasteful work. This woman does not have the same fears, weaknesses, and insecurities as other women, but believes herself to be and is, in fact, stronger emotionally than most men. Less of a woman in that she is less "feminine" and helpless, she is really *more* of a woman in that she is the embodiment of Mother Earth, the quintessential mother with infinite sexual, life-giving, and nurturing reserves. In other words, she is a superwoman.

Through the years this image has remained basically intact, unquestioned even by the occasional black woman writer or politician. In fact, if anything, time has served to reinforce it. Even now I can hear my reader thinking, *Of course she is stronger. Look what she's been through. She would have to be. Of course she's not like other women.* Even for me, it continues to be difficult to let the myth go. Naturally black women want very much to believe it; in a way, it is all we have.

But just imagine, for a moment, that you had a little girl and circumstances dictated that she be released in a jungle for a period of time to get along the best way she could. Would you want her to think she was invulnerable to the sting of the snake, the claws of the panther? Would you like her to believe that she could go without sleep and food indefinitely and that she needed no shelter? Or would you want her to know something of her actual capabilities and human weaknesses, not enough to make her give up before she had begun, but just enough to make her want to protect herself? How long do you think she'd survive if you deceived her? And, more importantly, in what state would she survive? Imagine further that she believed her wounds were just another proof of her strength and invulnerability.

Now I want you to picture a little black girl in a jungle that has no tigers and lions, but poverty, ignorance, welfare centers, tenements, rats, roaches, inadequate schools, malevolent teachers, pimps, Forty-second Streets, Eighth Avenues, heroin, hypodermic needles and methadone, opportunistic preachers and community leaders, a narrow range of career possibilities, always impending pregnancies, sterilization, poor medical services, corrupt lawyers, an insensitive and illogical court system, and two races of men who prey upon her as a sexual chattel and a beast of burden. And suppose that behind this black girl, there was a whole string of little black girls who had faced this same jungle with their imaginary advantages and been defeated. Would it not be an act of unkindness, of extreme injustice really, to tell her that she was a woman of special strengths, of exceptional opportunities?

I remember once I was watching a news show with a black male friend of mine who had a Ph.D. in psychology and was the director of an out-patient clinic. We were looking at some footage of a black woman who seemed barely able to speak English, though at least six generations of her family before her had certainly claimed it as their first language. She was in bed wrapped in blankets, her numerous small, poorly clothed children huddled around her. Her apartment looked rat-infested, cramped, and dirty. She had not, she said, had heat and hot water for days. My friend, a solid member of the middle class now but surely no stranger to poverty in his childhood, felt obliged to comment—in order to assuage his guilt, I can think of no other reason—"That's a *strong* sister," as he bowed his head in reverence.

■

In essence, the Negro community has been forced into a matriarchal structure which, because it is so out of line with the rest of American society, seriously retards the progress of the group as a whole, and imposes a crushing burden on the Negro male. . . . Obviously, not every instance of social pathology afflicting the Negro community can be traced to the weakness of family structure . . . [but] once or twice removed, it will be found to be the principal source of most of the aberrant, inadequate, or anti-social behavior that did not establish, but now serves to perpetuate the cycle of poverty and deprivation. (Daniel P. Moynihan, "The Negro Family: The Case for National Action," Washington, D.C.; U.S. Department of Labor, 1965.)

This is an often-quoted passage from Daniel Patrick Moynihan's 1965 report. An almost unanimous roar of protest was the response from the academic and policy-making segments of the black community. Moynihan was trying to take the responsibility for racism off white shoulders, where it belonged, and place it on blacks themselves. This would never do.

To anyone fairly knowledgeable about the history of the black community, Moynihan's argument was clearly ridiculous. For one thing, the numbers of fatherless black households did not become significantly large until, perhaps coincidentally, blacks began to be more successful economically in American society. Yet Moynihan's argument did not fade into the distance as did, say, Shockley's theory of the genetic inferiority of blacks. Despite the denials and protests, he had hit a responsive chord. Just as black men were busiest attacking Moynihan, they were equally busy attacking the black woman for being a matriarch. Although no one would admit it, Moynihan had managed to provide authoritative support for something a lot of black men wanted to believe anyway: that the black woman had substantial advantages over the black man educationally, financially, and in employment.

With fanatic compulsion Moynihan righteously and indignantly related the professional and educational advancements of the black woman to high juvenile delinquency levels, high crime levels, poor educational levels for black males. He paused every now and then to shake a finger at the black man. Your problem, buddy, he seemed to suggest, is this black woman of yours. You want to be equal but, if you're a man, you must do something about her first. He never actually said the black woman had *more*. That was left to black men who knew of the contents of the report through second- and third-hand sources. All Moynihan actually said was that she had too much.

Dr. Thompson reports that 70 percent of all applications for the National Achievement Scholarship Program financed by the Ford Foundation for outstanding Negro high school graduates are girls, despite special efforts by high school principals to submit the names of boys.

The finalists for this new program for outstanding Negro students were recently announced. Based on an inspection of the names, only about 43 percent of all the 639 finalists were male. (However, in the regular National Merit Scholarship program, males received 67 percent of the 1974 scholarship awards.)(Moynihan, "The Negro Family.")

Can't you just see one of Moynihan's researchers poring over a list of poor little black kids who won "Negro" scholarship awards, weeding the girls' names out from the boys'? "Now let's see, Willa Mae, girl, George, boy. . . ."

This report was probably the most publicized exercise in hairsplitting this country has ever seen. While Moynihan readily admitted, for example, that more black males attended college than black females, he seemed to think it extremely significant that in 1964 the average nonwhite female had completed .8 more years of school than the average nonwhite male. Specifically, the figures he cited were 9.2 years of school for the average nonwhite male as opposed to 10.0 years of school for the average nonwhite female.

The difference in educational attainment between nonwhite men and women in the labor force is even greater; men lag 1.1 years behind women.

The disparity in educational attainment of male and female youth age 16 to 21 who were out of school in February 1963 is striking. Among the nonwhite males, 66.3 percent were not high school graduates, compared with 55.0 percent of the females. A similar difference existed at the college level, with 4.5 percent of the males having completed 1 to 3 years of college compared with 7.3 percent of the females. (Moynihan, "The Negro Family".)

But Moynihan failed to give all the information needed to evaluate these facts. Not until 1974 did the educational attainment of all males in the labor force in the United States catch up to that of females in terms of school years completed at an average of 12.4. In 1952 the average American male, black or white, in the labor force, had completed 10.4 years of schooling, whereas the average number of years of schooling for all females in the labor force was 12.0. The vast majority of black women and white women are still not employed; nor have they ever been. Moynihan's figures on educational levels of black men versus black women in the labor force appear to prove only one thing—women need more education to obtain employment than do men.

As for the assertion that nonwhite women in general exceed nonwhite males in educational attainment in terms of the average number of years of schooling, Moynihan failed to point out that this "advantage" had never been by even as much as a whole year of schooling, always by some percentage of that, and that such an "advantage" did not translate into an economic advantage for black women. It did not even translate into a clearly reliable educational advantage.

For example, when Moynihan stated that a greater percentage of black women than black men completed one to three years of college in 1963, he had good reason for choosing precisely that category and that year. During the sixties the figures for the college enrollment of black males and females oscillated from year to year, alternately showing each to have the advantage. Further, women are much more likely to be engaged in one- and three-year degree programs because of such traditionally female occupations as nursing. As a matter of fact, white females also exceeded white males in the one- to three-year category for that year. Despite Moynihan's emphasis, a higher percentage of black men than black women continued to complete college throughout the sixties.

But the important thing is, as Jacqueline J. Jackson, Associate Professor of Medical Sociology at Duke University Medical Center, pointed out in her appraisal of black male versus black female educational attainment:

. . . The critical comparison . . . should not be between black females and males, but a comparison of both black females and black males with that group most likely to receive higher education in the United States, namely white males. When such comparisons are made, it is readily apparent that the greatest educational gains made during the 1960's were not those made by blacks at all, but those made especially by white males. Between 1960 and 1970, 1.8 percent more black females were likely to have received at least a bachelor's degree at the close of that decade than at the beginning. Corresponding data were 1.9 percent for black males, 4.9 percent for white females, and, highest of all, 5.2 percent for white males. (Jacqueline J. Jackson, "But Where Are the Men?" *Contemporary Black Thought: The Best from The Black Scholar*, ed. Robert Chrisman and Nathan Hare.)

Moynihan, however, seemed to think his argument particularly strong when it came to black female employment.

More important, it is clear that Negro females have established a strong position for themselves in white collar and professional employment, precisely the areas of the economy which are growing most rapidly, and to which the highest prestige is accorded. The President's Committee on Equal Employment Opportunity, making a preliminary report on employment in 1964 of over 16,000 companies with nearly 5 million employees, revealed this pattern with dramatic emphasis. In this work force, Negro males outnumber Negro females by a ratio of 4 to 1. Yet Negro males represent only 1.2 percent of all males in white collar occupations, while Negro females represent 3.1 percent of the total female white collar work force. Negro males represent 1.1 percent of all male professionals. . . . (Moynihan, "The Negro Family.")

According to the 1970 Census figures, the percentage of black female professional and technical workers was twice the percentage of black males in that category, but the males held the most prestigious and highest-paying jobs and the women were usually relegated to the more traditionally female, lower-paying, low-status professional occupations. Such discrepancies still exist in most official classifications of occupations in respect to female versus male employment. The very system relied upon to compare male and female career levels has incorporated discrimination into its methods of measurement.

113

For example, in the "service workers" category, females were cooks, waiters, hairdressers, chambermaids, household workers, whereas males in this category were firemen, guards, and policemen. Considering this, it is not surprising that, despite the manipulation of the job categories, the Census was also forced to note that in 1970 the average black male made about 1 1/2 times as much as the average black female, or about $2000 more.

Analyzing statistics and drawing conclusions from them is a devilish business. If one is selective about one's choice of figures, they can be made to support practically any thesis. What Moynihan was leading up to in the presentation of his "data" was his recommendation for the rehabilitation of the black family.

Most Americans who succeed, he offered, come from families with principal male providers. Black families have too many female providers and too many female heads (it was 23.7 percent in 1965), and therefore are not status quo. Thus, the female provider is the reason blacks are not successful.

In a sense he was right. The American family with a black female head is the most impoverished family in the country, because the black female has the lowest earning power. The logical solution to this problem would be to simply increase the earning power of the black woman. But this was not Moynihan's answer. His argument went as follows: If you increase the black *man's* educational and employment opportunities—the implication was that you would ignore the black woman, who had too much already—you will increase the numbers of black status quo families with principal male providers and thus eliminate or substantially diminish the problems of blacks—in other words, unemployment, juvenile delinquency, illiteracy, fatherless households.

Moynihan's theory was instrumental in ushering in a broad campaign to increase the opportunities for black males in the

sixties in respect to college admission; graduate and professional school admission; high-status professional, technical, and
business employment. And, in fact, the prospects for many
black men did improve.

There was an increase in the numbers of black male professionals, black males with college and graduate degrees and
technical skills, black males entering the middle class, and
there was even a slight decrease in the numbers of job holders
among married black women with husbands present (with a
corresponding drop in the median income of the black family,
by the way). But there were some problems.

The percentage of black families headed by females went up
from 23.7 percent in 1965 to 33.4 percent in 1976, which
represents an acceleration rate nearly four times that of the rate
previous to 1965. Only slightly less than half of all black children under eighteen were now totally dependent upon the
earnings of black women, women whose earning ability had
increased only slightly. (This number did not include the children of black women whose husbands are present and also
work.) This meant that despite the improvements, there were
still a great many poor black people. Jobs for black men did not
translate into more financially secure black families with male
heads.

Jacqueline Jackson maintains that the relatively large numbers of black female heads of families has always had a lot to
do with the black sex-ratio. As of 1976 the U.S. Census reported that there were about 80.7 black males for every 100
black females over twenty-four years of age. Moynihan wrote
the sex-ratio off as nonsense, blaming it on an undercount of
black men. He even suggested that the undercount of black
men might mean that there were even greater numbers of
black males unemployed and uneducated. Was he also suggesting that an influx of black male heads of families might come
from that quarter?

Besides the sex-ratio, there was another obstacle to the success of Moynihan's plan. The black males who were given access to employment and educational opportunities did not, for various reasons, automatically connect such opportunities with the imperative of family building. And even if a man did build a family of his own, it did not necessarily make him any more concerned with any other man's family.

Just as the existence of greater opportunities for a small elite of college-ready and/or upwardly mobile young black men had not had any profound effect upon the masses of underemployed, poorly educated, chronically incarcerated (and also predominantly unmarried) black males, it also had no positive effect upon the masses of black female poor. If anything, it increased the extent to which the black community focused on the success and gains of black males to the exclusion of black females; it focused most philanthropic, rehabilitative, and remedial efforts on behalf of black people away from the black woman, and made it that much more likely that she might see any efforts to improve herself as "counterrevolutionary," counterproductive, and emasculating.

Moynihan, and those who picked up where he left off, were using the black woman as a scapegoat. Rather than carve a piece of pie for the black man out of the white man's lion's share, they preferred to take away from the really very little that the black woman had and give that meager slice to him.

During the sixties it was not unusual for a successful black woman in a profession to feel extremely guilty, even to the point of sabotaging her own career or of pursuing a male to replace her. Some just simply quit their jobs and had babies. Black males thought nothing of saying, in reference to a black woman's job, "A brother should have that."

Employers and college administrators in the late sixties and early seventies did not hesitate to declare, openly if not officially, We are looking for men, not women; we want to improve conditions for black men, since black women already have enough.

▪

> There is a war going on between the black man and the black woman, which makes her the silent ally, indirectly but effectively, of the white man. The black woman is an unconsenting ally and she may not even realize it—but the white man sure does. That's why, all down through history, he has propped her up economically above you and me, to strengthen her hand against us. (Cleaver, "The Allegory of Black Eunuchs," *Soul on Ice.*)

Was this paranoia on Cleaver's part or a shortsightedness that came out of his combined reverence for maleness and his contempt for femaleness—in other words, sexism?

> The myth of the strong black woman is the other side of the coin of the myth of the beautiful dumb blonde. The white man turned the white woman into a weak-minded, weak-bodied, delicate freak, a sex pot, and placed her on a pedestal; he turned the black woman into a strong self-reliant Amazon and deposited her into his kitchen —that's the secret of Aunt Jemima's bandanna. The white man turned himself into the Omnipotent Administrator and established himself in the Front Office. And he turned the black man into the Supermasculine Menial and kicked him out into the fields. (Cleaver, *Soul on Ice.*)

It didn't seem to strike Cleaver as incongruous that a strong, self-reliant woman would allow herself to be deposited in someone's kitchen.

Cleaver, however, could see the white woman's weakness, in relation to men, quite clearly (and, by the way, I think he underestimated the strength and the willfulness in the role she played, just as he overestimated the white man's awareness of his own design) but the black woman, who is at the white woman's knees, under the black man's heel, and gets the back of the white man's hand, he described as an Amazon. Didn't he realize that Amazon meant female warrior? What warrior would have put up with that kind of abuse?

Although Cleaver was able to stand back a little from the prevailing mythology and see how black women and men were all manipulated against one another, some combination of male ego and disdain for the black woman superceded his reasoning abilities. She was only useful to him to the extent that she illustrated his own oppression. When he said she was strong, he meant strong for a black woman, given what had been done to her. When he said self-reliant, he meant self-reliant for a black woman, given what she had been through. Black women were second class in relation to everybody. That was a given. But even the black woman's second-class, worn-out, rickety old versions of strength and self-reliance were more than he preferred she have; they were still too great a threat to male dominance to be ignored.

And wasn't Moynihan saying the same thing? That the black woman had the temerity, the unmitigated gall to survive slavery—not to mention the hundreds of years of oppression that followed—is something that seems to upset a great many people.

■

To some extent, the white woman's newly acquired feminism has meant that she has become more aware of the oppression of the black woman, but she has done very little of a positive nature about that awareness. One will generally find that when she talks about the black woman, she also tends to support the myth.

Gerda Lerner, a white feminist, in the preface to her book *Black Women in White America* insists upon giving us her version of the black woman's dichotomy.

The question of black "matriarchy" is commonly misunderstood. The very term is deceptive, for "matriarchy" implies the exercise of power by women, and black women have been the most powerless group in our entire society. . . . Black women's wages, even today, are lowest of all groups. . . . But the status of black women can be viewed from two different viewpoints: one, as members of the larger society; two, within their own group. When they are considered as Blacks among Blacks, they have higher status within their own group than do white women in white society. (Gerda Lerner, ed., *Black Women in White America*, New York: Pantheon, 1972.)

What immediately came to my mind when I first read this was a confrontation Susan Brownmiller had with a black male librarian at the Harlem Schomburg Collection when she was doing her book *Against Our Will*. She asked him if she might see some information on black women and rape.

"Why did you come here?" he asked with caution.

"Because I thought this would be the best place to find historical stuff on the rape of black women. I'm writing a serious book." "Then you mean to ask about the lynching of black men."

"Sir, I know about that," I answered, "and I know where to find the material when I'm ready for it. At this point I really need to know about the rape of black women."

"I'm sorry, young lady. If you're serious about your subject you need to start with the historic injustice to black men. That must be your approach."

"That has been your approach, sir. I'm interested in the historic injustice to women."

"To black people, rape has meant the lynching of the black man," he said with his voice rising. (Brownmiller, *Against Our Will*.)

What could be more eloquent? To black people, rape means the lynching of a black man. Obsession with the lynching of the black man seems to leave no room in the black male consciousness for any awareness of the oppression of black women.

If a black female celebrity is pretty, or sexy, or is married to a white man, she is called a talentless whore. If she's elegant or highbrow or intellectual, she's pronounced funny-looking, uptight and in need of a good brutal fuck. If she happens to appeal to a white audience, she is despised. If she's independent, physical, or aggressive, she's called a dyke.

It is a mockery to say, as Gerda Lerner does, that black women have higher status in their community than white women in theirs. As far as I have been able to tell, black women have no status at all in the black community, particularly since the sixties. Their presence there is at best good-humoredly tolerated.

One would be hard pressed to make a list of any length of all the important, *recognized* black female filmmakers, politicians, playwrights, artists, athletes. One would be frustrated in trying to find equivalents in terms of status for Margaret Mead, Susan Sontag, Rosalynn Carter, Katharine Graham, Martha Graham, Greta Garbo, Jacqueline Kennedy, Lillian Hellman, Helen Hayes, Georgia O'Keeffe, Twyla Tharp, Carol Burnett, Lily Tomlin, Billy Jean King.

The black woman pays an enormous price to walk the streets of her community. Only after she is over sixty and weighs two hundred pounds is she given any peace. And even then at night she may be beaten up and have her pocketbook stolen. It is impossible for her to protect her children. Do you think it was her choice that drug addicts and winos should rule the streets? Any black woman who's got any sense treads lightly in Harlem.

Since I know that Lerner's statement does not reflect a true situation, I am inclined to conclude that it reflects some unacknowledged hostility. That white women should be hostile toward black women is not at all surprising. The myth was that we were strong and that they were weak. Somehow it turned into the myth that they were weak because we were strong.

In *Pentimento* Lillian Hellman relates a conversation between herself and her black maid, Helen, about one of Ms. Hellman's friends who had just sent Helen a coat and some money.

"Write him," she said. "Tell him my coat's fine and the money too."

All my life, beginning at birth, I have taken orders from black women, wanting them and resenting them, being superstitious the few times I disobeyed. So I did write about the money and the coat. ... (Lillian Hellman, *Pentimento: A Book of Portraits*, Boston: Little, Brown & Co., 1973.)

That Hellman was afraid of Helen or suspected her of special powers is perhaps true, but it seems most unlikely that a black woman could make Lillian Hellman do anything.

I don't mean to tamper with whatever fantasies white employers and black domestics like to entertain about the nature of their relationship, but there is an essential reality here. Their relationship is based upon the economic superiority of one over the other. It is based upon one woman being confined to a very limited range of ways of making a living and another woman having a greater range of possibilities.

The liberal white woman, who may do admirably well at suppressing and masking her prejudice against the black man, still has a difficult time with the black woman. When she says the black woman is strong, just as in the case of the black man and the white man, it is an expression of contempt. But in a way one can hardly blame her. After all, neither the Civil Rights Movement nor the Black Movement gave her any criteria for even identifying her prejudice against black women. For example, the white woman knows that it is not acceptable to assert, even though one may still believe it, that black men are infantile, happy-go-lucky, and predominantly sexual in orientation. But when it comes to the black woman it is still all right to assert that she is sexier, more maternal, more exotic, stronger.

In a very real sense the black woman was right to become suspicious when white feminists came along, patted her on the back, and declared themselves on her side. Before I even get into any discussion of the black woman's rather mindless rejection of feminism, I want to make it clear that if her cause had truly been the racism of white women, she would have had a just cause.

■

On the occasion of the First Modern Pan-African Congress in Atlanta in 1970, a black woman named Akiba ya Elimu made the following statement:

We understand that it is and has been traditional that the man is the head of the house. He is the leader of the house/nation because his knowledge of the world is broader, his awareness is greater, his understanding is fuller and his application of this information is wiser. . . . After all, it is only reasonable that the man be the head of the house because he is able to defend and protect the development of his home. . . . In a process of dehumanization resulting with our present condition of slavery, one of the various steps has been that of destroying the family. Black men and women were separated, given conflicting roles, and the creation of various myths assured our nation to be disunified. One of the most harmful myths was . . . the idea of the Black matriarchy. The Black woman's role was defined in such an intentional manner so as to emasculate our men and give them a limited responsibility, to guarantee broken Black homes. . . . The necessity of the acceptance of our roles, therefore our responsibilities, is essential in making the Black family whole again.

(Imamu A. Baraka [LeRoi Jones], ed., *African Congress: A Documentary of the First Modern Pan-African Congress,* New York: William Morrow, 1972.)

Armed with such an ideology, the young black woman of the sixties did herself a great deal of damage. Her guilt and her confusion were thorough. Not only had she had all of the advantages while the black man had none, she had actually been used by the oppressor against him.

The growing phenomenon in the late sixties of black men marrying and dating white women only served to reinforce the black woman's sense of shame. She had driven him away from her.

It is not surprising that the black woman's resistance to the Women's Movement was impassioned. There were two sides to her argument against it. First, she claimed she was already liberated. As Joyce Ladner put it in 1971 in her book on the black woman called *Tomorrow's Tomorrow:*

. . . women in American society are held to be the *passive* sex, but the majority of Black women have, perhaps, never fit this model, and have been liberated from any of the constraints the society has traditionally imposed on women. Although this emerged from forced circumstances, it has nevertheless allowed the Black woman the kind of emotional well-being that Women's Liberation groups are calling for. (Joyce A. Ladner, *Tomorrow's Tomorrow: The Black Woman,* New York: Doubleday, 1971.)

Or in the words of one black woman from the Midwest whom Inez Smith Reid quotes in her survey of black women,

. . . Black women have a movement going on that I couldn't very well call liberation because the average Black woman is trying to get back to her rightful position with her man. We have been liberated by slavery already. . . . (Inez S. Reid, *Together Black Women,* New York: Emerson Hall, 1972.)

The second part of the black woman's argument was that her oppression as a black was greater and more pressing than her oppression as a woman. On the subject of feminism, Smith goes on to say, "Examination, [black women] felt, would . . . reveal little or no time for women's liberation since the priority item is Black Liberation." As one of Reid's middle-class informants put it, "I recognize certainly that there is sex discrimination, nevertheless I don't think it affects Black women nearly as much as racism."

Although the two sides of this argument are contradictory, most black women combine them. That the black woman often sees herself as liberated merely involves an extension of the myth. As for racism being more important than sexism, she is only saying that she can't afford to work on her oppression as a woman because the black man's oppression is greater. I get an image of a Herculean woman who with one long muscular arm is holding the dogs that are nipping at her heels at bay, while with the other arm she is helping a fragile, tiny little man over the fence of racism.

Everyone knows that whites have traditionally been prejudiced against blacks, but what people do not know, or do not care to know, is the extent to which blacks are now prejudiced against each other. This intra-group prejudice takes many forms, but the one I would like to direct attention to is the prejudice black women have against black men. If the black man is nothing—and many black women believe that, despite all evidence to the contrary—then the black woman must be better. She also feels guilty about it. Her prejudice and guilt act as blinders to prevent her from seeing her own lamentable condition and so, naturally, she does not see a need for a liberation movement for herself.

There has also been a serious element of opportunism in the black woman's resistance to the Women's Movement. The Women's Movement made employment a primary goal of liberation. Employment may be loosely defined for women as labor which is performed for someone other than your husband and children. From the day the black woman first set foot on the American shore, she was involved in labor for someone other than her husband. This made her part of the first large group of women in America to "work." Even though, just like a housewife, she wasn't paid for the first three hundred years or more and hardly anything in the next hundred years, it was maintained that this represented a substantial bit of achievement on her part. Just like the woman in Inez Smith Reid's book said, "We have been liberated by slavery." But the fact was that the black woman's "Liberation" consisted of being bound to the most unpleasant, unrewarding kind of work, work that did not enlarge her universe or increase her fulfillment. The black woman had not chosen her work. It was something she had to do, either because of the whip or to keep her family from starving—a necessity, a drudgery. That she worked did not mean that she viewed herself outside a traditional female role but only that she had, because of the urgent demands of her life, expanded upon that role to include a few very circumscribed areas of employment—domestic, field, and factory work; or, if she was middle-class, teaching, nursing, secretarial work, and social work.

Janice Porter Gump and L. Wendell Rivers, sociologists, pointed out in their study, "A Consideration of Race in Efforts to End Sex Bias," that:

. . . the black woman's expectations for employment and actual participation in the labor force do not so much reflect an embracing of the achievement ethic, or simply economic need, as they reflect an initially imposed but presently incorporated sense of responsibility. It is not so much that the black woman has been able to escape the constraints of the traditional feminine role as that she has had to take on in addition aspects of the traditional masculine role. In fact, she appears to endorse the traditional view of the feminine role to a larger extent than does the white woman, believing that a woman's identity derives primarily from marriage and that a woman should be submissive to a man. (Esther Diamond, ed., *Issues of Sex Bias and Sex Fairness in Career Interest Measurement*, Washington, D.C.: Department of Health, Education, and Welfare, 1975.)

Before black women or white women said a word, there was a basic communication gap between them on this subject of work. When the middle-class white woman said "I want to work," in her head was a desk in the executive suite, while the black woman saw a bin of dirty clothes, someone else's dirty clothes. Something similar probably happened with the poor and lower-middle-class white woman. Her personal nightmare may have been a secretarial job or the kind of sales clerk job she had before she was married. When the white woman said, "Don't you want to work?" the black woman said, "Work? No thanks, I've already got more of that than I can use."

. . . Gurin and Katz (1966) found high aspiration in black college women inconsistent with subjects' conception of femininity. Turner (1972) found that half her sample of black college women actually wanted less work involvement than they anticipated, while almost half the white women wanted more; further, though high career expectations were related to competitive and egalitarian parental child-rearing values among the white women, for the black women high career expectations were related to what appeared to be perceptions of the expectations and desires of others. . . .

Many data have been presented that portray the black woman as more likely to enter the labor force than the white woman, more interested in doing so, more likely to work full time and continuously, and more necessary to the financial welfare of her family. . . . While such facts suggest a woman much less constricted by the traditional role than her white counterpart, they represent an incomplete portrait, for it is equally true that black women choose occupations traditional for women, are motivated perhaps more by a sense of responsibility than by achievement need, are much more traditional in their sex-role attitudes than are young white women, and to some extent seem burdened by the responsibility they carry. (Diamond, *Issues of Sex Bias.*)

Women's Liberation, the black woman reasoned, would chain her to Ms. Anne's stove forever. None of that for her. She wanted, she said, to stay home and have her man take care of her. A movement offering her that would be the only one in which she could be interested.

2

My mother was the smartest black woman in Eden. She was as quick as a flash of lightning, and whatever she did could not be done better. She could do anything. She cooked, washed, ironed, spun, nursed and labored in the fields. She made as good a field hand as she did a cook. I have heard Master Jennings say to his wife, "Fannie has her faults, but she can outwork any nigger in the country, I'd bet my life on that."

My mother certainly had her faults as a slave. . . . She said that she wouldn't be whipped, and when she fussed, all Eden must have known it. She was loud and boisterous, and it seemed to me that you could hear her a mile away. . . .

One day my mother's temper ran wild. For some reason Mistress Jennings struck her with a stick. Ma struck back and a fight followed. Mr. Jennings was not at home and the children became frightened and ran upstairs. For a half hour they wrestled in the kitchen. Mistress seeing that she could not get the better of ma, ran out in the road, with ma right on her heels. In the road, my mother flew into her again. . . . She suddenly began to tear Mistress Jennings' clothes off . . . . Poor mistress was nearly naked when the storekeeper got to them and pulled me off.

"Why, Fannie, what do you mean by that?" he asked. "Why, I'll kill her, I'll kill her dead if she ever strikes me again." . . .

Pa heard Mr. Jennings say that Fannie would have to be whipped by law. He told ma. Two mornings afterward, two men came in at the big gate, one with a long lash in his hand. . . . To my surprise, I saw her running around the house, straight in the direction of the men. . . . I should have known she wouldn't hide. . . . She swooped upon them like a hawk of chickens. I believe they were afraid of her or thought she was crazy. One man had a long beard which she grabbed with one hand, and the lash with the other. Her body was made strong with madness. She was a good match for them. Mr. Jennings came and pulled her away. . . . Ma did not see the gun until Mr. Jennings came up. On catching sight of it, she said, "Use your gun, use it and blow my brains out if you will." . . .

That evening Mistress Jennings came down to the cabin. "Well, Fannie," she said, "I'll have to send you away. You won't be whipped, and I'm afraid you'll get killed." . . . "I'll go to hell or anywhere else, but I won't be whipped," ma answered. "You can't take the baby, Fannie. . . ."

Mother said nothing to this. That night, ma and pa sat up late, talking over things, I guess. Pa loved ma, and I heard him say, "I'm going too, Fannie." . . .

Thus my mother and father were hired to Tennessee. The next morning they were to leave. I saw ma working around with the baby under her arms as if it had been a bundle of some kind. Pa came up to the cabin with an old mare for ma to ride, and an old mule for himself. Mr. Jennings was with them.

"Fannie, leave the baby with Aunt Mary," said Mr. Jennings very quietly.

At this, ma took the baby by its feet, a foot in each hand, and with the baby's head swinging downward, she vowed to smash its brains out before she'd leave it. Tears were streaming down her face. It was seldom that ma cried, and everyone knew that she meant every word. Ma took her baby with her. . . . (Ophelia S. Egypt, J. Masouka, and Charles Johnson, "Unwritten History of Slavery: Autobiographical Accounts of Ex-Slaves," *Black Women in White America*, ed. Gerda Lerner.)

It was slavery that gave us the myth of the superwoman, but the legends of Miss Anne and little Eva, young massa and Simon Legree, the Southern belle and the evil old mistress— of whites in all their mythic helplessness, softness, decadence, cruelty, and perversion—are as essential to our notion of the strong black woman as the existence of slavery and the general mythology of the inferiority of blacks.

To read much of the literature of the Black Movement, one would think that whites were simply a demon race of incalculable wealth who came to this country for the express purpose of making a mockery of democracy, and subjecting blacks to the basest kinds of torture and abuse. Perhaps for a time in the late sixties there was a certain usefulness for blacks in claiming a degree of moral superiority for themselves after centuries of an imposed sense of cultural inferiority. Perhaps it was even valid to depict whites as monsters for a brief period by way of compensation for the dashed hopes of the Civil Rights Movement.

But all of this is water under the bridge. At this point particularly, the sexual myths about white men, white women, black men, and black women are just an accumulation of waste —wasted hope and wasted cockiness, born of insecurity and anxiety, which help to keep us all in our respective places.

By the time slavery was introduced into America it had already existed in the world for as long as anyone cared to remember. Africans certainly had been enslaved before by Arabs, by their own people, by the Dutch, Portuguese, Spanish, and French. From the outset the primary difference between American slavery and every other kind of slavery the world had ever known was not its barbarity but the total impossibility of upward social mobility for the slave. The Southern colonies and the antebellum South had no free mulatto class with established rights such as in the Caribbean islands. The slave was not allowed to work his way up and distinguish himself as he had been in the Arab and African worlds and in Ancient Greece and Rome. The laws of the South dictated that the slave could not legally marry, inherit property, or sign contracts. He was permanently locked into his situation. Except in the rarest cases, his descendants were doomed to live as he had.

Blacks were among the first settlers of America. Since English law held that those who had been baptized could not be sold into slavery, the first blacks to arrive in Jamestown in 1619 were signed on as indentured servants, as were many poor whites who had been induced to come to the colonies. In the beginning, black bondsmen worked the prescribed number of years and earned their freedom, as did whites. They became farmers and artisans, accumulated land, voted, and even held servants and slaves.

But within twenty years black indentured servants were working longer terms of service than white indentured servants. As punishment for running away their terms might even be extended to life. By 1661, Virginia had established slavery as legal. In 1667 Virginia Law declared that the baptism of a black did not rule out his being enslaved. By the 1700s the number of white indentured servants willing to enlist for the strenuous work available in the Southern colonies dwindled, and slavery was well on its way to becoming a primary source of labor. Between 1680 and 1786, some 2,130,000 slaves, most of whom ended up in the South, made the voyage from Africa to America. By the time of the American Revolution, slaves made up two thirds of South Carolina's population and half of Virginia's.

But exactly how did the gap between blacks and whites, that we know as racism, develop? Yes, blacks were rather quickly singled out for a particularly exacting service. But then most whites in the South who were not wealthy and male labored in the service of those who were. Yes, Africans were brought in chains from their native land, packed into holds of ships like so much cargo, sold in slave markets like so much meat. But some of the first white indentured servants were also kidnapped from the streets of London and Bristol. They too suffered a harrowing middle passage:

. . . it was seven to twelve weeks of horror. Men and women were crowded into holds without ventilation, light, decent food, or sanitary facilities. As many as half the passengers died on the way, especially the children—and whole shiploads of children were sent over, beginning in 1618 with the first two hundred youngsters gathered off the London streets. (Barbara M. Wertheimer, *We Were There: The Story of Working Women in America*, New York: Pantheon 1977.)

Whites too were sold at market by the ship's captain. From one half to as many as two thirds of the immigrants who came to the New World, it has been estimated, came as indentured servants.

As Lerone Bennett points out in *Before the Mayflower*, "The racial situation, at this juncture, was fluid. . . ." Discrimination was clearly along class lines. Blacks and whites worked together in the fields, married, socialized with one another, and bore many children together. In fact the first group of free blacks were born of black fathers and white mothers who were mostly indentured servants.

The rulers of the early American colonies were not overly scrupulous about the color or national origin of their work force. Indian slavery was tried and abandoned. Many masters attempted to enslave white men and white women. When these attempts failed, the spotlight fell on the Negro. He was tried and he was found not wanting. Why were Negroes more acceptable than poor whites and poor Indians? White men, for one thing, were under the protection of strong governments; they could appeal to a monarch. White men, moreover, were white; they could escape and blend into the crowd. Indians, too, could escape; they knew the country and their brothers were only a hill or a forest away. Another element in the failure of Indian slavery was the fact that Indians tended to sicken and die. (Lerone Bennett Jr., *Before the Mayflower: A History of Black America*, Chicago: Johnson Publishing, 1969.)

African blacks were singled out for American slavery because white plantation owners needed labor, *lots of it*, fast and cheap, to develop the plentiful resources of their land. Beginning in 1444, Europeans had found it particularly advantageous to enslave Africans—because displaced Africans were disoriented by differences in culture, language, religion, terrain; because their bodies were strong and they labored well; because they had no protector in the Western world; because their color made them highly visible as runaways.

As America grew and the prosperity and mobility of the whites increased, the slave remained fixed in time. It was an eminently practical arrangement. White males could not be forced to labor. They had been induced to come to the colonies with promises of better land and religious freedom. No such inducement was necessary for blacks; the only necessary condition to ensure their labor was that they be forcibly held. It was cheaper to purchase a slave for life than to maintain an indentured servant for ten years. Slaves were not allowed to marry because such a bond might be interpreted as a restriction upon the owners' right to sell husbands away from wives and wives away from husbands.

The colonial South belonged to the rich white man. The poor white man had a tremendous stake in it because it provided him with opportunities to improve his situation. The slave had no stake in it at all, although that was not immediately apparent. As for the white woman, although she had a greater stake in her society than did the slave, she did not have the possibilities for self-determination of even the poorest white male, and like the slave she was viewed as genetically suited to service.

Religion conveniently confirmed this arrangement. If black skin was the mark of Cain, women would never escape the fatal error of Eve in the Garden of Eden. In the seventeenth century, women in the British Empire were not even accorded legal status:

... When a small brooke or little river incorporateth with Rhodanus, Humber, or the Thames, the poor rivulet looseth her name; it is carried and recarried with the new associate; it beareth no sway. ... I may more truly, farre away, say to a married woman, Her new self is her superior; her companion, her master. ... They make no laws, they consent to none, they abrogate none. All of them are understood either married, or to be married, and their desires are to their husbands. (Julia C. Spruill, "The Lawes Resolution of Women's Rights," *Women's Life and Work in the Southern Colonies*, New York: Norton, 1972.)

Like the slave, the white woman of the colonial South was perceived as property: the property of her father as long as she was underaged; the property of her husband once she married.

Once she married, all of her assets belonged to her husband, even if they had been left to her by a previous husband. Her wages also belonged to him, as did her clothing and jewelry and even her children. If there was a separation, both the courts and society took it for granted that the children would go to the father. She herself was not allowed to represent herself in court or to petition for divorce. If a husband felt that his wife spent too freely, he might place a notice in the newspapers informing the community that he would no longer pay her debts. If he felt she was not obedient enough, he was allowed by law to discipline her short of mutilation or death.

Her duty was to serve her husband in all things, to keep his house, to wait on him, and to bear his children unceasingly and without complaint. Birth control was virtually nonexistent. It was not unusual for a woman to marry at fifteen, have a dozen children, and die in childbirth in her mid-thirties. The husband invariably took another wife after a brief perfunctory period of mourning, often no longer than a month. In this way, a man often had four or more wives in his lifetime.

In addition to childbearing, cooking, cleaning, and sewing, a colonial housewife kept a dairy, a collection of livestock, a smokehouse, and a garden to supply her table. Although she had full responsibility for the care of the house, all supplies were chosen, ordered, and paid for by her husband.

The extent of her labors was determined by the wealth of her husband. A rich woman might have many servants and slaves. A poorer woman had to do much more for herself. The life of the frontier woman in particular was one of hard, unremitting labor. Not only did she work beside her husband in the fields. With spinning wheel, loom, and dyepots, she made all the clothing of the family, as well as the household linen, blankets, quilts, coverlets, curtains, rugs, and other furnishings. She made soap, and candles, and served as family doctor to an even greater extent than the plantation mistress or farmer's wife closer to town.

William Byrd wrote in 1710 of a well-to-do frontier woman who had entertained him and the other dividing-line commissioners: "She is a very civil woman and shews nothing of ruggedness, or Immodesty in her carriage, yett she will carry a gunn in the woods and kill deer, turkeys, &c., shoot down wild cattle, catch and tye hoggs, knock down beeves with an ax and perform the most manfull Exercises as well as most men in those parts." (Spruill, *Women's Life and Work in the Southern Colonies.*)

The Southern colonial woman, in fact, had a reputation for working hard and willingly and bearing the same hardships as her husband. The survival of the colonies depended upon her efforts. The frontier woman was praised for her "unfeminine" capabilities.

Lawson found them the "most industrious sex" in North Carolina. Byrd, writing of the outlying settlements in Virginia and Carolina, declared that the men, like the Indians, imposed all the work upon the women and were themselves "Sloathfull in everything but getting Children." . . . Brickell also found the wives of the poorer farmers "ready to assist their husbands in any Servile Work, as planting when the Season of the Year requires expedition." (Spruill, *Women's Life and Work in the Southern Colonies.*)

As the colonies became more prosperous, and the wealthy settlers began to keep slaves, the role of the white woman began to change. Although she continued to suffer in frequent childbirth, to marry young, to worship her husband as her master, and to serve him, her function became largely ornamental.

Early colonial men had needed partners in labor. Now the patriarchs of a plantation system needed a crown to their glory, a symbol of their success, a constant reminder of their strength and power. In the process the Southern woman was slowly transformed into an expensive, delicate, impractical pet.

By 1776 the legend of the Southern belle had come into being:

This marvelous creation was described as a submissive wife whose reason for being was to love, honor, obey, and occasionally amuse her husband, to bring up his children and manage his household. Physically weak, and "formed for the less laborious occupations," she depended upon male protection. To secure this protection she was endowed with the capacity to "create a magic spell" over any man in her vicinity. She was timid and modest, beautiful and graceful. . . .

Less endearing, perhaps, but no less natural, was her piety and her tendency to "restrain man's natural vice and immorality." She was thought to be "most deeply interested in the success of every scheme which curbs the passions and enforces a true morality." (Anne F. Scott, *The Southern Lady: From Pedestal to Politics 1830–1930*, Chicago: University of Chicago Press, 1972.)

As the function of the Southern white woman changed, the life of the black woman continued just as if the country were in its first stages of growth. She labored in the fields beside her husband, developed muscles in her arms, bore the lash and the wrath of her master. Her labor and trials became inextricably associated with her skin color, even though not so long before, the colonial woman had not been much better off.

Whether slavery would continue seemed in doubt during the Revolutionary War and immediately afterward. The truth is that the Revolutionary forces had enlistment problems. When the British offered blacks freedom if they fought with them, the Revolutionaries had no choice but to enlist blacks too. Five thousand blacks, in integrated and all-black regiments, fought in the Revolutionary War. They did so because they believed it would win them their freedom. The Rights of Man, they had reason to assume, would be extended to them. After the war, when many masters did not make good their promises, many blacks escaped to Canada and to other territories. Others sued for their freedom in the American courts and won. The new government seriously considered the abolition of slavery, but because of cotton and tobacco it was not to be.

Gradually a network of lies developed to justify the continuance of the master/slave relationship, the selling of children away from their mothers, the separation of wives and husbands, the breeding of slaves like animals. After the constitutional ban on slave importation, which took effect in 1808, the market required that a brutal emphasis be placed upon the stud capabilities of the black man and upon the black woman's fertility. The theory of the inferiority of blacks began to be elaborated upon and to take hold. It was at this point that the black woman gained her reputation for invulnerability. She was the key to the labor supply. No one wished to admit that she felt as any woman would about the loss of her children, or that she had any particularly deep attachment to her husband, since he might also have to be sold. Her first duty had to be to the master of the house.

She was believed to be not only emotionally callous but physically invulnerable—stronger than white women and the physical equal of any man of her race. She was stronger than white women in order to justify her performing a kind of labor most white women were now presumed to be incapable of. She had to be considered at least the physical equal of the black man so that he would not feel justified in attempting to protect her.

She was labeled sexually promiscuous because it was imperative that her womb supply the labor force. The father might be her master, a neighboring white man, the overseer, a slave assigned to her by her master; her marriage was not recognized by law.

Every tenet of the mythology about her was used to reinforce the notion of the spinelessness and unreliability of the black man, as well as the notion of the frivolity and vulnerability of white women. The business of sexual and racial definition, hideously intertwined, had become a matter of balancing extremes. That white was powerful meant that black had to be powerless. That white men were omnipotent meant that white women had to be impotent. But slavery produced further complications: black women had to be strong in ways that white women were not allowed to be, black men had to be weak in ways that white men were not allowed to be.

It has become a national belief that because the black

woman's master was the slaveowner, and not her husband, she became abusive to her husband, overly aggressive, bossy, domineering. But those who trace such characteristics in the contemporary black woman back to her slave ancestry will have to find some other basis for their arguments. So far as circumstances would permit, she was a loyal, faithful and dutiful wife and mother. In partnership with her slave husband, the black woman slave fought to preserve her family, and everything that she did can be seen in that light. Her family structure was simply different from that of whites; it had no fewer rules and allowed women no greater measure of equality.

If circumstances permitted, a slave woman often lived with a single man most of her life. If her husband was to be sold, he might assign a friend to look after his wife and children. Or after a time, the woman might take another husband. She would act just as if her previous husband were dead.

In choosing a husband, a woman might live with a succession of men, but once she had settled upon a mate, she would be faithful to him. Adultery was vigorously frowned upon by the slave community. Often she was pregnant before she settled down. Her behavior did not indicate what the slaveowners claimed was a unique immorality or moral devastation; it was a carryover from her African home, where it was fairly common behavior, just as it was in many agrarian societies. If the black woman could not get along with her husband, she was allowed to separate from him. These practices were all acceptable under the code the slaves devised for themselves and necessary to their survival. It is easy to see how slaveowners used them to support their contentions that slaves were amoral and socially chaotic.

The work of historian Herbert Gutman has revealed that the threat slavery posed to the black family did not prompt the slave to give up all hopes of family life but rather to value it above all else. For the black man and woman family life was their only daily refuge. It offered them companionship, some modicum of comfort, a positive and reinforcing view of themselves and a future. Gutman describes the slaves as having been considerably preoccupied not only with their husbands and wives and children but with their cousins, nieces and nephews, aunts and uncles and grandparents. Whenever it was possible, they maintained family ties across generations.

Eugene Genovese suggests that the reputation the slave woman had for beating her children might have resulted from her attempts to teach them to obey quickly that they might later avoid death at a white man's hand. Plantation owners had a habit of spoiling black children, allowing them to play and roam freely with white children until the age of twelve or thirteen. Then abruptly everything would change. The white children would go off to school and the black children would be sent to the fields. The black children would become subject to the whippings and plantation discipline administered to adults. Slave mothers evidently tried to minimize that transition. No precedent for harsh parental discipline existed in African society, where mothers traditionally indulge their younger offspring. It is also known that some black women slaves in America traveled much of the night in order to see their children on another plantation and arrive back home before dawn.

In many ways the black woman's plight in slavery was worse than the black man's, not because she fought against a traditional woman's role but because she willingly assumed it. In addition to her labors in the fields or in the big house, she also did the same work expected of early colonial women, and all poor women, in her own house. Certain rituals in which she participated, like the annual corn-shucking parties which Genovese cites in *Roll, Jordan, Roll,* indicated that she believed in the notion of the male slave as provider: The men shucked the corn, competed for prizes, while the women looked on and prepared the food.

In this and various other ways, the slaves showed that they had not forgotten what constitutes a desirable relationship between male and female. And no matter what the white master might whisper in the black woman's ear, she usually showed herself to have a mind of her own in matters that concerned her own people. For instance, although their mistresses encouraged them to shun the attentions of the field hands, black female house servants quite commonly married field hands. Whites had little success in effecting a division between house and field slaves like the one that developed in the West Indies.

Assimilation was simply not a possibility, much less a problem for the slave woman. Although she often lived in close proximity to whites, the emotional reality of her world remained distant from direct white influence. She was never able to relate freely to whites—the consciousness of the barrier was always there, even in bed with the master—and thus she was unable to absorb the intricate rationalizations for their racism and to adapt them to her image of herself. She had to depend upon her own people for her self-image.

▪

. . . O, ye happy women, whose purity has been sheltered from childhood, who have been free to choose the objects of your affection, whose homes are protected by law, do not judge the poor desolate slave girl too severely! If slavery had been abolished, I, also, could have married the man of my choice; I could have had a home shielded by the laws; and I should have been spared the painful task of confessing what I am now about to relate; but all my prospects had been blighted by slavery. I wanted to keep myself pure. . . .

. . . A white unmarried gentleman . . . often spoke to me in the street. . . . He expressed a great deal of sympathy, and a wish to aid me. He constantly sought opportunities to see me, and wrote to me frequently. I was a poor slave girl, only fifteen years old.

So much attention from a superior person was, of course, flattering; for human nature is the same in all. . . . By degrees, a more tender feeling crept into my heart. He was an educated and eloquent gentleman; too eloquent, alas, for the poor slave girl who trusted in him. Of course I saw whither all this was tending. I knew the impassable gulf between us; but to be an object of interest to a man who is not married, and who is not her master, is agreeable to the pride and feelings of a slave, if her miserable situation has left her any pride or sentiment. It seems less degrading to give one's self, than to submit to compulsion.

. . . I made a headlong plunge. Pity me, and pardon me, O virtuous reader! You never knew what it is to be a slave; to be entirely unprotected by law or custom; to have the laws reduce you to the condition of a chattel, entirely subject to the will of another. You never exhausted your ingenuity in avoiding the snares, and eluding the power of a hated tyrant; you never shuddered at the sound of his footsteps, and trembled within hearing of his voice. I know I did wrong. No one can feel it more sensibly than I do. The painful and humiliating memory will haunt me to my dying day. . . . (Linda Brent, *Incidents in the Life of a Slave Girl,* ed. L. Maria Child, New York: Harcourt Brace Jovanovich, 1973.)

That the slaves had their own standards for womanhood did not mean that slave women would entirely escape the influence of the standard the society imposed upon the white women. Though the slaves had adapted Christianity to meet their need for reaffirmation of community, as Christians some slave women absorbed Christian ideas of female purity and virtue. Although they never came to view "illegitimacy" with the kind of distaste characteristic of whites of that period, slave women who had consistent contact with whites increasingly sought to preserve the virginity of their daughters, and encouraged them to marry first and bear children later.

In slave narratives there can be found accounts of slaves, particularly house slaves, who began to admire and idealize the white skins and the lifestyles of their owners. It was the house servant who was most feared in the planning stages of a slave revolt, feared for her intimacy with the master's family. The extent to which the black female slave became unable to distinguish her own reality from the white view of that reality, and the extent to which she leaned toward the latter, were the measure of the beginnings of a process of psychic deterioration.

The situation of one slave named Harriet Brent Jacobs provides an example of the kind of torment this could precipitate.

Harriet Brent Jacobs was born in 1818 into a privileged class of slaves. Her people were mulattos who were craftsmen and house servants. Harriet's father was a skilled carpenter who maintained a successful business and such a pleasant home that Harriet was not aware she was a slave until she was six years old and her mother died. She lived the next six years in the home of her mother's mistress, who was very kind to her, did not overwork her, allowed her to run and play, and taught her to read and write. This woman had promised to free Harriet, but when she died, she left instructions that Harriet was to become the property of her five-year-old niece. Along with her younger brother Willie, Harriet went to live with the Flint family.

Many years later Harriet Jacobs would write a book under the name of Linda Brent, with the help of L. Maria Child, a famous abolitionist writer, about her experiences in the Flint home and her subsequent escape from slavery.

Dr. and Mrs. Flint were the prototypical cruel master and mistress. Whippings were common in their household, as well as unnecessary viciousness. If dinner was not served at exactly the appointed time on Sundays, Mrs. Flint would spit in the food after her family's portion had been dished out, in order to prevent the slaves from eating it. Dr. Flint took a carnal interest in Harriet. When Harriet wanted to marry a young black man, her request was denied. Dr. Flint pursued her unrelentingly. Harriet never gave in to him, but she did, in her torment, finally have sexual relations with another white man in the community who was kind to her. She bore this man two children, which much angered her master. Finally she hid for several months in an unused shed attached to her grandmother's house, and, disguising herself as a man, escaped from the South on a ship. The white man who had been her lover finally succeeded in purchasing Harriet's children, and, after some minor difficulties, they came to live with her in the North.

Particularly interesting, in this slave narrative, is the extent to which Harriet reflects the mores of the white middle class of that time. Despite her awareness that she was placed in an untenable situation by slavery and the cruelty of her master and mistress, she clearly spent a good portion of her life feeling guilty about having had sex outside of wedlock and having borne children as a result of it. "I know I did wrong," she says. "No one can feel it more sensibly than I do. The painful and humiliating memory will haunt me to my dying day. . . ." When she says, "do not judge the poor desolate slave girl too severely," she isn't being facetious. Although her sufferings were real and her actions justified, she seems to place as much blame upon herself as she does upon her tormentors. There is a definite note here of unnecessary agony, the agony of measuring herself against a standard which was not designed to fit her circumstances, and which could only work to destroy her image of herself.

■

Her interests were those of other intelligent girls reared in that calm Quaker city during its antebellum days; she read widely and with a catholic taste that embraced everything from the classics to sentimental poetry, attended lectures avidly, listened rapturously to the musical recitals of wandering artists, gazed worshipfully on the steel engravings that passed for art among unsophisticated Americans, and took mild pleasure in the ailments that were the stock in trade of all well-bred females during the Victorian era. Yet one thing distinguished Charlotte Forten from other Philadelphia belles. She was a Negro. . . . (Charlotte L. Forten, *The Journal of Charlotte L. Forten: A Free Negro in the Slave Era,* New York: Macmillan, 1961.)

Charlotte Forten of Philadelphia was one of the tiny minority of free, educated black women of the nineteenth century. She came from a middle-class family who did not differ appreciably from their well-off white neighbors in demeanor and values.

The Fortens were dedicated abolitionists, but the indignation felt about slavery was not prompted by a first-hand knowledge of the lash, forced labor, or poverty and deprivation, but rather by the difficulty of a situation in which they

had been barred from stores and denied service in restaurants. They had been forced to sit in segregated sections of omnibuses and railroad cars. They had been turned away from lectures and theaters. They had heard thoughtless white men refer to them as "niggers" without even realizing the insulting sting of that word. From behind drawn curtains in her grandfather's spacious Philadelphia home on Lombard Street the youthful Charlotte had watched terror-stricken as runaway slaves were hounded by mobs or returned in shackles to their masters. (Forten, *Journal.*)

The Fortens suffered most from their knowledge that although they had achieved equality in all of the visible ways, they were still not allowed to take their rightful places as Americans, and so in the end, their attempts to assimilate had been unsuccessful.

Black abolitionists like the Fortens were the principal means of communication between the enslaved blacks and the anti-slavery whites. Well meaning as such people were, they shaped their message according to their special concerns rather than the actual concerns of the slaves. Charlotte's grandfather was the founder and president of the American Moral Reform Society, an agency of Negro men dedicated to the "promotion of Education, Temperance, Economy and Universal Liberty." James Forten is remembered most for his fight against the American Colonization Society, which proposed to free the slaves and send them back to Africa at the society's expense. The colonization plan attracted the support of a great many liberal Northerners during the late eighteenth century and continued to enjoy a substantial, although diminished, popularity right through the Civil War. It was, in fact, Lincoln's favorite solution to the "Negro problem" right up until he died.

Not so with free black society in the North. In 1817, along with Reverend Richard Allen, Absolom Jones, Robert Douglass, and other prominent Philadelphia Negroes, Forten organized protest meetings, maintaining that colonization would "deprive the freed slave of the benefits of civilization and religious instruction. . . . Liberia would be 'the abode of every vice, and the home of misery.' " As part of their efforts to thwart the colonization plan, at one point they even decided to strike all references to Africa from the titles of their organizations and institutions.

The white pro-colonizers were far from pure of heart. They were motivated by a desire to rid their country of the odious presence of uncivilized blacks. Certainly Forten and his group reacted against their contemptuous attitude. But is it not possible that a great many blacks in bondage at the time would have welcomed the opportunity to return to Africa in order to escape slavery? Was not freedom in Africa better than slavery in America? Forten and his crowd did not seem to think so. And these members of the black middle class who were the ministers in black churches, the teachers and principals in black

schools, and the most influential members of the black community, had the full support of the poorer, less well educated, free
black population of the North.

In the West Indies a similar class of blacks had been created
but given more privileges, more stability, and a clear, established position in society which, while it did not make them
white men, did indisputably set them apart from other blacks.
The members of this class owned and abused slaves themselves
and even fought on the white side during slave uprisings. In the
United States in Forten's time it was not the feeling of an
ethnic bond with the common slave that turned men like
Forten against colonization or that made the average middle-
class black an ardent abolitionist, but the inability to break that
bond.

In 1854 when Charlotte went to Higginson Grammar
School, an integrated school in Salem, she began to keep a
diary. She maintained it right through her teaching career,
which began when she became the only black teacher at the
Epes Grammar School in Salem, and continued through her
participation in the attempt to educate freed men at Port
Royal in South Carolina during the Civil War. Throughout the
diary Charlotte emphasizes her commitment to education as
a means of proving that blacks could attain the intellectual
heights of whites.

Port Royal, with its hordes of freed slaves, was the site of an
experimental project which sent instructors to "the Negroes to
teach them all the necessary rudiments of civilization . . . until
they be sufficiently enlightened to think and provide for themselves." For Charlotte Forten this enterprise seemed to provide
the opportunity to prove once and for all that blacks were the
equals of whites. She had no doubt that the former slaves would
share her aspirations and her diary suggests that they were
careful not to disappoint her.

Although in her diary Charlotte Forten tended to dismiss

most matters that might give us some insight into the actual ordeal of a black woman of her class, with a "the less said of that the better," it is possible on occasion to read between the lines. The description of the following incident expresses a characteristic reaction:

[I] Went into the Commissary's Office to wait for the boat which was to take us to St. Helena's Island which is about six miles from B[eaufort]. 'Tis here that Miss Towne has her school, in which I am to teach. . . . While waiting in the Office we saw several military gentlemen (sic), *not* very creditable specimens, I sh'ld say. The little Commissary himself . . . is a perfect little popinjay, and he and a Colonel somebody who didn't look any too sensible, talked in a very smart manner, evidently for our special benefit. The word "nigger" was plentifully used, whereupon I set them down at once as *not* gentlemen (sic). . . . (Forten, *Journal.*)

She was clearly a woman who found it most debilitating to endure the thousands of trivial insults directed at a black in a bigoted and segregated society. Though she belonged to the most privileged class of her people, she seemed endlessly plagued by depressions, vague illnesses, and a profound insecurity. She constantly harangues herself for not being worthy, for not doing enough, for not being smart enough. On her twenty-fifth birthday she notes: "Tisn't a very pleasant thought that I have lived a quarter of a century, and am so very, very ignorant. Ten years ago, I hoped for a different fate at twenty-five. But why complain? The accomplishments, the society, the delights of travel which I have dreamed of and longed for all my life, I am now convinced can never be mine." This from a young woman who as an adolescent would commonly read a hundred books a year in addition to her other studies.

Her contemporaries described her as a handsome girl, delicate, slender, attractive, whereas she saw herself as hopelessly ugly. Yet is it any wonder that the repressed mind that would render judgments of racists in the restrained muted tone of "the word 'nigger' was plentifully used, whereupon I set them down at once as *not* gentlemen" would also find the rejection of whites nearly unbearable?

It would have been completely understandable if a woman like Charlotte Forten had wished to sever identification with a people whose existence caused her so much misery. But the middle-class nineteenth-century black woman was not allowed to do this. An ignorant white mob or a single drunken white might abruptly reduce her to a condition no more privileged than that of any black in slavery.

Such women formed organizations like the Afric-American Female Intelligence Society of Boston, which were meant to demonstrate through reading and other "cultured" activities that black women were not vulgar, crude, and promiscuous, as they were reputed to be. Perhaps because of the precariousness of their freedom and the continual reminders that they were second-class citizens, they rarely thought in terms of complete isolation from their race or even in terms of their own individual advancement above everything else. Even though they read European novels and attended violin recitals, even though they patterned themselves after upper-class whites, they made the central activity of their lives the abolitionist movement.

Yes, they wished to break their ties with Africa, but they understood that they could not improve their own position without improving the position of the entire race. The result was a kind of racial unity. Genuinely dedicated to the advancement of their race, they unwittingly desired to destroy all that defined them as a race in the name of betterment.

My friends, I am rejoiced that you are glad, but I don't know how you will feel when I get through. I come from another field—the country of the slave. They have got their liberty—so much good luck

149

to have slavery partly destroyed; not entirely. I want it root and branch destroyed. Then we will all be free indeed. I feel that if I have to answer for the deeds done in my body just as much as a man, I have a right to have just as much as a man. There is a great stir about colored men getting their rights, but not a word about the colored women; and if colored men get their rights, and not colored women theirs, you see the colored men will be masters over the women, and it will be just as bad as it was before. . . .

. . . I have done a great deal of work; as much as a man, but did not get so much pay. I used to work in the field and bind grain, keeping up with the cradler; but men doing no more, got twice as much pay. . . . We do as much, we eat as much, we want as much. I suppose I am about the only colored woman that goes about to speak for the rights of colored women. I want to keep the thing stirring, now that the ice is cracked. What we want is a little money. You men know that you get as much again as women, when you write, or for what you do. When we get our rights, we shall not have to come to you for money, for then we shall have money enough in our own pockets; and maybe you will ask us for money. But help us now until we get it. . . . ("Convention of the American Equal Rights Association, New York City, 1867—Sojourner Truth Speech," *Black Women in White America*, ed. Gerda Lerner.)

Although, today large, strong women are not appreciated by blacks, it was frequently boasted during slavery that such women were the equals of any men in their ability to perform physical labor. Their physical strength was highly prized, and they often seemed to couple strong bodies with rebellious natures. These women were neither rejected nor frowned upon by slave men. They did more than their share of work and this made the load lighter for everyone else.

As suffragette and abolitionist efforts mounted, the "strong" black woman became an increasingly threatening presence to the slaveholder. She endangered the prevailing notion of women as weak and helpless, and thus the whole system of the oppression of women. She doubled the potential strength of black men. Women like Harriet Tubman and Sojourner Truth were present in the front lines of every camp of escaped slaves.

Born in Maryland around 1820, Harriet Tubman was trained by her father to hunt game and to know the forest. An enthusiastic pupil of everything that involved the outdoors, she found sewing, as well as most indoor work, tedious. From the time she was a young girl, she was known among her fellow slaves as an excellent worker who could rival the men in the fields. At the age of fifteen she intervened in behalf of another slave and was struck in the head by an overseer with a metal weight. From then on Harriet Tubman suffered dizzy spells and sleeping seizures. But that didn't stop her from running away at the age of thirty when her young master died. She subsequently made nineteen trips to the North transporting hundreds of fugitive slaves. She prodded them on with the butt of her gun, and although there was a price of forty thousand dollars on her head, she was never caught and never lost a single slave.

Only illness prevented her from being with John Brown at Harper's Ferry. She served the Union Army during the Civil War as a scout, a spy, and a nurse; in one campaign she rescued 765 slaves on the Combahee River. The slaves called her Moses. Harriet Tubman was the living antithesis of everything women were supposed to be.

Harriet Tubman's contemporary, Sojourner Truth, was born a slave in New York State. Her early life was difficult; she suffered heavy farm work, cruel masters, and the sales of her children. She, like Harriet Tubman, had the reputation of being able to do as much work as a man.

Not long after the abolition of slavery in New York she became an itinerant preacher and a spokeswoman not only for the rights of blacks but the rights of black women.

Most black women who were educated or otherwise in the

position to maintain an opinion during the nineteenth century were for women's rights, particularly for black women's rights. Among the papers and speeches of black women during slavery one will continually find references to the necessity for education, freedom, achievement among black women. A good many black women supported the Women's Movement of the day.

When slavery was over, and the Fourteenth Amendment which would entitle black men to the vote was about to pass, white women tried to fight for the inclusion of female suffrage in that amendment. Yet most black women, who had previously been for the vote for women, backed down in favor of the vote for black men. It was generally felt that if the Amendment extended the franchise to women, it would endanger its passage through Congress, which it probably would have. Mrs. Francis Harper, a black feminist, orator, and abolitionist said,

Being black is more precarious and demanding than being a woman; being black means that every white, including every white working-class woman, can discriminate against you. (Catherine Stimpson, "Thy Neighbor's Wife, Thy Neighbor's Servants: Women's Liberation and Black Civil Rights," *Woman in Sexist Society: Studies in Power & Powerlessness,* ed. Vivian Gornick and Barbara K. Moran, New York: Basic Books, 1971.)

The one great exception was Sojourner Truth. She felt that black men would perpetuate gross injustices if they were allowed to advance beyond black women.

Such women as Sojourner Truth and Harriet Tubman stood at the opposite extreme from assimilationists like Charlotte Forten. They had experienced the very worst of slavery. They were not imitations of white women, nor did they show any inclination to become so. They stood on the brink of a new definition of woman's role—one which undoubtedly would have been an improvement over the way women were defined both in Africa and white America.

Until they died, both Tubman and Truth continued to be useful to their people. Harriet Tubman, who lived on a scant pension as a result of her husband's death (she was never paid for her role in the war), set up a home for the aged. Sojourner Truth could be found after the war petitioning the government for lands in the West for freedmen. The existence of a Sojourner Truth or a Harriet Tubman did not mean that black women were superwomen, any more than their counterparts were supermen. For every single slave woman like Harriet Tubman there were twenty who died in childbirth, went mad, or became old by the time they were thirty. It only meant that some unusually talented women had emerged despite a vicious and cruel system of human devastation. Women have often stood on the brink of redefinition after a national catastrophe such as a war, but they are almost always shoved back into line once conditions "improve," and so it was with black women.

The struggle of the women to define a feminine role for themselves and to strengthen their men's sense of their own masculinity came to fruition after the war when the women so readily deferred to their men without surrendering their own opinions and activities, which were often militant. Black people found themselves in a brutal battle for genuine freedom in a postwar world in which certain norms reigned. They knew that in order to win, they would have to accommodate to those norms—specifically, the norms according to which men, not women, controlled the political process and supported the family. The ease with which black men and women made that transition, when not prevented by forces beyond their control, demonstrates how well prepared they already were. (Genovese, *Roll, Jordan, Roll.*)

Despite the common interests of Negro and white women, however, the dichotomy of the segregated society has prevented them from cementing a natural alliance. Communication and cooperation between them have been hesitant, limited and formal. Negro women have tended to identify all discrimination against them as racial in origin and to accord high priority to the civil rights struggle. They have had little time or energy for consideration of women's rights. But as the civil rights struggle gathers momentum, they begin to recognize the similarities between paternalism and racial arrogance. They also begin to sense that the struggle into which they have poured their energies may not afford them rights they assumed would be theirs when the civil rights cause has triumphed.

Recently disquieting events have made imperative an assessment of the role of the Negro woman in the quest for equality. The civil rights revolt, like many social upheavals, has released powerful pentup emotions, cross currents, rivalries, and hostilities. . . . There is much jockeying for position as ambitious men push and elbow their way to leadership roles. Part of this upsurge reflects the Negro male's normal desire to achieve a sense of personal worth and recognition of his manhood by a society which has so long denied it. One aspect is the wresting of the initiative of the civil rights movement from white liberals. Another is the backlash of a new male aggressiveness against Negro women. (Dr. Pauli Murray, "The Negro Woman in the Quest for Equality," *Black Women in White America,* ed. Gerda Lerner.)

Black people emerged from slavery with two distinct female archetypes. The privileged woman who had either been free before the war or maintained a special position in the white household, sometimes as the mistress of the white master; and the woman who was bigger, stronger, tougher, more rebellious, and usually poor. The first category we will call the Black Lady, the second the Amazon.

The great majority of women were somewhere in between. That is, they desired the ease, comfort, and respectability in the eyes of the white world that being a Black Lady to some extent provided; at the same time they realized the immediate necessity of preserving many of their Amazonian qualities.

Yet the deterioration and neutralization of the Amazon was inevitable. As her mythical strength gained in importance, her actual accomplishments diminished. The myth carried with it certain self-destructing mechanisms. The average woman believed that the Amazon was also a ballbreaker—unfeminine and hard hearted. As blacks increasingly began to accept the things whites said about them, they began to blame their problems on one another. Although the Amazonian woman was terribly important to the process of keeping food on the table and clothes on the children's backs, the black man slowly began to believe that if she were weaker, he might mysteriously become more powerful.

Nevertheless, until our own day, the hostility between the sexes was never total. Only infrequently did the masses of blacks engage in the masochistic exercise of comparing themselves to whites. Most of the time they were too occupied with struggling to survive. As long as their oppression was out in the open and severe, it remained very clear to them that they needed their own rules in order to get by. Their families were solid and close-knit, despite the problems of unemployment and underemployment that plagued both black men and women.

Through the post-Civil War period and during the early twentieth century, blacks frequently lived in an extended family which had at its core a solid nuclear family. Despite the morality of the prevailing society, young black women continued to become pregnant and have children out of wedlock, but most of these women were married before they were thirty. And until they did marry, they invariably lived with their families of origin. Most black women who worked outside of the home as maids were single and young. Married women with children tended to work as washerwomen so that they could be available to their children.

Blacks had their music, their dance, their cooking, their way of talking and walking, their culture. In every aspect of their being they struggled for a repudiation of the image of their inferiority which whites force-fed them through textbooks and newspapers, through segregated public facilities, through the Klan's nightrides. Yet it was an impoverished culture, dependent upon the white majority even for its survival-level subsistence. Ironically, perhaps it was also dependent upon the clarity of oppression.

Blacks did not deny their blackness but they did not delude themselves into thinking that black was a good thing to be in white America. The positive aspects of their culture they took for granted. Slowly, very slowly, however, as the hopes that accompanied the Emancipation Proclamation began to dwindle and die, they began to believe that even these positive aspects were the signs of inferiority that whites proclaimed them to be.

Meanwhile the movement of club women which had begun with the intellectual societies formed before the war by Northern free women progressed and expanded under the guidance of middle-class and even lower-middle-class black women. These women, the descendants of the Black Ladies, inherited the obsessions of their forebears with white standards. One of the fundamental goals of these organizations was to uplift the black woman to the white woman's level. To achieve this, it seemed necessary to make her more of a lady, more clean, more proper than any white woman could hope to be. As if to blot out the humiliation of working in the white woman's kitchen all day, of being virtually defenseless before the sexual advances of white men, black women enacted a charade of teas, cotillions, and all the assorted paraphernalia and pretensions of society life. It was a desperate masquerade which seemed to increase in frenzy as time went on. As the reaffirmation of their womanhood from black men became less certain, more and more black women began to turn their heads in Charlotte Forten's direction, even if their economic circumstances prevented them from imitating her standard of living. Many fewer looked to the examples of Harriet Tubman and Sojourner Truth, whom no man in his right mind would want except, perhaps, patient old Uncle Tom. These middle-class women were struggling for a positive identity in the only way left open to them by the society. At the same time, they put their bodies and their hearts behind every effort to benefit, to "uplift" the race; they built schools, hospitals, and fought against the lynching in the South.

The Amazon made her last convincing appearances during the Civil Rights Movement, in the form of Rosa Parks, who refused to move from the front of the bus one day in 1955 in Montgomery, Alabama; in the form of Fannie Lou Hamer and the countless other black women in the South who contributed to the struggle for equal rights. It was the Civil Rights Movement, however, that also made it clear that a gap was developing between black men and women. Although usually grudgingly respected by men for the contribution they made to the movement's work, black women were never allowed to rise to the lofty heights of a Martin Luther King or a Roy Wilkins, or even a John Lewis. Not a single black woman was allowed to make one of the major speeches or to be part of the delegation of leaders that went to the White House during the March on Washington. And there was yet another price the black women of the Civil Rights Movement had to pay for their competence. After hours, their men went off with white women. Given the time (the commencement of one of the greatest human rights movements the world has ever seen) and the place (the deep South), black women couldn't help but take this as a personal rejection. An increasing paranoia was inevitable.

The black woman had not failed to be aware of America's

standard of beauty nor the fact that she was not included in it; television and motion pictures had made this information very available to her. She watched as America expanded its ideal to include Irish, Italian, Jewish, even Oriental and Indian women. America had room among its beauty contestants for the buxom Mae West, the bug eyes of Bette Davis, the masculinity of Joan Crawford, but the black woman was only allowed entry if her hair was straight, her skin light, and her features European; in other words, if she was as nearly indistinguishable from a white woman as possible. The black man noticed this too. It was also clear that, whether he wished it or not, he was risking his life for his reputed lust for white women. Could he fail to get the message? The black woman had no value. He projected his self-hatred onto her. She reminded him of his oppression, of his mythic inability to assert himself as a man. Even if he allowed himself to be with her, he was reluctant to supply her with the kind of reinforcement and approval she craved. In a thousand little ways he made it clear to her that he would rather have Kim Novak.

The black woman approached the Black Movement of the sixties unsure of her womanhood, desperate for the approval of black men, more than ever impressed with and dependent upon white interpretations of herself. Yes, there were women who were reasonably certain of themselves, who had men who loved and adored them, but these would not be the women who determined the future.

The black community had for quite some time been plagued by color discrimination. The upper echelons of black society in particular tended to rate beauty and merit on the basis of the lightness of the skin and the straightness of the hair and features. White features were often a more reliable ticket into this society than professional status or higher education. Interestingly enough, this was more true for women than it was for men.

And there was another side of the coin. The black woman was not entirely unprejudiced in respect to the black man. The saying "a black man ain't shit" was never more popular than in the fifties. We shouldn't, however, forget some other popular sayings of the times: "There's two things I've never seen, green snow and an ugly white woman," and, "There's only one thing a black woman can do for me, and that's to show me where that pretty little white gal went."

The tendency to internalize one's oppression was nothing new. In 1835 Maria Stewart, the first black woman to speak in public, seemed to reflect the thinking of her class and times when she said,

. . . I would strongly recommend to you, to improve your talents; let not one lie buried in the earth. Show forth your powers of mind. Prove to the world, that

> Though black your skins as shades of night,
> Your hearts are pure, your souls are white.

(Bert J. Loewenberg and Ruth Bogin, ed., *Black Women in Nineteenth-Century American Life: Their Words, Their Thoughts, Their Feelings,* Pennsylvania: Pennsylvania State University Press, 1976.)

The Civil Rights Movement was the great test of the theory that whites could be persuaded of the equality of blacks. The theory that self-improvement was the cure-all turned out to be only one step away from self-contempt.

3

As the organization grew stronger, the truly committed cadres were being separated from the staff members who wanted the credit but not the responsibility for building SNCC. On the original central staff there had been six men and three women. The three women on the staff—Bobbie, Rene and myself—always had a disproportionate share of the duties of keeping the office and the organization running. . . .

Some of the brothers came around only for staff meetings (sometimes), and whenever we women were involved in something important, they began to talk about "women taking over the organization" —calling it a matriarchal coup d'etat. . . . By playing such a leading role in the organization, some of them insisted, we were aiding and abetting the enemy, who wanted to see Black men weak and unable to hold their own. . . .

Later, when Margaret came, and saw me all huddled up in the blanket, freezing above a water-logged floor, her mouth fell open. "They must be kidding!" she said. "I've been inside a lot of jails, but this beats them all."

Her outrage made me feel a little better. For a while, I had been wondering whether I was overreacting. And then I thought of the descriptions George [Jackson] had given of the many dungeons they had thrown him into over the last decade. This place couldn't be as bad as O Wing in Soledad or the Adjustment Center in San Quentin or solitary in Folsom or any of the other cells where they had tried to squeeze the will and determination out of George. (Angela Davis, *An Autobiography*, New York: Random House, 1974.)

In the spring of 1969 black students took over the south campus of the City College of New York for nearly two weeks. Although I was still in high school, I spent a lot of time there. My mother originally sent me with food for the students. I ended up attending a good many of their meetings. I remember one meeting especially well. The president of the black student organization, a tall, handsome Haitian, was begging the black female students to stop picking fights with white male students on North campus. It seemed the black female students were so amazed and delighted by the new notion that black male students would come to their defense that they kept starting fights with white males on North campus in order to witness this miracle again and again.

The previous year I had attended the National Black Theatre, an organization founded by Barbara Ann Teer, a black actress with unusual magnetism and organizational ability. The membership spent much of its time talking about what a shame it was that a man could not be found to take her place.

Misogyny was an integral part of Black Macho. Its philosophy, which maintained that black men had been more oppressed than black women, that black women had, in fact, contributed to that oppression, that black men were sexually and morally superior and also exempt from most of the responsibilities human beings had to other human beings, could only be detrimental to black women. But black women were determined to believe—even as their own guts were telling them it was not so—that they were finally on the verge of liberation from the spectre of the omnipotent blonde with the rosebud lips and the cheesecake legs. They would no longer have to admire another woman on the pedestal. The pedestal would be theirs. They would no longer have to do their own fighting.

They would be fought for. The knight in white armor would ride for them. The beautiful fairy princess would be black.

The women of the Black Movement had little sense of the contradictions in their desire to be models of fragile Victorian womanhood in the midst of a revolution. They wanted a house, a picket fence around it, a chicken in the pot, and a man. As they saw it, their only officially designated revolutionary responsibility was to have babies.

Precious few black women were allowed to do anything important in the Black Movement. Those few who did manage to exercise some kind of influence did not concern themselves with the predicament of black women. In that sense, they were ahistorical, compared to the club-society women, activists and career women, black abolitionists, and feminists who were their predecessors.

Angela Davis, a member of the Communist Party and a professor at the University of California, was probably the best-known female activist. Davis grew up in Birmingham, Alabama. Her father owned a service station and her mother was a teacher. She attended the segregated schools of Birmingham until she was fifteen, when she gained admission to a program that enabled her to live with a white family in New York and attend the private, progressive Elisabeth Irwin High School. She claims that her interest in the Communist Party, in socialism, and in liberation struggles began at this time and continued through her undergraduate years at Brandeis and her graduate study in Frankfurt. In 1967 she went to California to teach and participate in the ongoing Black Revolution. Three years later, not long after being removed from her post as professor of philosophy at the University of Southern California because of her affiliation with the Communist Party, Davis was arrested and charged with conspiracy, murder, and kidnapping.

Early in 1969 she had become involved in the case of the Soledad Brothers. Their story, Davis tells us, began in Soledad Prison during an integrated exercise period. Unaccompanied by guards, black and white prisoners had filed into the yard. A general melee ensued during a fight between a black inmate and a white inmate. O.G. Miller, an expert marksman stationed in the gun tower, shot down three men, all of whom were black. The court ruled that it was "justifiable homicide." Black prisoners protested, and a white guard was pushed over a railing and killed. George Jackson, John Clutchette, and Fleeta Drumgo, who reportedly had reputations in the prison as "militants," were charged with the guard's murder.

Deeply impressed by George Jackson's political theories, Angela Davis became a prime mover in the committee to free the Soledad Brothers. She subsequently became friendly with George Jackson's brother Jonathan, who was seventeen, and began to correspond with George Jackson. Although she had only seen him briefly in his courtroom appearance, she fell in love with him. Such things were not uncommon in the sixties.

On August 7, 1970, Jonathan Jackson attended the trial of James McClain, a prisoner at San Quentin who was a friend of George's. At an early point during the proceedings young Jackson stood up. He had a carbine in his hand and, as in all the good movies, he ordered everyone in the courtroom to freeze. McClain, as well as Ruchell Magee and William Christmas, also prisoners at San Quentin who were present in order to testify, joined Jonathan. They left the courtroom with Judge Harold Haley, Assistant DA Gary Thomas, and several jurors, and got into a waiting van. A San Quentin guard fired on them, and a general shoot out followed, leaving three of the prisoners and Judge Haley dead, Thomas, Magee and one of the jurors wounded. It was called a revolt.

Davis, who immediately went into hiding, was captured by police and FBI in a motel in New York. She was charged with conspiracy with Jonathan Jackson and giving him the gun. Therefore, under California law, she was also guilty of murder and kidnapping.

Davis's passionate love for George Jackson was cited by the prosecution as a motive for her involvement with the events of August seventh. Davis said she had known nothing about what Jonathan Jackson intended to do. The gun that Jonathan had used had come from a collection of weapons that the Che-Lumumba Club, the branch of the Communist Party to which Angela Davis belonged, had used for target practice and were available to any member.

Perhaps the largest campaign of its kind was launched to set Angela free. On June 4, 1972, she was cleared of all the charges against her. During the two years that she was confined without bail she became one of the most important figures in the Black Movement and certainly the key figure in the movement to free black political prisoners. As she wrote in her autobiography, it was to this movement that she planned to dedicate the rest of her life.

Angela Davis had grown up surrounded by the bigotry and poverty of the South, yet her family had been comfortably middle class. Just at the height of the Civil Rights Movement (during which a childhood friend of her sister's died in a church bombing), she went off to a private school in New York. As the Black Movement and the urban riots were getting under way she was in Frankfurt studying Hegel and Marx. Throughout her life she had always been unmistakably removed from the struggles of her people, by education, money, and opportunities. When she finally plunged herself into Movement activity, she reached right over all of the possible issues that might have been considered relevant to her own experience to the issue of the plight of the black male "political prisoner." She even fell in love with a man who had made it eminently clear that he considered black women enslaving.

It always starts with mama, mine loved me. As testimony of her love, and her fear for the fate of the manchild all slave mothers hold, she attempted to press, hide, push, capture me in the womb. The conflicts and contradictions that will follow me to the tomb started right there in the womb. The feeling of being captured . . . this slave can never adjust to it. (George Jackson, *Soledad Brother: The Prison Letters of George Jackson,* New York: Bantam Books, 1970.)

But I understand Angela Davis's choice much better than I often care to admit. When I read George Jackson's *Soledad Brother* and Gregory Armstrong's book about him, *The Dragon Has Come* (New York: Harper and Row, 1974.) everything I was doing with my own life seemed meaningless measured against the sufferings that had been inflicted upon him. I think of Angela Davis as a person driven by a sense of mission— totally committed to alleviating some of the pain inflicted upon people in this world.

I met her once waiting for an elevator at Random House, where I worked as a typist. Immediately she wanted to know who I was, what I was doing there. I was struck by her directness, her openness, her innocence, her rawness. Although I was only twenty-one and painfully insecure, I felt strangely protective of this handsome, statuesque, very famous young woman.

What I am getting to is that there are two ways to look at Angela Davis. I admire her immensely as an individual for turning her feelings of guilt toward a constructive purpose— something privileged black women have rarely done. It is the use of her image by the Black Movement that I rebel against. Angela Davis, a brilliant, middle-class black woman, with a European education, a Ph.D. in philosophy, and a university appointment, was willing to die for a poor, uneducated black male inmate. It was straight out of Hollywood—Ingrid Bergman and Humphrey Bogart.

For all her achievements, she was seen as the epitome of the selfless, sacrificing "good woman"—the only kind of black woman the Movement would accept. She did it for her man, they said. A woman in a woman's place. The so-called political issues were irrelevant.

Nikki Giovanni, a kind of nationalistic Rod McKuen, was the reigning poetess of the Black Movement during the sixties. Most of us remember her best for poems like this one written in 1968:

Nigger
Can you kill
Can you kill
Can a nigger kill
Can a nigger kill a honkie
Can a nigger kill the Man
Can you kill nigger
Huh? nigger can you
kill
Do you know how to draw blood
Can you poison
Can you stab-a-jew
Can you kill huh? Nigger
Can you kill
Can you run a protestant down with your
'68 El Dorado
(that's all they're good for anyway)
Can you kill
Can you piss on a blond head
Can you cut it off
Can you kill. . . .

(Nikki Giovanni, "The True Import of Present Dialogue: Black vs. Negro," *Black Feeling, Black Talk, Black Judgement*, New York: William Morrow, 1970.)

She attached herself to a black poets' movement in New York that had been started by LeRoi Jones. The poems generally exhorted blacks to return to their roots and to partake in revolutionary action like killing honkies. There were a great many men and very few women involved; Giovanni was one of the few that lasted.

She had a remarkable facility for riding the tide of public opinion. When it became obvious that (1) the black male poets were going to shut her out and that (2) she could not depend upon a black female audience as long as her poems advocated outright violence, she began to speak positively of the church and to focus more on having babies and loving the black man. Her albums sold quite well. She herself had a baby and refused to disclose the name of the father. Early in the seventies she told young black women to become mothers because they needed something to love. She also told young black people that school was useless and a waste of time—despite her own years of education at Fisk University. Soon after, she backed away from these positions, amending her original statement about having babies to you-should-only-have-one-if-you-could-afford-to-take-care-of-it-like-she-could, and actually encouraging blacks to go back to school. Concomitantly, she began to make a lot of money on the college lecture circuit. She received an award for her work with youth from the *Ladies' Home Journal.* It was presented by Lynda Bird Johnson on national television.

Both Davis and Giovanni represented the very best black women had to offer, or were allowed to offer, during the Black Movement. They carved out two paths for women who wished to be active. Davis's was Do-it-for-your-man. Giovanni's was Have-a-baby. Neither seemed to have any trouble confining herself to her narrow universe.

Unfortunately, and I believe unintentionally, Davis set a precedent for black female revolutionary action as action that could never be self-generated. When I visited Riker's Island several years ago, I met a few female revolutionaries suffering the consequences of that example. The run-of-the-mill female prisoner was there because of her man—her pimp, her dope supplier, or the man she had accompanied on a stickup. The political women were there for the same reason.

But only the most adventurous were ready to follow Angela Davis's lead. The majority took Nikki Giovanni much more seriously. She was the guiding light for those who had been left behind in the flurry and chaos of the revolution. No doubt she prompted many by word and deed to have babies so that they could have "something to love." By the time she advised them later to first make sure they had enough income to support the child, a lot of women were already on welfare. Giovanni did her bit to encourage the view of black men as sex symbols.

> Beautiful Black Men
> (With compliments and
> apologies to all not
> mentioned by name)
>
> i wanta say just gotta say something
> bout those beautiful beautiful beautiful outasight
> black men
> with they afros
> walking down the street
> is the same ol danger
> but a brand new pleasure
>
> sitting on stoops, in bars, going to offices
> running numbers, watching for their whores
> preaching in churches, driving their hogs
> walking their dogs, winking at me
> in their fire red, lime green, burnt orange
> royal blue tight tight pants that hug
> what i like to hug . . .
>
> (Giovanni, *Black Feeling.*) (1968)

Yet she could also write, in "Woman Poem":

> you see, my whole life is tied up to unhappiness . . .
> it's having a job
> they won't let you work
> or no work at all
> castrating me
> (yes it happens to women too)
> it's a sex object if you're pretty
> and no love
> or love and no sex if you're fat
> get back fat black woman be a mother
> grandmother strong thing but not woman
> gameswoman romantic woman love needer
> man seeker dick eater sweat getter
> fuck needing love seeking woman. . . .
>
> (Giovanni, *Black Feeling*.)

Although she rarely chose to reflect it in her work, Giovanni did realize the black woman's dilemma to some extent. A line from one of her later poems is unfortunately more typical: "what i need to do/is sit and wait/cause i'm a woman . . . " (Nikki Giovanni, "All I Gotta Do," *The Women and the Men*, New York: William Morrow, 1975.)

As we can see in Giovanni's "Woman Poem" there was some low-key directionless complaining and grumbling among black women in the sixties. But they put more energy into their fight against Women's Liberation than into anything else. Hardly a week passed during the late sixties and early seventies when there wasn't an article on how black women felt that Women's Liberation was irrelevant to them because they were already liberated.

The black woman had been rendered invisible. She was not allowed to participate in political planning. She was also not allowed to go to the hairdresser or church, to attend most clubs, or to participate in sororities, all of which had been declared counterrevolutionary. It could only be said with certainty that she hated white women, hated Women's Liberation, that she was having babies for the revolution, and that she wanted a man who would provide for her and keep her in a manner to which she had never been accustomed. She became a distinctly reactionary creature. She sat silently by as Eartha Kitt, who had spoken out in the White House against the Vietnam War, and two other politically minded singers, Nina Simone and Miriam Makeba, were virtually banned from performing in this country. It was Aretha Franklin who read her mind: "I don't want nobody always sitting right there looking at me and that man." (Aretha Franklin and Ted White, "Dr. Feelgood [Love Is a Serious Business]," *Aretha Franklin in Paris,* Atlantic Records, 1968.) And that included *all* women, black or white.

She seemed to think this suicidal course would win her black man back. It drove him further away. In the past the black woman had always provided the black man with an atmosphere in which he was treated as the equal of any man. That included resisting him when he was wrong. Now the black woman was making excuses for him, treating him like a very bad child and herself like a doormat. What use had he for her now? She seemed to make his inferiority a certainty by her very existence.

They were always there. . . . Those classifying signs that told you who you were, what to do. More than those abrupt and discourteous signs one gets used to in this country—the door that says "Push," the towel dispenser that says "Press," the traffic light that says "No"—these signs were not just arrogant, they were malevolent: "White Only," "Colored Only," or perhaps just "Colored," permanently carved into the granite over a drinking fountain. But there was one set of signs that was not malevolent; it was, in fact, rather reassuring in its accuracy and fine distinctions: the pair that said "White Ladies" and "Colored Women."

The difference between white and black females seemed to me an eminently satisfactory one. White females were *ladies*, said the sign maker, worthy of respect. And the quality that made ladyhood worthy? Softness, helplessness and modesty—which I interpreted as a willingness to let others do their labor and their thinking. Colored females, on the other hand, were *women*—unworthy of respect, independent and immodest. (Toni Morrison, "What the Black Woman Thinks About Women's Lib," *The New York Times Magazine*, August 22, 1971.)

dark phrases of womanhood/ of never havin been a girl half-notes scattered/ without rhythm no tune distraught laughter fallin/ over a black girl's shoulder it's funny it's hysterical/ the melody-less-ness of her dance don't tell nobody don't tell a soul she's dancin on beer cans & shingles this must be the spook house/ another song with no singers lyrics, no voices & interrupted solos/ unseen performances are we ghouls?/ children of horror? the joke?/ don't tell nobody don't tell a soul are we animals? have we gone crazy? i can't hear anything/ but maddening screams & the soft strains of death/ & you promised me you promised me . . . / . . . you promised me somebody/ anybody/ sing a black girl's song bring her out/ to know herself/ to know you but sing her rhythms/carin/ struggle/ hard times sing her song of life/ she's been dead so long closed in silence so long/ she doesn't know the sound of her own voice/ her infinite beauty she's half-notes scattered/ without rhythm no tune sing her sighs/ sing the song of her possibilities sing a righteous gospel/ let her be born let her be born. . . . (Ntozake Shange, *For Colored Girls Who Have Considered Suicide When the Rainbow is Enuf: A Choreopoem,* New York: Macmillan, 1977.)

The black woman never really dealt with the primary issues of the Black Movement. She stopped straightening her hair. She stopped using lighteners and brighteners. She forced herself to be submissive and passive. She preached to her children about the glories of the black man. But then, suddenly, the Black Movement was over. Now she has begun to straighten her hair again, to follow the latest fashions in *Vogue* and *Mademoiselle,* to rouge her cheeks furiously, and to speak, not infrequently, of what a disappointment the black man has been. She has little contact with other black women, and if she does, it is not of a deep sort. The discussion is generally of clothes, makeup, furniture, and men. Privately she does whatever she can to stay out of that surplus of black women (one million) who will never find mates. And if she doesn't find a man, she might just decide to have a baby anyway.

Although black women have been having babies outside of marriage since slavery, there are several unusual things about the current trend among black women. Whereas unmarried black women with babies have usually lived with extended families, these women tend to brave it alone. Whereas the black women of previous generations have generally married soon after the baby was born, these women may not and often say they do not wish to. Whereas the practice of having babies out of wedlock was generally confined to the poorer classes of black women, it is now not uncommon among middle-class, moderately successful black women. A woman may pick a man she barely knows, she may not even tell him he is going to be a father or permit him to ever see the child. While I don't believe that anything like a majority of black women are going in for this, it is worth finding out why so many black women have, why so many are saying, "Well, if I don't marry by the time I am thirty, I'll have a baby anyway."

It certainly can't be for love of children. I am inclined to believe it is because the black woman has no legitimate way of coming together with other black women, no means of self-affirmation—in other words, no women's movement, and therefore no collective ideology. Career and success are still the social and emotional disadvantages to her that they were to white women in the fifties. There is little in the black community to reinforce a young black woman who does not have a man or a child and who wishes to pursue a career. She is still considered against nature. It is extremely difficult to assert oneself when there remains some question of one's basic identity.

The Women's Movement redefined womanhood for white women in a manner that allowed them to work, to be manless, but still women. White women replaced some of their traditional activities with new ones—consciousness raising, feminist meetings and demonstrations, the Women's Political Caucus, campaigns for Bella Abzug and other feminist politicians, antidiscrimination suits against employers, and the pursuit of an entirely new range of careers. And some white women dragged their men right along with them, not to mention a good many black men.

But the black woman, who had pooh-poohed the Women's Movement, was left with only one activity that was not considered suspect: motherhood. A baby could counteract the damaging effect a career might have upon her feminine image. A baby could even be a substitute for a man. A baby clarified a woman's course for at least the next five years. No need for her to bother with difficult decisions about whether or not she ought to pursue promotion or return to school for an advanced degree, both of which might attract even more hostility from black men. Her life had been simplified. Instead of confronting the problems that are presently repressing the black family, instead of battling with her fear of success, she could pursue her individual course which would allow her to make a provisional peace with herself. Never mind the bad odds under which her baby entered the world. In her less than serious moments she could even imagine that there was something liberated about what she had done.

I have a friend whose cousin is at Howard University now. She says that Howard men still insist that their women be light and have long hair. Whereas white women begin to complain about all the decent men being married when they reach their thirties, black women begin this complaint upon graduation from college.

Some young black women are beginning to be honest about seeing themselves as victims rather than superwomen. The pain and isolation set forth in Ntozake Shange's play *For Colored Girls Who Have Considered Suicide* was recognized by many as the bitter truth about their condition. Having decided not to play the role society has alloted them, an alarming number of black women go one disastrous step further. They become angry with black men, black people, blackness; it is simply a new way of blaming someone else for their underdevelopment. It rarely occurs to them that if things are not going well, they ought to take a leadership role in correcting them. The first impulse of upwardly mobile black women to pursue an advanced education, a higher salary, to become a professional, is not motivated by a desire to improve the lot of their race, but by a desire to break away from all its accessories of humiliation and guilt.

Their problems arise from the fact that they are living in the transformed world of the liberated woman at the same time they continue to scorn liberation. But liberation is nothing more than responsibility, responsibility for setting the tone of one's own life and standing by it.

When I was a newborn infant, my mother used to wonder why I was always scratching. It wasn't long before the cause became evident: I had eczema, a then incurable skin condition which causes peeling, flaking, and scabs. As I got older, it got worse. I was uglier than anyone or anything; I was positive of that. Other children were afraid to touch me. I greeted new schoolmates with "Don't worry, it isn't contagious." Boys treated me like a leper. It was probably the reason, I now realize, I always preferred to stay inside and read, to be near my mother.

As I approached puberty, it spread to my face. I was the only kid in the seventh grade who didn't have eyebrows. Because I was always chip dry, I had to put a lot of creams on my skin, couldn't go swimming or tumble around in the dirt. There wasn't a single moment of my life that I wasn't acutely aware of my skin, not only because of its effect on my social life but also because it was constantly itching, burning; I always felt dirty and uncomfortable. It was my excuse for everything—even for why I didn't do my homework.

When I was thirteen, I was sent to a famous dermatologist, who cured me completely in three weeks. My skin was not only clear, it seemed perfect. I remember people used to stop me on the street to ask me what I used on my skin. Suddenly I was beautiful, but my perception of myself had not adjusted to the change in my appearance.

I had grown up feeling wounded, marked, victimized, scarred, and the mere removal of my eczema had not altered that sensibility. The sense of being handicapped, of having a right to special considerations, never left me. When people complained about my lateness or my seeming lack of a sense of responsibility, I was always baffled and hurt. Didn't they understand that I couldn't be expected to perform as if I were healthy?

I think that the black woman thinks of her history and her condition as a wound which makes her different and therefore special and therefore exempt from human responsibility. The impartial observer may look at her and see a beautiful, healthy, glowing, vigorous woman but none of that matters. What matters is what she feels inside. And what she feels inside is powerless; she feels powerless to do anything about her condition or anyone else's. Her solution is to simply not participate, or to participate on her own very limited basis.

Yes, it is very important that we never forget the tragedy of our history or how racist white people have been or how the black man has let us down. But all of that must be set in its proper perspective. It belongs to the past and we must belong to the future. The future is something we can control. When I began this book, I thought it would be about what the black woman is, but this book has turned out to be about what has happened to her. She has yet to become what she is.

Lately I've noticed the appearance of a number of black women's organizations and conferences. The middle-class black woman in particular is beginning to address herself to feminist issues. But everything I've seen so far has been an imitation of what white feminists have done before. I now hear students refer casually to a Black Women's Movement. But I haven't seen black women make any meaningful attempt to differentiate between their problems and the problems of white women and, most important, there seems to be no awareness of how black women have been duped by the Myth of the Superwoman. Some black women have come together because they can't find husbands. Some are angry with their boyfriends. The lesbians are looking for a public forum for their sexual preference. Others notice that if one follows in the footsteps of the white feminists, a lucrative position or promotion may come up before long.

These women have trouble agreeing on things. Their organizations break up quickly and yet more keep forming. Every now and then someone still mentions that white women are going to rip them off if they join the Women's Movement—that is, white women will use their support to make gains and then not share with the black women. Unfortunately, this is probably true. It would be true of any movement the black woman joined in her present condition, that is, without some clear understanding of her priorities. The black woman needs an analysis. She belongs to the only group in this country which has not asserted its identity.

Early in 1978 there was a series of articles in *The New York*

Times on the changes in the black community since 1968. It covered the Civil Rights Movement, the Black Movement, the economic and social situation for blacks today. Never once did it mention the contribution black women made to the Civil Rights Movement. The article spoke of three Americas: one white, one middle-class black, one poor black. No particular notice was given to the fact that that poor black America consists largely of black women and children. It was as if these women and children did not exist.

The history of the period has been written and will continue to be written without us. The imperative is clear: Either we will make history or remain the victims of it.

Selected Bibliography

179

1. Afro-American Literary Criticism

Andrews, William L., ed., *Black Women's Slave Narratives*, New York: Oxford University Press, 1987.

Baker, Houston A. Jr., *Blues, Ideology, and Afro-American Literature*, Chicago: University of Chicago Press, 1984.

—— *Modernism and the Harlem Renaissance*, Chicago: University of Chicago Press, 1987.

—— and P. Redmon, eds, *Afro-American Literary Study in the 90s*, Chicago: University of Chicago Press, 1990.

Bell, Roseann Pope, Bettye J. Parker, and Beverly Guy-Sheftall, eds, *Sturdy Black Bridges: Visions of Black Women in Literature*, New York: Anchor Books, 1979.

Bowles, Juliet, ed., *In the Memory and Spirit of Frances, Zora and Lorraine: Essays and Interviews Relating to Black Women and Writing*, Washington, DC: Howard University Institute for the Arts and Humanities, 1975.

Braxton, Joanne M., *Black Women Writing Autobiography: A Tradition Within a Tradition*, Philadelphia: Temple University Press, 1989.

—— and Andree Nicola McLaughlin, eds, *Wild Women in the Whirlwind: Afra-American Culture and the Contemporary Literary Renaissance*, New Brunswick, NJ: Rutgers University Press, 1990.

Brown-Guillory, Elizabeth, *Their Place on the Stage: Black Women Playwrights in America*, Westport, Conn.: Greenwood Press, 1988.

Carby, Hazel V., *Reconstructing Womanhood: The Emergence of the Afro-American Novelist,* New York: Oxford University Press, 1987.

Christian, Barbara, *Black Feminist Criticism: Perspectives on Black Women Writers,* New York: Pergamon Press, 1985.

—— *Black Women Novelists: The Development of a Tradition 1892–1976,* Westport, Conn.: Greenwood Press, 1980.

Cone, James, *The Spirituals and the Blues: An Interpretation,* New York: Seabury Press, 1972.

Dearborn, Mary V., *Pocahontas's Daughters: Gender and Ethnicity in American Culture,* New York: Oxford University Press, 1986.

Dendridge, Rita, 'Male Critics/Black Women's Novels', *CLA Journal,* vol. 23, no. 1, September 1979.

—— 'On Novels By Black American Women: A Bibliographical Essay', *Women's Studies Newsletter,* vol. 6, no. 3, Summer 1978, pp. 28-30.

Evans, Mari, ed., *Black Women Writers 1950–1980: A Critical Evaluation,* Garden City, NY: Anchor Press/Doubleday, 1984.

Exum, Pat, *Contemporary Black Women Writers,* Deland, Fla.: Everett/Edwards, 1976.

Fisher, Dexter, and Robert E. Stepto, eds, *Afro-American Literature: The Reconstruction of Instruction,* New York: Modern Language Association of America, 1979.

Gates, Henry Louis Jr., ed., *Black Literature and Black Literary Theory,* New York and London: Methuen, 1984.

—— ed., *The Classic Slave Narratives,* New York: Mentor/New American Library, 1987.

—— *Figures in Black: Words, Signs, and the 'Racial' Self,* New York: Oxford University Press, 1987.

—— ed., *Reading Black/Reading Feminist: A Critical Anthology,* New York: Meridian/New American Library, 1990.

Giovanni, Nikki, and James Baldwin, *A Dialogue: James Baldwin and Nikki Giovanni,* Philadelphia: Lippincott 1973.

—— and Margaret Walker, *A Poetic Equation: Conversations between Nikki Giovanni and Margaret Walker,* Washington DC: Howard University Press, 1974.

Hammonds, Evelyn, 'Toward a Black Feminist Aesthetic', *Sojourner,* October 1980.

Harley, Sharon, and Roslyn Terborg-Penn, eds, *The Afro-American Woman: Struggle and Images*, Port Washington, NY: Kennikat Press, 1978.

Harris, Trudier, 'Folklore in the Fiction of Alice Walker: A Perspective of Historical and Literary Traditions', *Black American Literature Forum* 2, Spring 1977, pp. 3-8.

—— *From Mammies to Militants: Domestics in Black American Literature*, Philadelphia: Temple University Press, 1982.

Hernton, Calvin, *The Sexual Mountain and Black Women Writers*, New York: Anchor/Doubleday, 1987.

Honey, Maureen, ed., *Shadowed Dreams: Women's Poetry of the Harlem Renaissance*, New Brunswick, NJ: Rutgers University Press, 1989.

Hull, Gloria T., *Color, Sex and Poetry: Three Women Writers of the Harlem Renaissance*, Bloomington: Indiana University Press, 1987.

—— Patricia Bell Scott, and Barbara Smith, eds, *All the Women Are White, All the Blacks Are Men, But Some of Us Are Brave: Black Women's Studies*, Old Westbury, NY: The Feminist Press, 1982.

Johnson, Barbara, *Give Us Each Day: The Diary of Alice Dunbar-Nelson*, New York: W.W. Norton, 1985.

—— *A World of Difference*, Baltimore: Johns Hopkins University Press, 1987.

Lee, Robert A., *Black Fiction: New Studies in the Afro-American Novel Since 1945*, New York: Barnes and Noble, 1980.

McDowell, Deborah E., 'New Directions for Black Feminist Criticism', in Elaine Showalter, ed., *The New Feminist Criticism*, New York: Pantheon Books, 1985.

—— and Arnold Rampersad, *Slavery and the Literary Imagination*, Baltimore, MD: Johns Hopkins University Press, 1988.

O'Neale, Sondra, 'Inhibiting Midwives, Usurping Creators: The Struggling Emergence of Black Women in Fiction', in Teresa de Lauretis, ed., *Feminist Studies/Critical Studies*, Bloomington: Indiana University Press, 1986.

Pryse, Marjorie, and Hortense Spillers, eds, *Conjuring: Black Women, Fiction and the Literary Tradition*, Bloomington: Indiana University Press, 1985.

Sadoff, Diane F., 'Black Matrilineality: The Case of Alice Walker and Zora Neale Hurston', *Signs* 11, Autumn 1985, pp. 4-26.

Shockley, Ann Allen, *Afro-American Women Writers, 1746–1933: An Anthology and Critical Guide*, Boston: G.K. Hall, 1989.

Sims, Rudine, *Shadow and Substance: Afro-American Experience in Contemporary Children's Fiction*, Urbana: National Council of Teachers of English, 1982.

Smith, Barbara, 'Toward a Black Feminist Criticism', in Elaine Showalter, ed., *The New Feminist Criticism*, New York: Pantheon Books, 1985.

Smith, Valerie, *Self-Discovery and Authority in Afro-American Narratives*, Cambridge, Mass: Harvard University Press, 1987.

Smitherman, Geneva, *Talkin and Testifyin: The Language of Black America*, Detroit: Wayne State University Press, 1986.

Spelman, Elizabeth V., 'Theories of Race and Gender: The Erasure of Black Women', *Quest* 5, 1979, p. 42.

Spillers, Hortense, 'Interstices: A Small Drama of Words', in Carole S. Vance, ed., *Pleasure and Danger: Exploring Female Sexuality*, New York: Routledge and Kegan Paul, 1984.

Stepto, Robert B., *From Behind the Veil: A Study of Afro-American Narrative*, Urbana: University of Illinois Press, 1979.

Tate, Claudia, ed., *Black Women Writers At Work*, New York: Continuum, 1983.

Wade-Gayles, Gloria, *No Crystal Stair: Visions of Race and Sex in Black Women's Fiction*, New York: Pilgrim Press, 1984.

Wall, Cheryl, 'Poets and Versifiers, Singers and Signifiers: Women of the Harlem Renaissance', in Kenneth W. Wheeler and Virginia Lee Lussier, eds, *Women, the Arts, and the 1920s in Paris and New York*, New Brunswick, NJ: Transaction Press/ Rutgers University, 1982.

—— ed., *Changing Our Own Words: Essays on Criticism, Theory, and Writing by Black Women*, New Brunswick, NJ: Rutgers University Press, 1988.

Watson, Carole M., *Prologue: The Novels of Black American Women 1891–1965*, Westport, Conn. and London: Greenwood Press, 1985.

White, Jack, 'The Black Person in Art: How Should S/he Be

Portrayed?', *Black American Literature Forum*, no. 21, Spring/
Summer 1987, pp. 19-22.

Willis, Susan, 'Black Women Writers: Taking a Critical Perspec-
tive', in Gayle Green and Coppelia Kahn, eds, *Making a
Difference: Feminist Literary Criticism*, New York and London:
Methuen, 1985.

—— *Specifying: Black Women Writing the American Experience*,
Madison, WI: University of Wisconsin Press, 1988.

Yellin, Jean Fagan, *Women and Sisters: Antislavery Feminists in
American Culture*, New Haven: Yale University Press, 1990.

—— 'Written By Herself: Harriet Jacobs's Slave Narrative',
American Literature no. 53, November 1981, pp. 479-86.

2. Collections of Writing by Afro-American Women

Andrews, William L., intro., *Six Women's Slave Narratives*, New
York: Oxford University Press (Schomburg Library of Nineteenth-Century Black Women Writers), 1988.

Anzaldua, Gloria, and Cherrie Moraga, eds, *This Bridge Called My
Back: Writings by Radical Women of Color*, Latham, NY: Kitchen
Table Press, 1981, 1983.

Bambara, Toni Cade, ed., *The Black Woman: An Anthology*, New
York: New American Library, 1970.

Baraka, Amina and Amiri Baraka, eds, *Confirmations: An Anthology
of African-American Women*, New York: William Morrow, 1983.

Bathelemy, Anthony G., intro., *Collected Black Women's Narratives*,
New York: Oxford University Press (Schomburg Library of
Nineteenth-Century Black Women Writers), 1988.

Exum, Pat, *Keeping the Faith: Writings by Contemporary Black Women*,
Greenwich, Conn.: Fawcett Publications, 1974.

Gaptooth Girlfriends, eds, *Gaptooth Girlfriends: An Anthology*,
Brooklyn, NY: Gaptooth Girlfriends Publications, 1981.

—— *Gaptooth Girlfriends: The Third Act*, New York: Third Act
Press, 1985.

Giovanni, Nikki, ed., *Night Comes Softly: An Anthology of Black*

Female Voices, Newark, NJ: Medic Press, 1970.

Hatch, James V., *Black Theatre, USA: Forty-five Plays by Black Americans, 1847–1974*, New York: Free Press, 1974.

Houchins, Sue E., intro., *Spiritual Narratives*, New York: Oxford University Press (Schomburg Library of Nineteenth-Century Black Women Writers), 1988.

Lotus Press, ed., *Blacksong Series I: Four Poetry Broadsides by Black Women*, Detroit: Lotus Press, 1977.

Perkins, Kathy A., ed., *Black Female Playwrights: An Anthology of Plays Before 1950*, Bloomington: Indiana University Press, 1989.

Plato, Ann, *Essays*, New York: Oxford University Press (Schomburg Library of Nineteenth-Century Black Women Writers), 1988.

Portland State University Center for Black Students, eds, *An Anthology of Black Women Poets of Oregon*, Portland, Ore.: Portland State University, 1980.

Sherman, Joan R., ed., *Collected Black Women's Poetry*, New York: Oxford University Press (Schomburg Library of Nineteenth-Century Women Writers), 1988.

Smith, Barbara, ed., *Home Girls: A Black Feminist Anthology*, Latham, NY: Kitchen Table Press, 1983.

Stetson, Erlene, ed., *Black Sister: Poetry by Black American Women, 1746–1980*, Bloomington: Indiana University Press, 1981.

Walker, Alice, ed., *I Love Myself When I Am Laughing ... and Then Again When I Am Looking Mean and Impressive: A Zora Neale Hurston Reader*, New York: Feminist Press, 1979.

Washington, Mary Helen, ed., *Black-Eyed Susans: Classic Stories by and about Black Women*, New York: Anchor/Doubleday, 1975.

—— ed., *Midnight Birds: Stories of Contemporary Black Women Writers*, New York: Anchor/Doubleday, 1980.

—— ed., *Invented Lives: Narratives of Black Women 1860–1960*, New York: Anchor Press, 1987; London: Virago, 1989.

Wilkerson, Margaret B., ed., *Nine Plays by Black Women*, New York: Mentor, 1986.

3. Afro-American Feminist Studies

Anderson, S.E., and Rosemari Mealy, 'Who Originated the Crises? A Historical Perspective', *The Black Scholar*, no. 10, May/June 1979, pp. 40-44.

Aptheker, Bettina, *Women's Legacy: Essays on Race, Sex, and Class in American History*, Amherst, Mass.: University of Massachusetts Press, 1982.

Barrett, Michèle, *Women's Oppression Today: The Marxist/Feminist Encounter*, revised edn., London: Verso, 1988.

Brownmiller, Susan, *Against Our Will*, New York: Simon and Schuster, 1975.

Cantarow, Ellen, with Susan G. O'Malley and Sharon Hartman Strom, *Moving the Mountain: Women Working for Social Change*, Old Westbury, NY: Feminist Press/McGraw-Hill, 1980.

Carby, Hazel V., '"On the Threshold of Woman's Era": Lynching, Empire, and Sexuality in Black Feminist Theory', *Critical Inquiry*, Autumn 1985, pp. 262-78.

—— 'It Just Be Dat Way Sometime: The Sexual Politics of Women's Blues', *Radical America*, vol. 20, no. 4, June/July 1986, pp. 9-22.

—— 'White Woman Listen! Black Feminism and the Boundaries of Sisterhood', in Centre for Contemporary Cultural Studies, University of Birmingham, eds, *The Empire Strikes Back: Race and Racism in 70s Britain*, London: Hutchinson in Association with the Centre for Contemporary Cultural Studies, University of Birmingham, 1982.

Chisholm, Shirley, 'Racism and Anti-Feminism', *The Black Scholar*, 1970, pp. 40-45.

Cole, Johnetta, *All-American Women: Lines That Divide, Ties That Bind*, New York: Free Press, 1985.

—— 'Militant Black Women in Early US History', *The Black Scholar*, no. 9, April 1978, pp. 38-45.

Collier-Thomas, Bettye, *Black Women in America: Contributors to Our Heritage*, Washington, DC: Bethune Museum Archives, 1983.

—— *Black Women: Organizing for Social Change 1800–1920*,

Washington, DC: Bethune Museum Archives, 1984.

—— *National Council of Negro Women, 1935–1980*, Washington, DC: Bethune Museum Archives, 1981.

Daniels, Bonnie, 'For Colored Girls ... A Catharsis', *The Black Scholar*, no. 10, May/June 1979, pp. 61-2.

Davidson, Sara, *Loose Change: Three Women of the 60s*, Garden City, NY: Doubleday, 1977.

Davis, Angela, 'Reflections of the Black Woman's Role in the Community of Slaves', *The Black Scholar*, no. 3, December 1971, pp. 2-15.

—— *Violence Against Racism and the Ongoing Challenge to Racism*, Latham, NY: Kitchen Table Press, 1987.

—— *Women, Race and Class*, New York: Random House, 1981.

—— *Women, Culture and Politics*, New York: Random House, 1989.

—— and Bettina Aptheker, eds, *If They Come in the Morning: Voices of Resistance*, New York: New American Library, 1971.

Deutrich, Mable E., and Virginia C. Purdy, eds, *Clio Was A Woman: Studies in the History of American Women*, Washington, DC: Howard University Press, 1980.

Diamond, Esther, ed., *Issues of Sex Bias and Sex Fairness in Career Interest Measurement*, Washington, DC: Dept. of Health, Education and Welfare, 1975.

Dill, Bonnie, 'The Dialectics of Black Womanhood', *Signs*, no. 4, Spring 1979, pp. 543-55.

Echols, Alice, *Daring to Be Bad: Radical Feminism in America*, Minneapolis: University of Minnesota Press, 1989.

Edwards, Harry, 'A Time To Listen', *The Black Scholar*, no. 10, May/June 1979, pp. 59-61.

Fabio, Sarah Webster, 'Blowing the Whistle on Some Jive', *The Black Scholar*, no. 10, May/June 1979, pp. 56-8.

Giddings, Paula, *In Search of Sisterhood: Delta Sigma Theta and the Challenge of the Black Sorority Movement*, New York: William Morrow, 1988.

—— *When and Where I Enter: The Impact of Black Women on Race and Sex in America*, New York: William Morrow, 1984.

Giovanni, Nikki, *Sacred Cows and Other Edibles*, New York: William Morrow, 1988.

Gornick, Vivian, and Barbara K. Moran, *Woman in Sexist Society: Studies in Power and Powerlessness*, New York: Basic Books, 1971.

Harrison, Daphne Duval, *Black Pearls: Blues Queens of the 1920s*, New Brunswick, NJ: Rutgers University Press, 1988.

Hine, Darlene Clarke, *When the Truth is Told: a History of Black Women's Culture and Community in Indiana, 1875–1958*, Indianapolis: National Council of Negro Women Indiana Section, 1981.

Hood, Elizabeth, 'Black Women, White Women, Different Paths to Liberation', *The Black Scholar*, no. 9, April 1978, pp. 45-56.

Hooks, Bell, *Ain't I a Woman?: Black Women and Feminism*, Boston: South End Press, 1981.

—— *Feminist Theory: From Margin to Center*, Boston: South End Press, 1984.

—— *Talking Back*, Boston: South End Press, 1989.

Horton, James Oliver, 'Freedom's Yoke: Gender Conventions Among Antebellum Free Blacks', *Feminist Studies*, vol. 12, no. 1, Spring 1986, pp. 51-76.

Jackson, Jacquelyne J., *Black Women: Their Problems and Power*, New York: Barrons, 1974.

Jaggar, Alison M., and Paula S. Rothenberg, eds, *Feminist Frameworks: Alternative Theoretical Accounts of the Relations Between Men and Women*, New York: McGraw-Hill, 1984.

Jones, Jacquelyn, *Labor of Love, Labor of Sorrow: Black Women, Work, and the Family from Slavery to the Present*, New York: Basic Books, 1985.

Jones, Terry, 'The Need To Go Beyond Stereotypes', *The Black Scholar*, no. 10, May/June 1979, pp. 48-9.

Jordan, June, 'Black Women Haven't Got It All', *The Black Scholar*, no. 10, May/June 1979, pp. 39-40.

—— *Civil Wars*, Boston: Beacon Press, 1981.

—— *On Call: Political Essays*, Boston: South End Press, 1985.

Joseph, Gloria, and Jill Lewis, *Common Differences: Conflicts in Black and White Feminist Perspectives*, New York: Anchor/Doubleday, 1981.

Karenga, M. Ron, 'On Wallace's Myths: Wading Thru Troubled Waters', *The Black Scholar*, no. 10, May/June 1979, pp. 36-9.

Lader, Joyce, *Tomorrow's Tomorrow: The Black Woman*, New York: Doubleday, 1971.

Lerner, Gerda, ed., *Black Women in White America: A Documentary History*, New York: Vintage Books, 1973.

—— *The Majority Finds Its Past: Placing Women in History*, New York: Oxford University Press, 1979.

Lewis, Diane K., 'A Response to Inequality: Black Women, Racism, and Sexism', in Sheila Ruth, ed., *Issues in Feminism: A First Course in Women's Studies*, Boston: Houghton Mifflin, 1980.

Lieb, Sandra, *Mother of the Blues: A Study of Ma Rainey*, Amherst: The University of Massachusetts Press, 1971.

Lorde, Audre, *A Burst of Light*, Ithaca, NY: Firebrand; London: Sheba, 1988.

—— *The Cancer Journals*, San Francisco, Calif.: Spinster Aunt Lute, 1980; London: Sheba, 1985.

—— 'Feminism and Black Liberation: The Great American Disease', *The Black Scholar*, no. 10, May/June 1979, pp. 17-20.

—— *Uses of the Erotic: The Erotic as Power*, New York: Out and Out Press, 1978.

—— *Sister Outsider: Essays and Speeches*, Trumansberg, NY.: Crossing Press, 1984.

Malveaux, Julianne, 'Political and Historical Aspects of Black Male/Female Relationships: the Sexual Politics of Black People: Angry Black Women, Angry Black Men', *The Black Scholar*, no. 10, May/June 1979, pp. 32-5.

McCluskey, Audrey T., ed., *Women of Color: Perspectives on Feminism and Identity*, Bloomington: Women's Studies Program, 1985.

Noble, Jeanne, *Beautiful Also Are the Souls of My Black Sisters: A History of Black Women in America*, Englewood Cliffs, NJ: Prentice-Hall, 1978.

Omolade, Barbara, 'Black Women and Feminism', in Hester Eisenstein and Alice Jardine, eds, *The Future of Difference*, New Brunswick, NJ: Rutgers University Press, 1985.

—— *It's a Family Affair: Black Single Mothers*, Latham, NY: Kitchen Table Press, 1987.

Poussaint, Alvin F., 'White Manipulation and Black Oppression',

The Black Scholar, no. 10, May/June 1979, pp. 52-5.

Reid, Inez Smith, '*Together' Black Women*, New York: Emerson, 1971.

Rich, Adrienne, *Blood, Bread, and Poetry: Selected Prose, 1979–1985*, New York: W.W. Norton, 1986.

—— *On Lies, Secrets, and Silences: Selected Prose, 1966–1978*, New York: W.W. Norton, 1979.

Rodgers-Rose, La Frances, ed., *The Black Women*, Beverly Hills, Calif.: Sage, 1980.

Sanchez, Sonia, *Crisis in Culture: Two Speeches by Sonia Sanchez*, New York: Black Liberation Press, 1983.

Shange, Ntozake, 'is not so gd to be born a girl (1)', *The Black Scholar*, no. 10, May/June 1979, pp. 28-9.

—— 'otherwise i would think it odd to have rape prevention week (2)', *The Black Scholar*, no. 10, May/June 1979, pp. 29-30.

—— *See No Evil: Prefaces, Essays, and Accounts*, San Francisco: Momo's Press, 1984.

Sojourner, Sabrina, 'The Perpetuation of Myths', *The Black Scholar*, no. 10, May/June 1979, pp. 31-2.

Spillers, Hortense, 'A Day in the Life of Civil Rights', *The Black Scholar*, no. 9, May/June 1978, pp. 20-27.

Spruill, Julia C., *Women's Life and Work in the Southern Colonies*, New York: Norton, 1972.

Staples, Robert, *The Black Woman in America: Sex, Marriage and the Family*, Chicago: Nelson Hill, 1973.

—— 'The Myth of Black Macho: A Response to Angry Black Feminists', *The Black Scholar*, no. 10, March/April 1979, pp. 26-7.

—— 'A Rejoinder: Black Feminism and the Cult of Masculinity: The Danger Within', *The Black Scholar*, no. 10, May/June 1979, pp. 63-7.

Steady, Filomena Chioma, *The Black Woman Cross-Culturally*, Cambridge, Mass.: Schenkman, 1981.

Sterling, Dorothy, ed., *We Are Your Sisters: Black Women in the Nineteenth Century*, New York: W. W. Norton, 1985.

Stone, Pauline Terrelonge, 'The Limitation of Reformist Feminism', *The Black Scholar*, no. 10, May/June 1979, pp. 24-7.

Toure, Askia M., 'Black Male/Female Relations: A Political Overview of the 1970s', *The Black Scholar*, no. 10, May/June 1979, pp. 45-8.

Walker, Alice, *In Search of Our Mothers' Gardens: Womanist Prose*, New York: Harcourt Brace Jovanovich, 1983; London: Women's Press 1984.

Watkins, Mel, 'An Interview With Ishmael Reed', *Southern Review*, no. 21, July 1985, pp. 603-14.

—— 'Sexism, Racism, and Black Women Writers', *The New York Times Book Review*, June 15, 1986, pp. 1, 35.

Wertheimer, Barbara M., *We Were There: The Story of Working Women in America*, New York: Pantheon Books, 1977.

Williams, Ora, ed., *American Black Women in the Arts and Social Sciences: A Bibliographical Survey*, Metuchen, NJ: Scarecrow Press, 1973; revised and expanded edn, 1978.

Williams, Sherely A. 'Cultural and Interpersonal Aspects of Black Male/Female Relationships: Comments From the Curb', *The Black Scholar*, no. 10, May/June 1979, pp. 49-51.

Ya Salaam, Kalamu, 'Revolutionary Struggle/Revolutionary Love', *The Black Scholar*, no. 10, May/June 1979, pp. 20-24.

4. Afro-American History

Allen, Robert L., *Black Awakening in Capitalist America: An Analytic History*, Garden City, NY: Anchor Books, 1969.

Aptheker, Bettina, ed., *The Unfolding Drama: Studies in US History*, New York: International Publishers, 1979.

Aptheker, Herbert, *To Be Free: Studies in American Negro History*, New York: International Publishers, 1948.

—— ed., *And Why Not Every Man? Documentary Story of The Fight Against Slavery in the US*, New York: International Publishers, 1970.

Armstrong, Gregory, *The Dragon Has Come*, New York: Harper and Row, 1974.

Ballard, Allen, *The Education of Black Folk: The Afro-American*

Struggle for Knowledge in White America, New York: Harper and Row, 1974.

Baraka, Immamu A., ed., *African Congress: A Documentary of the First Modern Pan-African Congress*, New York: William Morrow, 1972.

Barbour, Floyd, B., ed., *The Black Power Revolt*, Boston: Sargeant Press, 1968.

Bennett, Lerone Jr., *Before the Mayflower: A History of Black America*, Chicago: Johnson Publishing Co., 1969.

Billingsley, Andrew, *Black Families in White America*, Englewood Cliffs, NJ: Prentice Hall, 1968.

Blassingame, John W., *The Slave Community: Plantation Life in the Antebellum South*, New York: Oxford University Press, 1972.

—— ed., *New Perspectives on Black Studies*, Urbana: University of Illinois Press, 1971.

Bogle, Donald, *Toms, Coons, Mulattoes, Mammies, and Bucks: An Interpretive History of Blacks in American Films*, New York: Viking Press, 1973.

Bond, Julian, *A Time to Speak, A Time to Act: The Movement in Politics*, New York: Simon and Schuster, 1972.

Bracey, John H. Jr., August Meier, and Elliott Rudwick, eds, *Black Nationalism in America*, Indianapolis and New York: Bobbs-Merrill, 1970.

Branch, Taylor, *Parting the Waters: America in the King Years 1954–63*, New York: Simon and Schuster, 1988.

Breitman, George, ed., *By Any Means Necessary: Speeches, Interviews and a Letter by Malcolm X*, New York: Merit, 1970.

Brown, H. Rap., *Die Nigger Die!*, New York: Dial, 1969.

Carmichael, Stokely, and Charles Hamilton, *Black Power: The Politics of Liberation in America*, New York: Random House, 1967.

Carson, Clayborne, *In Struggle: SNCC and the Black Awakening of the 1960s*, Cambridge, Mass.: Harvard University Press, 1981.

Cleaver, Eldridge, ed. Robert Sheer, *Post-Prison Writings and Speeches*, New York: Random House, 1969.

—— *Soul on Ice*, New York: McGraw-Hill, 1968.

Cruse, Harold, *The Crisis of the Negro Intellectual*, New York: William Morrow, 1967.

—— *Rebellion or Revolution?*, New York: William Morrow, 1968.

Davis, David Brion, *From Homicide to Slavery: Studies in American Culture*, New York: Oxford University Press, 1986.

—— *Slavery and Human Progress*, New York: Oxford University Press, 1984.

DuBois, W.E.B., *Black Reconstruction In America, 1860–1880*, New York: Atheneum, 1969.

—— *The Souls of Black Folk: Essays and Sketches*, New York: Random House, 1989.

Elkins, Stanley, *Slavery: A Problem in American Institutional and Intellectual Life*, Chicago: University of Chicago Press, 1959.

Evans, Sara, *Personal Politics: The Roots of Women's Liberation in the Civil Rights Movement and the New Left*, New York: Vintage Books, 1980.

Foner, Philip S., ed., *The Black Panthers Speak*, Philadelphia: J.B. Lippincott, 1970.

Fox-Genovese, Elizabeth, *Within the Plantation Household: Black and White Women of the Old South*, Chapel Hill: University of North Carolina Press, 1988.

Franklin, John Hope, *From Slavery to Freedom: A History of Negro Americans*, 3rd edn, New York: Vintage Books, 1969.

Frazier, E. Franklin, *The Negro Church in America*, New York: Schocken Books, 1963.

—— *The Negro in the United States*, New York: Macmillan, 1949.

Genovese, Eugene D., *In Red and Black: Marxian Explorations in Southern and Afro-American History*, New York: Vintage Books, 1971.

—— *Roll, Jordan, Roll: The World That Slaves Made*, New York: Vintage Books, 1974.

—— *The World That the Slaveholders Made*, New York: Vintage Books, 1977.

Gitlin, Todd, *The Sixties: Years of Hope, Days of Rage*, New York: Bantam Books, 1987.

Grant, Joanne, ed., *Black Protest: History, Documents and Analyses 1619 to the Present,* New York: Fawcett/Premier Books, 1968.

Gutman, Herbert G., *The Black Family in Slavery and Freedom, 1750–1925,* New York: Pantheon Books, 1976.

Hansberry, Lorraine, *Movement: Documentary of a Struggle for Equality,* New York: Simon and Schuster, 1964.

Harding, Vincent, *The Other American Revolution,* Los Angeles: Center for Afro-American Studies, University of California, Los Angeles, 1980.

—— *There is a River: The Black Struggle for Freedom in America,* New York: Harcourt Brace Jovanovich, 1981.

Hare, Nathan, and Robert Chrisman, *Contemporary Black Thought: The Best From The Black Scholar,* New York: Bobbs-Merrill, 1973.

Henri, Florette, *Black Migration: Movement North, 1900–1920,* Garden City, NY: Anchor Press/Doubleday, 1975.

Hernton, Calvin C., *Sex and Racism in America,* New York: Grove Press, 1966.

Huggins, Nathan I., *Black Odyssey: The Afro-American Ordeal in Slavery,* New York: Pantheon Books, 1977.

Jackson, George, *Soledad Brothers: The Prison Letters of George Jackson,* New York: Bantam Books, 1970.

Jones, LeRoi, *Blues People,* New York: William Morrow, 1963.

—— *Home,* New York: William Morrow, 1966.

Jordan, Winthrop D., *White Over Black: American Attitudes toward the Negro, 1550–1812,* Baltimore: Penguin Books, 1969.

King, Mary, *Freedom Song: A Personal Story of the 1960s Civil Rights Movement,* New York: William Morrow, 1987.

Kofsky, Frank, *Black Nationalism and the Revolution in Music,* New York: Pathfinder Press, 1970.

Kovel, Joel, *White Racism,* New York: Columbia University Press, 1984.

Kruger, Barbara, and Phil Mariani, *Remaking History,* Seattle: Bay Press, 1989.

Lester, Julius, *Revolutionary Notes,* New York: R.W. Barton, 1969.

Levine, Lawrence, W., *Black Culture and Black Consciousness: Afro-American Folk Thought from Slavery to Freedom,* New York:

Oxford University Press, 1977.

Lewis, David, *King: A Biography*, 2nd edn, Urbana: University of Illinois Press, 1978.

Litwack, Leon F., *Been in the Storm So Long: The Emergence of Black Freedom in the South*, New York: Knopf, 1979.

Lomax, Louis E., *The Negro Revolt*, New York: Harper, 1963.

Louis, Debbie, *And We Are Not Saved: A History of the Movement as People*, Garden City, NY: Anchor Press, 1970.

Malcolm X, *The Autobiography of Malcolm X*, New York: Grove Press, 1965.

—— *Malcolm X on Afro-American History*, New York: Pathfinder Press, 1970.

Marable, Manning, *Black American Politics: From the Washington Marches to Jesse Jackson*, London: Verso, 1985.

—— *Blackwater: Historical Studies in Race, Class Consciousness and Revolution*, Dayton, Ohio: Black Praxis Press, 1981.

—— *From the Grassroots: Social and Political Essays Towards Afro-American Liberation*, Boston: South End Press, 1980.

—— *How Capitalism Underdeveloped Black America: Problems in Race, Political Economy and Society*, Boston: South End Press, 1983.

—— *Race, Reform and Rebellion: The Second Reconstruction in Black America 1945–1982*, Jackson, MI: University Press of Mississippi, 1984.

Meier, August, and Elliott Rudwick, *CORE: A Study of the Civil Rights Movement, 1942–1968*, New York: Oxford University Press, 1973.

Morgan, Edmund S., *American Slavery, American Freedom: The Ordeal of Colonial Virginia*, New York: W.W. Norton, 1975.

Morris, Aldon D., *The Origins of the Civil Rights Movement*, New York: Free Press, 1984.

Moynihan, Daniel Patrick, *The Negro Family: The Case for National Action*, Washington, DC: Superintendent of Documents, US Government Printing Office, 1965.

Murray, Albert, *Stompin the Blues*, New York: McGraw-Hill, 1976.

NAACP, ed., *Thirty Years of Lynching in the United States*, New York: Arno Press, 1970.

Perry, Lewis, and Michael Fillman, eds, *Antislavery Reconsidered:*

Fourteen New Essays, Baton Rouge: Louisiana State University Press, 1979.

Powell, Adam Clayton Jr., *Marching Blacks: An Interpretive History of the Rise of the Black Common Man*, revised edn, New York: Dial, 1973.

Quarles, Benjamin, *The Black Abolitionists*, New York: Oxford University Press, 1969.

Raines, Howell, *My Soul is Rested: The Story of the Civil Rights Movement in the Deep South*, New York: Viking/Penguin Books, 1983.

Rainwater, Lee, and William L. Yancy, eds, *The Moynihan Report and the Politics of Controversy: A Transaction Social Sciences and Public Policy Report*, Cambridge: MIT Press, 1967.

Ransom, Roger L., and Richard Sutch, *One Kind of Freedom: The Economic Consequences of Emancipation*, New York: Cambridge University Press, 1977.

Robert, J. Deotis, *A Black Political Theology*, Philadelphia: Westminster Press, 1974.

Ross, Andrew, *No Respect: Intellectuals and Popular Culture*, New York: Routledge, 1989.

Scott, Anne Firor, *The Southern Lady: From Pedestal to Politics*, Chicago: Chicago University Press, 1970.

Seale, Bobby, *Seize the Time*, New York: Vintage, 1970.

Silberman, Charles E., *Crisis in Black and White*, New York: Random House, 1964.

Smuts, Robert W., *Women and Work in America*, New York: Columbia University Press, 1959.

Stromberg, Ann H. and Shirley Harkess, eds, *Women Working: Theories and Facts in Perspective*, Palo Alto, Calif.: Mayfield Publishing Co., 1978.

West, Cornel, *Prophesy Deliverance!: An Afro-American Revolutionary Christianity*, Philadelphia: Westminster Press, 1982.

Williams, Juan, *Eyes on the Prize: America's Civil Rights Years 1954–1965*, New York: Penguin, 1987.

Willie, Charles V., ed., *The Family Life of Black People*, Columbus, Ohio: Charles B. Merrill, 1970.

Wilson, William Irving, *Power, Racism, and Privilege: Race Relations in Theoretical and Sociohistorical Perspectives*, New York: Macmillan, 1973.

—— *The Truly Disadvantaged: The Inner City, the Underclass, and Public Policy*, Chicago: University of Chicago Press, 1987.

—— *The Declining Significance of Race: Blacks and Changing American Institutions*, 2nd edn, Chicago: University of Chicago Press, 1980.

Wilmore, Gayraud S., *Black Religion and Black Radicalism: An Interpretation of the Religious History of the Afro-American People*, Maryknoll, NY: Orbis Books, 1983.

5. Post-Colonial Criticism

Ashcroft, Bill, et al., eds, *The Empire Writes Back: Theory and Practice in Post-Colonial Literature*, New York: Routledge, Chapman and Hall, 1989.

Bhabha, Homi, ed., *Nation and Narration*, Routledge.

Fanon, Frantz, trans. Charles Lam Markham, *Black Skin, White Masks*, New York: Grove Press, 1967.

—— *A Dying Colonialism*, New York: Grove Press, 1965.

—— trans. Haakon Chevalier, preface Jean-Paul Sartre, *Toward the African Revolution: Political Essays*, New York: Grove Press, 1969.

—— trans. Constance Farrington, *The Wretched of the Earth*, New York: Grove Press, 1968.

Jameson, Fredric, 'Third World Literature in the Era of Multinational Capitalism', *Social Text*, no. 15 (Fall 1986) 5:3, pp. 65-88.

Mannoni, Oscar, *Prospero and Caliban*, New York: Frederick A. Praeger, 1956.

Memmi, Albert, *The Colonizer and the Colonized*, Boston: Beacon Press, 1965.

—— *Dominated Man*, New York: Orion Press, 1968.

Minh-ha, Trinh T., *Women, Native, Other: Writing Postcoloniality and Feminism*, Bloomington: Indiana University Press, 1989.

Mohammed, Abdul Jan, *Manichean Aesthetics: The Politics of Liter-*

ature in Colonial Africa, Amherst, MA: University of Massachusetts Press, 1983.

Said, Edward, *Orientalism*, New York: Pantheon Books, 1978.

—— *The World, the Text, and the Critic*, Cambridge: Harvard University Press, 1983.

Spivak, Gayatri Chakravorty, 'Can The Subaltern Speak?' *Marxism and The Interpretation of Culture*, eds. Cary Nelson and Larry Grossberg, 1983, p. 61.

—— *In Other Worlds: Essays in Cultural Politics*, New York: Methuen, 1987.

6. Biographies/Autobiographies/Memoirs of Afro-American Women

Adams, Elizabeth Laura, *Dark Symphony*, New York: Sheed and Ward, 1942.

Anderson, Marian, *My Lord What a Morning*, New York: Viking Press, 1956.

Andrews, William L., ed., *Sisters of the Spirit: Three Black Women's Autobiographies of the Nineteenth Century*, Bloomington: Indiana University Press, 1986.

Angelou, Maya, *I Know Why the Caged Bird Sings*, New York: Random House, 1970; London: Virago, 1984.

—— *Gather Together in My Name*, New York: Random House, 1974; London: Virago, 1985.

—— *Singin' and Swingin' and Gettin' Merry Like Christmas*, New York: Random House, 1976; London: Virago, 1985.

—— *Heart of A Woman*, New York: Random House, 1981; London: Virago, 1986.

—— *All God's Children Need Traveling Shoes*, New York: Random House, 1986; London: Virago, 1987.

Ashbaugh, Carolyn, *Lucy Parsons: American Revolutionary*, Chicago: Kerr, 1976.

Bailey, Pearl, *Talking to Myself*, New York: Harcourt Brace Jovanovich, 1971.

Baker, Josephine, and Jo Bouillon, *Josephine*, New York: Harper and Row, 1977.

Barlow, Leila Mae, *Across the Years: Memoirs*, Montgomery, Ala.: Paragon Press, 1959.

Bates, Daisy, *The Long Shadow of Little Rock*, New York: David McKay, 1962.

Beckles, Frances N., *Twenty Black Women: A Profile of Contemporary Black Maryland Women*, Baltimore: Gateway Press, 1978.

Brooks, Gwendolyn, *Report from Part One*, Detroit: Broadside Press, 1972.

Brown, Hallie Q., *Homespun Heroines and Other Women of Distinction*, intro. Randall K. Burkett, New York: Oxford University Press (Schomburg Library of Nineteenth-Century Black Women Writers), 1988.

Browne, Rose Butler, *Love My Children*, New York: Meredith, 1969.

Cherry, Gwendolyn and others, *Portraits in Color: The Lives of Colorful Negro Women*, New York: Pageant Press, 1962.

Chisholm, Shirley, *Unbought and Unbossed*, Boston: Houghton Mifflin, 1973.

—— *The Good Fight*, New York: Harper and Row, 1973.

Clark, Septima, *Ready From Within: Septima Clark and the Civil Rights Movement*, Navarro, Calif.: Wild Trees Press, 1986.

Clifton, Lucille, *Generations*, New York: Random House, 1970.

Cooper, Anna Julia, *A Voice from the South by a Black Woman of the South*, intro. Mary Helen Washington, New York: Oxford University Press (Schomburg Library of Nineteenth-Century Black Women Writers), 1988.

Cornwell, Anita, *Black Lesbian in White America*, Tallahassee, Fla.: Naiad Press, 1983.

Darden, Norma Jean, and Carole Darden, *Spoonbread and Strawberry Wine: Recipes and Reminiscences of a Family*, New York: Fawcett Book Group, 1980.

Davis, Angela, *Angela Davis: An Autobiography*, New York: Random House, 1974.

DeVeaux, Alexis, *Don't Explain: A Song of Billie Holiday*, New York: Harper and Row, 1980.

Dunham, Katherine, *Touch of Innocence*, New York: Cassell, 1960.

Dunnigan, Alice, *A Black Woman's Experience from Schoolhouse to White House*, Philadelphia: Dorrance, 1974.

Gabel, Leona C., *From Slavery to the Sorbonne and Beyond: The Life and Writings of Anna J. Cooper*, Northampton, Mass.: Smith College Publications, 1982.

Gibson, Althea, *I Always Wanted to Be Somebody*, New York: Harper and Row, 1958.

Giovanni, Nikki, *Gemini: An Extended Autobiographical Statement*, New York: Bobbs-Merrill, 1971.

Golden, Martina, *Migrations of the Heart: A Personal Odyssey*, New York: Anchor Press, 1983.

Griffiths, Mattie, *Autobiography of a Female Slave*, New York: Negro Universities Press, 1857.

Grimke, Charlotte Forten, *The Journals of Charlotte Forten Grimke*, Brenda Stevenson, ed., New York: Oxford University Press, (Schomburg Library of Nineteenth-Century Black Women Writers), 1988.

Green, Mildred Denby, *Black Women Composers: A Genesis*, Boston, Twayne Publishers, 1983.

Guffy, Ossie, *The Autobiography of a Black Woman*, New York: Bantam Books, 1972.

Hansberry, Lorraine, *To Be Young, Gifted and Black: Lorraine Hansberry in Her Own Words*, adapt. Robert Nemiroff, intro. James Baldwin, Englewood Cliff, NJ: Prentice-Hall, 1969.

Hedgeman, Anna (Arnold), *The Trumpet Sounds*, New York: Holt Rinehart and Winston, 1964.

Hemenway, Robert, *Zora Neale Hurston: A Literary Biography*, Urbana: University of Illinois Press, 1977.

Holiday, Billie, *Lady Sings the Blues*, New York: Doubleday, 1956.

Humez, Jean M., ed., *Gifts of Power: The Writings of Rebecca Jackson, Black Visionary, Shaker Eldress*, Amherst, Mass.: University of Massachusetts Press, 1981.

Hunt, Annie Mae, *I Am Annie Mae: An Extraordinary Woman in Her Own Words: The Personal Story of a Black Texan Woman*, Austin, Tex.: Rosegarden Press, 1983.

Hunter, Jane Edna, *A Nickel and a Prayer*, Nashville: Parthenon Press, 1940.

Hurston, Zora Neale, *Dust Tracks on a Road*, Philadelphia: J.B. Lippincott, 1942.

Keckley, Elizabeth, *Behind the Scenes. Or, Thirty Years a Slave, and Four Years in the White House*, intro. James Olney, New York: Oxford University Press (Schomburg Library of Nineteenth-Century Black Women Writers), 1988.

Kennedy, Adrienne, *People Who Led to My Plays*, New York: Alfred A. Knopf, 1987.

King, Coretta Scott, *My Life with Martin Luther King, Jr.*, New York: Holt Rinehart and Winston, 1969.

Kitt, Eartha, *Alone With Me*, Chicago: Henry Regnery Co., 1976.

Larison, Cornelius Wilson, *Silvia Dubois: a Biografy of the slav who whipt her mistres and gand her fredom*, trans. and intro. Jared C. Lobdell, New York: Oxford University Press (Schomburg Library of Nineteenth-Century Black Women Writers), 1988.

Lawson, Ellen McKenzie, and Marlene D. Merrill, eds, *The Three Sarahs: Documents of Antebellum Black College Women*, New York: Mellen, 1984.

Loewenberg, Bert James, and Ruth Bogin, eds, *Black Women in Nineteenth-Century American Life: Their Words, Their Thoughts, Their Feelings*, University Park: Pennsylvania State University Press, 1976.

Lorde, Audre, *Zami: A New Spelling of My Name*, Trumansberg, NY: Crossing Press, 1982; London: Sheba, 1984.

Marteena, Constance, *The Lengthening Shadow of a Woman: A Biography of Charlotte Hawkins Brown*, New York: Exposition Press, 1977.

Mebane, Mary, *Mary*, New York: Fawcett, 1982.

—— *Mary, Wayfarer*, New York: Viking, 1983.

Moody, Anne, *Coming of Age in Mississippi*, New York: Dell, 1968.

Mossell, N.F., *The Work of the Afro-American Woman*, intro. Joanne Braxton, New York: Oxford University Press (Schomburg Library of Nineteenth-Century Black Women Writers), 1988.

Moutoussamy-Ashe, Jeanne, *Viewfinders: Black Women Photographers 1839–1985*, New York: Dodd, Mead, 1986.

Murray, Pauli, *Sing in a Weary Throat: An American Pilgrimage*, New York: Harper and Row, 1982.

Ortiz, Victoria, *Sojourner Truth: A Self-Made Woman*, New York: Lippincott, 1974.

Petry, Ann, *Harriet Tubman, Conductor on the Underground Railroad*, New York: Crowell, 1955.

Robinson, Jo Ann, *The Montgomery Bus Boycott and the Women Who Started It: The Memoir of Jo Ann Gibson Robinson*, Knoxville: University of Tennessee Press, 1987.

Roses, Lorraine Elena, and Elizabeth Ruth Randolph, *Harlem Renaissance and Beyond: Literary Biographies of 100 Black Women Writers, 1900–1945*, Boston: G.K. Hall and Co., 1989.

Seacole, Mary, *The Wonderful Adventures of Mrs Seacole in Many Lands*, intro. Willima L. Andrews, New York: Oxford University Press (Schomburg Library of Nineteenth-Century Black Women Writers), 1988.

Shakur, Assata, *Assata: An Autobiography*, Westport, Conn.: Lawrence Hill, 1987.

Shepperd, Gladys, *Mary Church Terrell, Respectable Person*, Baltimore: Human Relations Press, 1951.

Simonsen, Thordis, ed., *You May Plow Here: The Narrative of Sara Brooks*, New York: W.W. Norton, 1986.

Smith, Amanda, *An Autobiography: The Story of the Lord's Dealings with Mrs Amanda Smith the Colored Evangelist*, intro. Jualynne E. Dodson, New York: Oxford University Press (Schomburg Library of Nineteenth-Century Black Women Writers), 1988.

Sterling, Dorothy, *Black Foremothers: Three Lives*, New York: Feminist Press, 1988.

Tarry, Ellen, *The Third Door: The Autobiography of an American Negro Woman*, New York: McKay, 1955.

Terrell, Mrs Mary Church, *A Colored Woman in a White World*, Washington, DC: Ransdell, 1940.

Thompson, Era Bell, *American Daughter*, Chicago: University of Chicago Press, 1946.

Walker, Margaret, *How I Wrote Jubilee*, Detroit: Broadside Press, 1971.

Waters, Ethel, *To Me It's Wonderful*, New York: Harper and Row, 1972.

Wells, Ida B., *Crusade for Justice: The Autobiography of Ida B. Wells*,

Alfreda Duster, ed., Chicago: University of Chicago Press, 1970.

Williams, Rose Berthena Clay, *Black and White and Orange*, New York: Vantage Press, 1961.

Wilson, Emily, *Hope and Dignity: Older Black Women of the South*, Philadelphia: Temple University Press, 1983.

7. Literature by Afro-American Women Writers

I. *Poetry*

Ai (Florence Ai Ogawa), *Cruelty*, Boston: Houghton Mifflin, 1973.

—— *Killing Floor*, Boston: Houghton Mifflin, 1979.

—— *Sin*, Boston: Houghton Mifflin, 1986.

Amini, Johari (Jewel Latimore), *Let's Go Somewhere*, Detroit: Third World Press, 1970.

Angelou, Maya, *And I Still Rise*, New York: Random House, 1978; London: Virago, 1986.

—— *Just Give Me a Cool Drink of Water 'fore I Die*, New York: Random House, 1971; London: Virago, 1986.

—— *Oh Pray My Wings Are Gonna Fit Me Well*, New York: Random House, 1975.

—— *Poems*, New York: Bantam, 1986.

—— *Shaker Why Don't You Sing*, New York: Random House, 1983.

Baraka, Amina, and Amiri Baraka, *The Music: Reflections on Jazz and Blues*, New York: William Morrow, 1987.

Bernadine, *Seeds of Ourselves*, New York: Women for Racial and Economic Equality, 1984.

Bogus, S. Diane, *I'm Off to See the Goddam Wizard Alright*, San Francisco: The Author, 1976.

—— *Woman in the Moon*, San Francisco: Soap Box Publishing, 1977.

Brand, Dionne, *Chronicles of the Hostile Sun*, Toronto: Williams-Wallace, Int'l., 1984.

—— *Earth Magic*, Toronto: Kids Can Press, 1980.

—— *'Fore Day Morning*, Toronto: Khiosan Artists, 1978.

—— *Primitive Offensive*, Toronto: Williams-Wallace Int'l., 1982.
—— *Rivers Have Sources, Trees Have Roots*, Toronto: Cross-Cultural Communication Centre, 1986.
—— *Winter Epigrams*, Toronto: Williams-Wallace Int'l., 1983.
Braxton, Jodi, *Sometimes I Think of Maryland*, New York: Sunbury Press, 1977.
Brooks, Gwendolyn, *Aloneness*, Detroit: Broadside Press, 1971.
—— *Annie Allen*, New York: Harper, 1949.
—— *The Bean Eaters*, New York: Harper, 1960.
—— *Beckonings*, Detroit: Broadside Press, 1975.
—— *Bronzeville Boys and Girls*, New York: Harper, 1956.
—— *Family Pictures*, Detroit: Broadside Press, 1970.
—— *Riot*, Detroit: Broadside Press, 1969.
—— *Selected Poems*, New York: Harper, 1960.
—— *A Street in Bronzeville*, New York: Harper, 1945.
—— *The Tiger Who Wore White Gloves, or, What You Really Are You Are*, Detroit: Broadside Press, 1974.
—— *The World of Gwendolyn Brooks*, Detroit: Broadside Press, 1971.
Chase-Riboud, Barbara, *From Memphis and Peking: Poems*, New York: Random House, 1974.
—— *Portraits of a Nude Woman as Cleopatra*, New York: William Morrow, 1987.
Clarke, Cheryl, *Living as a Lesbian*, Ithaca, NY: Firebrand Press, 1986.
—— *Narratives: Poems in the Tradition of Black Women*, Latham, NY: Kitchen Table Press, 1982.
Clifford, Carrie, *The Widening Light*, Boston: Walter Reid, 1922.
Clifton, Lucille, *Good News About the Earth: New Poems*, New York: Random House, 1972.
—— *Good Times*, New York: Random House, 1970.
—— *An Ordinary Woman*, New York: Random House, 1974.
—— *Two-Headed Woman*, Amherst, Mass.: University of Massachusetts Press, 1980.
Clinton, Gloria, *Trees Along the Highway*, New York: Comet Press, 1953.
Collins, Merle, *Because the Dawn Breaks! Poems Dedicated to the*

Grenadian People, London: Karia Press, 1985.

Cortez, Jayne, *Coagulations: New and Selected Poems*, New York: Thunder's Mouth Press, 1984; London: Pluto, 1986.

—— *Festivals and Funerals*, New York: Bola Press, 1971.

—— *Firespitter*, New York: Bola Press, 1982.

—— *Merveilleux Coup de Foudre: Poetry of Jayne Cortez and Ted Joans*, Paris: Handshake Editions, 1982.

—— *Mouth on Paper*, New York: Bola Press, 1977.

—— *Scarifications*, New York: Bola Press, 1973.

Danner, Margaret, *Impressions of African Art Forms*, Detroit: Broadside Press, 1968.

Das, Mahadai, *Bones*, Leeds, Yorkshire, UK: Peepal Tree Press, 1988.

Davis, Thulani, *All the Renegade Ghosts Rise*, Washington, DC: Anemone Press, n.d.

—— *Playing the Changes*, Middletown, Conn.: Wesleyan University Press, 1985.

Dee, Ruby, *My One Good Nerve*, Chicago: Third World Press, 1986.

Derricotte, Toi, *The Empress of the Death House*, Detroit: Lotus Press, 1978.

—— *Natural Birth: Poems*, Trumansberg, NY: Crossing Press, 1983.

DeVeaux, Alexis, *Blue Heat: a Portfolio of Poems and Drawings*, New York: Diva Publishing Associates, 1985.

Dove, Rita, *Museum*, Pittsburgh: Carnegie-Mellon University Press, 1983.

—— *Thomas and Beulah*, Pittsburgh: Carnegie-Mellon University Press, 1986.

—— *The Yellow House on the Corner*, Pittsburgh: Carnegie-Mellon University Press, 1980.

Evans, Mari, *I Am a Black Woman*, New York: William Morrow, 1970.

—— *Where Is All the Music*, London: Paul Breman, 1968.

Fabio, Sarah, *A Mirror: A Soul*, San Francisco: Julian Richardson, 1967.

Fordham, Mary Weston, *Magnolia Leaves: Poems*, Tuskegee, Ala.: Walker, Evans, Cogswell, 1897.

Giovanni, Nikki, *Black Feeling, Black Talk, Black Judgement*, New York: William Morrow, 1970.

—— *Cotton Candy on a Rainy Day*, New York: William Morrow, 1978.

—— *Ego Tripping and Other Poems for Young Readers*, New York: Lawrence Hill, 1973.

—— *My House: Poems*, New York: William Morrow, 1972.

—— *Poems for Angela Yvonne Davis*, Newark, NJ: Nikton, 1970.

—— *ReCreation*, Detroit: Broadside Press, 1970.

—— *Spin Soft Black Song*, New York: Hill and Wang, 1971.

—— *Those Who Ride the Night Winds*, New York: William Morrow, 1983.

—— *Vacation Times: Poems for Children*, New York: William Morrow, 1980.

Gomez. Jewel, *Flamingoes and Bears*, New Brunswick, NJ: Grace Publications, 1986.

Goodison, Lorna, *I Am Becoming My Mother*, London: New Beacon, 1986.

—— *Heartease*, London: New Beacon, 1988.

Gossett, Hattie, *Presenting... Sister NoBlues*, Ithaca, NY: Firebrand Press, 1988.

Greenfield, Elouise, *Honey I Love You and Other Poems*, New York: Harper and Row, 1978.

Harper, Frances Ellen Watkins, *Complete Poems of Frances E. W. Harper*, Maryemma Graham, ed., New York: Oxford University Press (Schomburg Library of Nineteenth-Century Black Women Writers), 1988.

Hunt, Evelyn Tooley, *Toad-Song: A Collection of Haiku and Other Small Poems*, New York: Apple Press, 1966.

Ifetayo, Femi Funmi, *We the Black Woman*, Detroit: Fine Arts Publications, 1970.

Jackson, Angela, *The Greenville Club, in Four Black Poets*, St Louis: BK MK, 1977.

—— *Solo in the Boxcar Third Floor E.*, Chicago: Obahouse, 1986.

—— *Voo Doo/Love Magic*, Chicago: Third World Press, 1974.

Jones, Gayl, *The Hermit Woman*, Detroit: Lotus Press, 1983.

—— *Song for Anninho*, Detroit: Lotus Press, 1981.

—— *Xarque and Other Poems*, Detroit: Lotus Press, 1985.

Jones, Patricia, *Mythologizing Always: 7 Sonnets*, Guilford, Conn.: Telephone Books, 1981.

Jordan, June, *Living Room*, New York: Thunder's Mouth Press, 1985.

—— *Some Changes*, New York: E.P. Dutton, 1971.

—— *New Days: Poems of Exile and Return*, New York: Emerson Hall, 1973.

—— *Passion: New Poems 1977–1980*, Boston: Beacon Press, 1981.

—— *Things That I Do in the Dark: Selected Poems*, New York: Random House, 1977.

Kim, Willyce, *Eating Artichokes*, San Francisco: Women's Press Collective.

Lane, Pinkie Gordon, *I Never Scream: New and Selected Poems*, Detroit: Lotus Press, 1985.

—— *The Mystic Female*, Little Rock, Ark.: South and West, 1978.

—— *Wind Thoughts*, Little Rock, Ark.: South and West, 1972.

Latimore, Jewel C., *Images in Black*, Chicago: Third World Press, 1967.

Loftin, Elouise (Hanna Ecrit), *Barefoot Necklace: Poems*, New York: Jafmina, 1975.

Lorde, Audre, *Between Ourselves*, San Francisco: Eidolon Editions, 1976.

—— *The Black Unicorn*, New York: W.W. Norton, 1978.

—— *Cables to Rage*, London: Breman, 1970.

—— *Chosen Poems: Old and New*, New York: W.W. Norton, 1982.

—— *Coal*, New York: W.W. Norton, 1978.

—— *The First Cities*, New York: Poets, 1967.

—— *From a Land Where Other People Live*, Detroit: Broadside Press, 1973.

—— *New York Head Shop and Museum*, Detroit: Broadside Press, 1974.

—— *Our Dead Behind Us*, New York: W.W. Norton, 1986; London: Sheba, 1987.

Madgett, Naomi Long, *Exits and Entrances*, Detroit: Lotus Press, 1978.

—— *One and the Many*, New York: Exposition Press, 1956.

—— *Pink Ladies in the Afternoon*, Detroit: Lotus Press, 1972.

—— *Star by Star*, Detroit: Harlo Press, 1965.

Mahone, Barbara, *Sugarfield Poems*, Detroit: Broadside Press, 1970.

Miller, May, *The Clearing and Beyond*, Washington, DC: Charioteer Press, 1974.

—— *Dust of an Uncertain Journey*, Detroit: Lotus Press, 1975.

—— *Halfway to the Sun*, Washington, DC: Writers Pub. House, 1980.

—— *Not That Far*, Washington, DC: Charioteer Press, 1973.

—— *The Ransomed Wait*, Detroit: Lotus Press, 1983.

Moore, La Nese B., *Can I Be Right?* New York: Vantage Press, 1971.

Morejon, Nancy, *Where the Island Sleeps Like a Wing: Selected Poetry*, San Francisco: Black Scholar Press, 1985.

Murphy, Beatrice M., and Nancy L. Arnez, *The Rocks Cry Out*, Detroit: Broadside Press, 1969.

Murray, Pauli, *Dark Testament*, Comstock, Ill.; Norwalk, Conn.: Silvermine, 1970.

Nicholes, Marion, *Life Styles*, Detroit: Broadside Press, 1971.

Nichols, Grace, *The Fat Black Woman's Poems*, London: Virago Poets, 1985.

Parker, Pat, *Child of Myself*, San Francisco: Diana Press, 1972.

—— *Jonestown and Other Madness: Poetry*, Ithaca, NY: Firebrand Press, 1985.

—— *Movement in Black: The Collected Poetry of Pat Parker*, San Francisco: Diana Press, 1978.

—— *Pit Stop*, San Francisco: Diana Press, 1973.

—— *Womanslaughter*, San Francisco: Diana Press, 1978.

Parkerson, Michelle, *Waiting Rooms*, Washington, DC: Common Ground Press, 1983.

Penn, Verna, *The Essence of Life*, Tortola, BWI: Caribbean Printing, 1976.

Pollard, Velma, *Crown Point and Other Poems*, Leeds, Yorkshire, UK: Peepal Tree Press, 1988.

Ray, Henrietta Cordella, *Poems*, New York: Grafton Press, 1910.

Richards, Elizabeth Davis, *The Peddlar of Dreams and Other Poems*, New York: W.A. Bodler, 1928.

Richards, Novella, *Tropic Gems*, New York: Vantage Press, 1971.

Rodgers, Carolyn, *For Flip Wilson*, Detroit: Broadside Press, 1971.

—— *The Heart as Evergreen*, New York: Doubleday, 1978.

—— *How I Got Ovah*, New York: Doubleday, 1976.

—— *Love Raps*, Chicago: Third World Press, 1969.

—— *Now Ain't That Love*, Detroit: Broadside Press, 1970.

—— *Songs of a Black Bird*, Chicago: Third World Press, 1969.

Sanchez, Sonia, *The Adventures of Fathead, Smallhead, and Square-head*, Chicago: Third World Press, 1973.

—— *A Blue Book for a Magical Woman*, Detroit: Broadside Press, 1974.

—— *Homecoming*, Detroit: Broadside Press, 1970.

—— *Homegirls and Handgrenades*, New York: Thunder's Mouth Press, 1984.

—— *Ima Talkin Bout the Nation of Islam*, New York: TruthDel, 1972.

—— *It's a New Day: Poems for Young Brothas and Sistuhs*, Detroit: Broadside Press, 1971.

—— *I've Been a Woman*, San Francisco: Black Scholar Press, 1978.

—— *Love Poems*, Chicago: Third World Press, 1973.

—— *A Sound Investment*, Chicago: Third World Press, 1980.

—— *Under a Soprano Sky*, New Brunswick, NJ: Africa World Press, 1987.

—— *We a BaddDDD People*, Detroit: Broadside Press, 1971.

Schwartz-Bart, Simone, *Between Two Worlds*, New York: Harper and Row, 1981.

Shange, Ntozake, *A Daughter's Geography*, New York: St. Martin's Press, 1983; London: Methuen, 1984.

—— *for colored girls who have considered suicide when the rainbow is enuf*, New York: Macmillan, 1975; London: Methuen, 1978.

—— *From Okra to Greens: Poems*, St. Paul, Minn.: Coffeehouse Press, 1984.

—— *Nappy Edges*, New York: St. Martin's Press, 1978; London: Methuen, 1978.

—— *Riding the Moon in Texas: Word Paintings*, New York: St. Martin's Press, 1987.

—— *Some Men*, n.p., n.d.

Simmons, Judy, *Indecent Intentions*, New York: Blind Beggar Press, 1984.

Stephany, *Moving Deep*, Detroit: Broadside Press, 1969.

Taylor, Gloria Lee, *Dreams for Sale*, New York: Exposition Press, 1953.

Thomas, Elean, *Word Rhythms from the Life of a Woman*, London: Karia Press, 1986.

Thomas, Joyce Carol, *Bittersweet*, Berkeley, Calif.: Firesign, 1973.

—— *Black Child*, New York: Zamani, 1981.

—— *Blessing*, Berkeley, Calif.: Jocato, 1975.

—— *Crystal Breezes*, Berkeley, Calif.: Firesign, 1974.

—— *Inside the Rainbow*, Palo Alto, Calif.: Zikawuna, 1982.

Thompson, Dorotheina Tinsley, *Three Slices of Black*, Chicago: Free Black Press, 1972.

Turner, Sherile, *Jamaica Chat*, London: Akira Press, 1986.

Walker, Alice, *Five Poems*, Detroit: Broadside Press, 1972.

—— *Goodnight Willie Lee, I'll See You in the Morning*, New York: Dial, 1979; London: Women's Press, 1987.

—— *Horses Make a Landscape Look More Beautiful*, New York: Harcourt Brace Jovanovich, 1984; London: Women's Press, 1985.

—— *Revolutionary Petunias and Other Poems*, New York: Harcourt Brace Jovanovich, 1973; London: Women's Press, 1985.

Walker, Margaret, *October Journey*, Detroit: Broadside Press, 1973.

—— *Prophets for a New Day*, Detroit: Broadside Press, 1970.

Wallace, Susan, *Bahamian Scene*, Philadelphia: Dorrance and Company, 1975.

Wheatley, Phillis, *The Collected Works of Phillis Wheatley*, John C. Shields, ed., New York: Oxford University Press (Schomburg Library of Nineteenth-Century Black Women Writers), 1988.

White, Paulette Childress, *Love Poem to a Black Junkie*, Detroit: Lotus Press, 1975.

—— *The Watermelon Dress: Portrait of a Woman*, Detroit: Lotus Press, 1984.

Williams, Sherley Anne, *One Sweet Angel Child*, New York: William Morrow, 1982.

—— *The Peacock Poems*, Middletown, Conn.: Wesleyan University Press, 1975.

Wright, Sarah, and Lucy Smith, *Give Me a Child*, Philadelphia: Kraft Publishing Company, 1955.

Yvonne, *Iwilla-Scourge: Vol. II*, New York: Chameleon, 1986.

II. *Drama*

Carroll, Vinette, and Micki Grant, *Don't Bother Me, I Can't Cope*, New York: Samuel French, 1972.

Childress, Alice, *Let's Hear It for the Queen*, New York: Coward McCann and Geoghegan, 1976.

—— *Mojo: A Black Love Story*, New York: Dramatist Play Service, 1971.

—— *String*, New York: Dramatist Play Service, 1969.

—— *String and Mojo: A Black Love Story*, New York: Dramatist Play Service, 1971.

—— *Wedding Band: A Love/Hate Story in Black and White*, New York: Samuel French, 1973.

—— *When the Rattlesnake Sounds*, New York: Coward McCann and Geoghegan, 1975.

—— *Wine in the Wilderness*, New York: Dramatist Play Service, 1973.

Franklin, J.E., *Black Girl*, New York: Dramatist Play Service, 1971.

Gibson, P.J., *Long Time Since Yesterday*, New York: Samuel French, 1984.

Graham, Shirley, *Track Thirteen*, Boston: Expression Company, 1940.

Grimke, Angelina, *Rachel*, Boston: Cornshill Company, 1920.

Hansberry, Lorraine, *Les Blancs: The Collected Last Plays of Lorraine Hansberry*, Robert Nemiroff, ed., New York: Random House, 1972.

—— *A Raisin in the Sun*, New York: Signet, 1959.

—— *The Sign in Sidney Brustein's Window*, New York: Signet, 1966.

—— *To Be Young, Gifted and Black: A Portrait of Lorraine Hansberry in Her Own Words*, Robert Nemiroff, adapt. New York: Samuel French, 1971.

Kennedy, Adrienne, *Adrienne Kennedy in One Act*, Minneapolis:

University of Minnesota Press, 1988.

King, Ramona, *Steal Away*, New York: Samuel French, 1981.

Lee, Leslie, *Between Now and Then*, New York: Samuel French, 1984.

—— *Colored People's Time*, New York: Samuel French, 1983.

—— *The First Breeze of Summer*, New York: Samuel French, 1975.

Mason, Judi Ann, *Livin' Fat*, New York: Samuel French, 1974.

Molette, Barbara, and Carlton Molette, *Rosalee Pritchett*, New York: Dramatist Play Service, 1973.

Shange, Ntozake, *for colored girls who have considered suicide when the rainbow is enuf*, New York: Macmillan, 1977; London: Methuen, 1978.

—— *From Okra to Greens/a Different Kinda Love Story*, New York: Samuel French, 1983.

—— *A Photograph: Lovers in Motion*, New York: Samuel French, 1981.

—— *Spell #7*, New York: St. Martin's Press, 1981.

—— *Three Pieces*, New York: St. Martin's Press, 1981.

Spencer, Eulalie, *Fool's Errand*, New York: Samuel French, 1927.

III. *Fiction*

Adisa, Opal Palmer, *Bake-Face and Other Guava Stories*, Berkeley, Calif.: Kelsey Street Press, 1986.

Albert, Octavia V. Rogers, *The House of Bondage, or, Charlotte Brooks and Other Slaves*, intro. Frances Smith Foster, New York: Oxford University Press (Schomburg Library of Nineteenth-Century Black Women Writers), 1988.

Allfrey, Phyllis S., *The Orchid House*, Washington, DC: Three Continents Press, 1985.

Austin, Doris Jean, *After the Garden*, New York: NAL, 1987.

Bambara, Toni Cade, *Gorilla My Love*, New York: Random House, 1972; London: Women's Press, 1984.

—— *The Salt Eaters*, New York: Random House, 1980; London: Women's Press, 1982.

—— *The Sea Birds Are Still Alive*, New York: Random House, 1977;

London: Women's Press, 1984.

Birtha, Becky, *For Nights Like This One: Stories of Love and Women*, San Francisco: Frog in the Well, 1983.

—— *Lover's Choice*, Seattle: Seal Press, 1987; London: Women's Press, 1988.

Brodber, Erna, *Jane and Louisa Will Soon Come Home*, London: New Beacon Press, 1980.

—— *Myal—A Novel*, London: New Beacon Press, 1988.

Brooks, Gwendolyn, *Maude Martha*, New York: Farrar, Straus and Giroux, 1969.

Brown, Linda Jean, *Jazz Dancin wif Mama*, New York: Iridian Press, 1982.

—— *Kiwi*, New York: Iridian Press, 1977.

—— *Rainbow River*, New York: Iridian Press, 1980.

Buford, Barbara, *The Threshing Floor*, London: Sheba Feminist Publishers, 1986.

Butler, Octavia, *Adulthood Rites*, New York: Warner Books; London: Gollancz, 1987.

—— *Clay's Ark*, New York: St. Martin's Press, 1984.

—— *Dawn*, New York: Warner Books, 1987; London: Gollancz, 1988.

—— *Kindred*, Garden City, NY: Doubleday, 1979; London: Women's Press, 1988.

—— *Mind of My Own*, Garden City, NY: Doubleday, 1977.

—— *Pattermaster*, Garden City, NY: Doubleday, 1976.

—— *Survivor*, Garden City, NY: Doubleday, 1978.

—— *Wild Seed*, Garden City, NY: Doubleday, 1980.

Cambridge, Joan, *Clarise Cumberbach Wants to Go Home*, New York: Ticknor and Fields, 1987.

Campbell, Hazel D., *The Rag Doll and Other Stories*, Mona, Jamaica, BWI: Savacou Cooperative, 1978.

—— *Woman's Tongue*, Mona, Jamaica, B.W.I.: Savacou Publications, 1985.

Cancryn, Addeliyu, *Man of Vision*, St. Thomas, V.I.: Val Hill Enterprises, 1975.

Chase-Riboud, Barbara, *Sally Hemings*, New York: Viking, 1979.

—— *Valide*, New York: William Morrow, 1986.

Childress, Alice, *A Hero Ain't Nothing But a Sandwich*, New York: Coward McCann and Geoghegan, 1973.

—— *Like One of the Family*, Brooklyn: Independence Publishers, 1956.

—— *Rainbow Jordan*, New York: Coward McCann and Geoghegan, 1981.

—— *A Short Walk*, New York: Coward McCann and Geoghegan, 1979.

Cliff, Michelle, *ABENG: A Novel*, Trumansberg, NY: Crossing Press, 1984.

—— *Claiming an Identity They Taught Me to Despise*, Boston: Persephone Press, 1980.

—— *The Land of Look Behind*, Ithaca, NY: Firebrand Press, 1985.

—— *No Telephone to Heaven*, New York: E.P. Dutton, 1987; London: Methuen, 1988.

Conde, Maryse, *Moi, Tituba, Sorciere, Noire de Salem/I, Tituba, Sorceress, Black Woman of Salem*, Paris: Mercure de France, 1986.

Cooper, California, *Homemade Love*, New York: St. Martin's Press, 1986.

—— *A Piece of Mind*, Navarro, Calif.: Wild Trees Press, 1984.

—— *Some Soul to Keep*, New York: St. Martin's Press, 1987.

DeVeaux, Alexis, *The Adventures of the Dred Sisters*, New York: The Author, n.d.

—— *Spirits in the Streets*, New York: Anchor/Doubleday, 1973.

Dove, Rita, *Fifth Sunday*, Charlottesville: University of Virginia Press, 1985.

Dunbar-Nelson, Alice Moore, *The Works of Alice Dunbar-Nelson*, Gloria T. Hull, ed., New York: Oxford University Press (Schomburg Library of Nineteenth-Century Black Women Writers), 1988.

Edgell, Zee, *Beka Lamb*, London: Heinemann, 1982.

Fauset, Jessie Redmon, *The Chinaberry Tree*, New York: Frederick A. Stokes, 1931.

—— *Comedy, American Style*, New York: Frederick A. Stokes, 1933.

—— *Plum Bun*, New York: Frederick A. Stokes, 1929.

—— *There is Confusion*, New York: Boni and Liveright, 1924.

Finch, Amanda, *Black Trail: A Novella of Love in the South*, New York: William-Frederick Press, 1951.

Fleming, Sarah Lee Brown, *Hope's Highway*. New York: Neale, 1917.

Gilroy, Beryl, *Frangipani House*, London: Heinemann Caribbean Writers Series, 1986.

Golden, Martina, *Migration of the Heart*, New York: Anchor, 1983.

—— *A Woman's Place*, New York: Doubleday, 1986; London: Methuen, 1988.

Guy, Rosa, *Bird at My Window*, Philadelphia: J.B. Lippincott, 1966.

—— *The Disappearance*, New York: Delacorte, 1979; London: Gollancz, 1980.

—— *Edith Jackson*, New York: Viking; London: Gollancz, 1979.

—— *The Friends*, New York: Holt, Rinehart and Winston, 1973; London: Gollancz, 1974.

—— *A Measure of Time*, New York: Holt, Rinehart and Winston, 1983; London: Virago, 1984.

—— *My Love, My Love, or, the Peasant Girl*, New York: Holt, Rinehart and Winston, 1985; London: Virago, 1987.

—— *New Guys Around the Block*, London: Gollancz, 1983.

—— *Paris, Pee Wee, and Big Dog*, New York: Delacorte; London: Gollancz, 1984.

—— *Ruby: A Novel*, New York: Viking, 1976; London: Gollancz, 1979.

Hamilton, Virginia, *Avilla Sun Down*, New York: Greenwillow, 1976.

—— *Dustland*, New York: Avon, 1981.

—— *The Gathering*, New York: Avon, 1981.

—— *Jadhu*, New York: Greenwillow, 1980.

—— *Junius Over Far*, New York: Harper and Row, 1985.

—— *Justice and Her Brothers*, New York: Avon, 1981.

—— *Little Love*, New York: Philomel Boones, 1984; London: Gollancz, 1985.

—— *The Magical Adventures of Pretty Pearl*, New York: Harper and Row, 1983.

—— *MC Higgins the Great*, New York: Macmillan, 1974.

—— *The People Could Fly: Afro-American Folktales*, New York:

Alfred A. Knopf, 1985; London: Walker Books, 1986.

—— *Sweet Whispers Brother Rush*, New York: Philomel Boones, 1982; London: Walker Books, 1987.

—— *Time Ago Lost Tales of Jadhu*, New York: Macmillan, 1973.

—— *Willie Bea and the Time the Martians Landed*, New York: Greenwillow, 1983.

Hanson, Joyce, *The Gift Giver*, Boston: Houghton Mifflin, 1980.

—— *Homeboy*, Boston: Houghton Mifflin, 1982.

—— *Which Way Freedom*, New York: Walker Books, 1986.

—— *Yellowbird and Me*, New York: Ticknor and Fields, 1986.

Harper, Frances Ellen Watkins, *Iola LeRoy, or, Shadows Uplifted*, intro. Frances Smith Foster, New York: Oxford University Press (Schomburg Library of Nineteenth-Century Black Women Writers), 1988.

Hodge, Merle, *Crick Crack, Monkey*, London: Heinemann, 1981.

Hopkins, Pauline E., *Contending Forces: A Romance Illustrative of Negro Life North and South*, intro. Richard Yarborough, New York: Oxford University Press (Schomburg Library of Nineteenth-Century Black Women Writers), 1988.

—— *The Magazine Novels of Pauline E. Hopkins*, intro. Hazel V. Carby, New York: Oxford University Press (Schomburg Library of Nineteenth-Century Black Women Writers), 1988.

Hunter, Helen, *Magnificent White Men*, New York: Vantage Press, 1964.

Hunter, Kristin, *Boss Cat*, New York: Avon Books, 1981.

—— *God Bless the Child*, Washington, DC: Howard University Press, 1987.

—— *The Landlord*, New York: Avon Books, 1977.

—— *The Laketown Rebellion*, New York: Charles Scribners' Sons, 1978.

—— *Lou in the Limelight*, New York: Charles Scribners' Sons, 1981.

—— *The Soul Brother and Sister Lou*, New York: Avon Books, 1968.

Hurston, Zora Neale, *Jonah's Gourd Vine*, Philadelphia: J.B. Lippincott, 1934.

—— *Moses, Man of the Mountain*, Philadelphia: J.B. Lippincott, 1935.

—— *Mules and Men*, Philadelphia: J.B. Lippincott, 1938.

—— *Seraphs on the Suwanee*, New York: Charles Scribners' Sons, 1948.

—— *Spunk: The Selected Stories of Zora Neale Hurston*, Berkeley, Calif.: Turtle Island Foundation, 1985.

—— *Tell My Horse*, Philadelphia: J.B. Lippincott, 1938.

—— *Their Eyes Were Watching God*, Philadelphia: J.B. Lippincott, 1937.

Johnson, A.E., *Clarence and Corinne, or, God's Way*, intro. Hortense J. Spillers, New York: Oxford University Press (Schomburg Library of Nineteenth-Century Black Women Writers), 1988.

—— *The Hazeley Family*, intro. Barbara Christian, New York: Oxford University Press (Schomburg Library of Nineteenth-Century Black Women Writers), 1988.

Jones, Gayl, *Corregidora*, New York: Bantam Books, 1975; London: Camden Press, 1988.

—— *Eva's Man*, New York: Random House, 1976.

—— *White Rat*, New York: Random House, 1977.

Jones, Marion Patrick, *J'Ouvert Morning*, Port of Spain, Trinidad: Columbus, 1976.

—— *Pan Bean*, Port of Spain, Trinidad: Columbus, 1973.

Kelley-Hawkins, Emma Dunham, *Four Girls at Cottage City*, intro. Deborah E. McDowell, New York: Oxford University Press (Schomburg Library of Nineteenth-Century Black Women Writers), 1988.

—— *Medga*, intro. Molly Hite, New York: Oxford University Press (Schomburg Library of Nineteenth-Century Black Women Writers), 1988.

Kincaid, Jamaica, *At the Bottom of the River*, New York: Farrar Straus and Giroux, 1983; London: Picador, 1984.

—— *Annie John*, New York: Farrar Straus and Giroux; London: Picador, 1985.

Larsen, Nella, *Passing*, New York: Alfred A. Knopf, 1929.

—— *Quicksand*, New York: Alfred A. Knopf, 1928.

Lee, Andrea, *Russian Journal*, New York: Random House, 1981.

—— *Sarah Phillips*, New York: Random House, 1984; London: Faber, 1986.

Lee, Audrey, *The Clarion People*, New York: McGraw-Hill, 1968.

McMillian, Terry, *Mama*, Boston: Houghton Mifflin, 1987.

Marshall, Paule, *Brown Girl, Brownstones*, New York: Random House, 1959.

—— *The Chosen Place; The Timeless People*, New York: Harcourt Brace and World, 1969.

—— *Praisesong for the Widow*, New York: Putnam; London: Virago, 1983.

—— *Reena and Other Stories*, New York: Feminist Press, 1983.

Mathis, Sharon Bell, *Listen for the Fig Tree*, New York: Viking, 1974.

—— *Teacup Full of Roses*, New York: Viking, 1972.

Meriwether, Louise, *Daddy Was a Numbers Runner*, Englewood Cliffs, NJ: Prentice Hall, 1970.

Mohr, Nicholasa, *El Bronx Remembered*, New York: Harper and Row, 1975.

—— *Felita*, New York: Dial, 1977.

—— *Going Home*, New York: Dial, 1986.

—— *In Nueva York*, New York: Dial, 1977.

—— *Nilda*, New York: Harper and Row, 1973.

—— *Rituals of Survival: A Woman's Portfolio*, Houston, Tex.: Arte Publico Press, 1985.

Morrison, Toni, *Beloved*, New York: Alfred A. Knopf; London: Chatto, 1987.

—— *The Bluest Eye*, New York: Holt Rinehart and Winston, 1970; London: Chatto; 1980.

—— *Song of Solomon*, New York: Alfred A. Knopf, 1977; London: Chatto, 1980.

—— *Sula*, New York: Alfred A. Knopf, 1974; London: Chatto, 1980.

—— *Tar Baby*, New York: Alfred A. Knopf; London: Chatto, 1981.

Naylor, Gloria, *Linden Hills*, New York: Ticknor and Fields, 1985; London: Methuen, 1986.

—— *Mama Day*, New York: Ticknor and Fields; London: Hutchinson, 1988.

—— *The Women of Brewster Place*, New York: Viking, 1982; London: Methuen, 1987.

Nelson, Annie Greene, *After the Storm*, Columbia, SC: Hampton, 1942.

—— *The Dawn Appears*, Columbia, SC: Hampton, 1944.

Nichols, Grace, *Whole of a Morning Sky*, London: Virago Poets, 1986.

Nunez-Harrell, Elizabeth, *When Rocks Dance*, New York: G.P. Putnam's Sons, 1986.

Petry, Ann, *Country Place*, Boston: Houghton Mifflin, 1947.

—— *Miss Muriel and Other Stories*, Boston: Houghton Mifflin, 1971.

—— *The Narrows*, Boston: Houghton Mifflin, 1953.

—— *The Street*, New York: Pyramid Books, 1961.

Potter, Valaida, *Sunrise Over Alabama*, New York: Comet Press Books, 1959.

Randall, Florence E., *The Almost Year*, New York: Atheneum, 1971.

Riley, Joan, *The Unbelonging*, London: The Women's Press, 1988.

—— *Waiting in the Twilight*, London: The Women's Press, 1986.

Roberson, Sadie, *Killer of the Dream*, New York: Carleton, 1963.

Rosebrough, Dorothy, *Wasted Travail*, New York: Vantage Press, 1951.

Saunders, Rubie, *Marilyn Morgan, R.N.*, New York: New Amsterdam Library, 1969.

Shange, Ntozake, *Betsey Brown: A Novel*, New York: St. Martin's Press, 1985; London: Methuen, 1985.

—— *Sassafrass, Cypress, and Indigo*, New York: St. Martin's Press, 1982; London: Methuen, 1984.

Shaw, Letty M., *Angel Mink*, New York: Comet Books Press, 1937.

Shinebourne, Janice, *The Last English Plantation*, Leeds, Yorkshire, UK: Peepal Tree Press, 1988.

—— *Timepiece*, Leeds, Yorkshire, UK: Peepal Tree Press, 1986.

Shockley, Ann Allen, *The Black and White of It*, Tallahassee, Fla.: Naiad Press, 1980.

—— *Loving Her*, New York: Bobbs-Merrill, 1974.

—— *Say Jesus and Come to Me*, New York: Avon, 1982.

Southerland, Ellease, *Let the Lion Eat Straw*, New York: Charles Scribner, 1979; London: Dent, 1980.

—— *The Magic Sun Spins*, London: Paul Breman, 1975.

Spencer, Mary Etta, *The Resentment*, Philadelphia: A.M.E. Book Concern, 1921.

Taylor, Mildred, *The Friendship*, New York: Dial, 1987.
—— *Gold Cadillac*, New York: Dial, 1987.
—— *Let the Circle Be Unbroken*, New York: Bantam, 1981; London: Gollancz, 1982.
—— *Roll of Thunder, Hear My Cry*, New York: Bantam, 1976; London: Gollancz, 1977.
—— *Song of the Trees*, New York: Dial, 1975.
Tennant, Emma Blake, *Marina*, London: Faber, 1985.
Thomas, Joyce Carol, *Bright Shadow*, New York: Avon, 1983.
—— *Journey*, New York: Scholastic, 1988.
—— *Marked by Fire*, New York: Avon, 1982.
Vaught, Estella U., *Vengeance is Mine*, New York: Comet Books Press, 1959.
Vroman, Mary Elizabeth, *Esther*, New York: Bantam Books, 1963.
—— *Harlem Summer*, New York: Berkeley, 1968.
Walker, Alice, *The Color Purple*, New York: Harcourt Brace and Jovanovich, 1982; London: Women's Press, 1983.
—— *In Love and Trouble: Stories of Black Women*, New York: Harcourt Brace and Jovanovich, 1973; London: Women's Press, 1982.
—— *Meridian*, New York: Harcourt Brace and Jovanovich, 1976; London: Women's Press, 1982.
—— *The Third Life of Grange Copeland*, New York: Harcourt Brace and Jovanovich, 1970.
—— *You Can't Keep a Good Woman Down*, New York: Harcourt Brace and Jovanovich, 1981; London: Women's Press, 1982.
Walker, Margaret, *Jubilee*, Boston: Houghton Mifflin, 1966.
Walker, Mildred Pitts, *Because We Are*, New York: Lothrop Lee and Shepard, 1983.
—— *Brother to the Wind*, New York: Lothrop Lee and Shepard, 1985.
Wallace, Elizabeth West, *Scandal at Daybreak*, New York: Pageant Press, 1954.
Washington, Doris, *Yulan*, New York: Carleton, 1964.
West, Dorothy, *The Living is Easy*, Boston: Houghton Mifflin, 1948.
Williams, Sherley Anne, *Dessa Rose*, New York: William Morrow, 1986.

Wilson-Cartier, Xam, *Bebop Rebop*, New York: Ballantine Books, 1987.

Wood, Lillian E., *Let My People Go*, Philadelphia: A.M.E. Book Concern, 1922.

Woods, Odella Phelps, *High Ground*, New York: Exposition Press, 1945.

Wright, Sarah E., *This Child's Gonna Live*, New York: Delacorte, 1969.

Wright, Zara, *Black and White Tangled Threads*, Chicago, Privately printed, 1920.

8. Literature by Men

Baldwin, James, *Another Country*, New York: Dial, 1960.

—— *The Fire Next Time*, New York: Dial, 1963.

—— *Go Tell It On the Mountain*, New York: Knopf, 1953.

—— *If Beale Street Could Talk*, New York: Dial, 1974.

—— *Nobody Knows My Name*, New York: Dial, 1961.

—— *No Name in the Street*, New York: Dial, 1972.

—— *Notes of a Native Son*, Boston: Beacon Press, 1955.

Baraka, Amiri, *The Dutchman and the Slave: Two Plays*, New York: William Morrow, 1964.

—— *The Dead Lecturer*, Poems by LeRoi Jones, New York: Grove Press, 1964.

—— *Preface to a Twenty Volume Suicide Note*, New Haven, CT: Corinth Books, 1961.

—— *Selected Poetry of Amiri Baraka/LeRoi Jones*, New York: Morrow Quill Paperbacks, 1979.

Douglass, Frederick, *Narrative of the Life of An American Slave, Written by Himself* (1845), New York: Signet, 1968.

Dubois, W.E.B., *The Souls of Black Folk* (1903), New York: New American Library, 1982.

Ellis, Trey, *Platitudes*, NY: Vint, 1988.

Ellison, Ralph, *Invisible Man*, New York: Random House, 1952.

—— *Shadow and Act*, New York: Random House, 1964.

BIBLIOGRAPHY

King, Jr., Martin Luther, *Why We Can't Wait*, New York: Signet, 1964.

Mailer, Norman, *The White Negro*, San Francisco: City Lights, 1957.

—— *Existential Errands*, New York: New American Library, 1973.

—— *The Fight*, Boston: Little Brown, 1975.

Reed, Ishmael, *The Last Days of Louisiana Red*, New York: Random House, 1974.

—— *Mumbo Jumbo*, New York: Doubleday, 1972.

—— *Flight to Canada*, New York: Random House, 1976.

—— *Reckless Eyeballing*, New York: St. Martin's Press, 1987.

Williams, John A., *The Man Who Cried I Am/Sissie*, New York: Doubleday, 1969.

Wolfe, Tom, *Radical Chic and Mau-Mauing the Flak Catchers*, New York: Farrar, Straus and Giroux, 1970.

Wright, Richard, *Black Boy*, New York: Harper & Row, 1945.

—— *Native Son*, New York: Harper & Row, 1940.

Index